MEDIEVAL WOMEN AND THE LAW

The question of women's status within medieval society has generated much interest concerning their social position, education, piety and relationships, and women's autonomy within these arenas. This volume unites all these issues in its exploration of the legal agency of the medieval woman.

Essays focus upon women's control over property and testamentary bequests, over living arrangements, guardianship and over their own bodies. While some of the conclusions question women's ability to act in law, other essays reveal that some, certainly, had an understanding of their legal rights, and of wider legal procedures enabling them to exercise a degree of legal autonomy.

NOËL JAMES MENUGE completed her D.Phil. in medieval studies at the University of York.

MEDIEVAL WOMEN
AND THE LAW

EDITED BY
NOËL JAMES MENUGE

THE BOYDELL PRESS

First published 2000
The Boydell Press, Woodbridge
Reprinted 2001
Reprinted in paperback 2003

ISBN 978 0 85115 775 7 hardback
ISBN 978 0 85115 932 4 paperback

Transferred to digital printing

The Boydell Press is an imprint of Boydell & Brewer Ltd
PO Box 9, Woodbridge, Suffolk IP12 3DF, UK
and of Boydell & Brewer Inc.
668 Mt. Hope Avenue, Rochester NY 14620, USA
website: www.boydellandbrewer.com

A CIP catalogue record for this title is available
from the British Library

This book is printed on acid-free paper

Contents

For Adam,
for everything

List of Contributors

P.J.P. Goldberg is a lecturer in history at the University of York. He is the author of *Women, Work and Life Cycle in a Medieval Economy: Women in York and Yorkshire c. 1300–1520, Women in England c. 1275–1525*, and the editor of *Women in Medieval English Society*. He has published numerous articles on medieval women.

Victoria Thompson lectures in medieval history for New York University's London Study abroad programme. Her book, *Dying and Death in Later Anglo-Saxon England*, is forthcoming from Boydell & Brewer.

Jennifer Smith gained her doctorate from the University of Western Australia. She currently teaches literature in a secondary college.

Cordelia Beattie completed her doctorate on single women in the late Middle Ages at the Centre for Medieval Studies at the University of York; she is now lecturer in history at the University of Edinburgh.

Katherine J. Lewis is a lecturer in history at the University of Huddersfield. She has published a book on the cult of St Katherine of Alexandria as well as several articles on saints' cults in fifteenth-century England. She is currently co-editing *A Companion to Margery Kempe* for Boydell.

Noël James Menuge works for the Heritage Lottery Fund in Cambridge. She has published on wardship in romance and law, and on landscape history. Her book on English wardship appeared from Boydell in 2002.

Corinne Saunders is lecturer in English at the University of Durham. She has published several articles on romance and law, and has authored a book on the forest in medieval romance. Her book on the history of medieval rape was published by Boydell in 2001.

Kim M. Phillips is a lecturer in history at the University of Auckland and holds a D.Phil. in Medieval Studies from the University of York on the topic of young womanhood in late medieval England. She has published on young womanhood, and gesture in romance and conduct literature.

Emma Hawkes completed her doctorate in history at the University of Western Australia in 1998. Her work examines the connections between family position, gender and the law, and her subsequent work has focused on the history of medieval rape. She currently works at the University of Western Australia.

Introduction

There is hardly need to apologise for a collection of scholarly essays on the theme of women and law in the Middle Ages, especially when the work contained herein is entirely the product of new research. Although it is possible to identify a number of individual articles, and indeed in a few cases monographs, that relate to particular issues explored in this collection, there is little that pertains to the theme more broadly. We may note, for example, the excellent collection edited by Sue Sheridan Walker entitled *Wife and Widow in Medieval England*, but this is focused specifically on issues relating to marriage and widowhood. Also of interest is a collection, jointly edited by Jenny Kermode and Garthine Walker, under the title *Women, Crime and the Courts in Early Modern England*, but as the title reveals, the chronological focus is post-medieval. Where this present collection differs from these, however, is in its interdisciplinary approach. The essays here bring together literary and historical sources in a methodologically sophisticated way that offers both a more rounded view of the past and, at times, a more demanding view of the past. There are, moreover, certain themes that link the essays. The focus is not on women as trangressors against the law, but on the way legal discourses constructed women and the way women attempted to exercise agency even within the patriarchal constraints of different legal systems. There is a particular emphasis on the experience of aristocratic women and a shared concern to read behind legal discourses to discover women's voices and women's feelings. What follows is an attempt to signal some of the particular themes that are the subject of this lively collection.

'Cherchez la femme.' That is the problem that so frequently confronts the medievalist. Women are not notable for their visibility in historical records, even in a later medieval context. Women exercising agency or giving voice to their own will are still more rarely observed. One would be tempted to conclude that women were in a minority in medieval societies and that they played little part in those societies. Jennifer Smith, in this present collection, writes that women are not much noticed in the customs of Occitan cities of the High Middle Ages. Even where they are found, they appear as wives, daughters, widows – dependents on males and presented as objects of male agency: daughters have to be provided for in marriage; wives supervised in the making of their wills. Her observations are hardly unusual. Rather they constitute the *leitmotif* of writing on the subject of women in legal sources. The temptation is to look elsewhere, especially to literature. Here women are much more numerous. They also appear much more real because located in a realm of feelings, emotion, imagined landscapes, and even speech. But here also we are confronted by optical illusions. Smith's article is again illustrative of the point. The apparently exulted status allowed to the lady or *domna* of the Occitan lyric, from which a supposedly 'golden interlude' for women in the half century from 1180 has been surmised, appears on closer inspection to be elusive. Smith argues that by locating the *domna* in an imaginary 'landscape of love', she is actually distanced from real power or agency. If anyone is exulted, indeed, it is by proxy the lord, her husband. This may reflect an anxiety about women's control of land and hence power, but it hardly constitutes a simple mirror of social practice.

Literature here thus serves to give expression to something of the concerns and anxieties largely invisible from more conventional historical records. This understanding also informs the essays by Noël James Menuge and Corinne Saunders. For Menuge, romances are the place where anxieties about the role of mothers as guardians in aristocratic society are played out. So far as the mother may stand in the way of the feudal ideal of the transmission of landed property from father to son, she is constructed as a threat both in legal treatises and in romances such as *William of Palerne* or *Beues of Hamtoun*. Particularly feared and hence vilified were the re-marrying widow and the step-mother. But for the evidence from the courts themselves, the nurturing role that many mothers of feudal wards may in practice have exercised is thus obscured. For Saunders, romances serve to highlight a fear of social dislocation that is a consequence of a breakdown in law, and in particular the sense that the crown should protect its subjects by enforcing laws against rape. *Havelok*, for example, looks back nostalgically to an imaged pre-Conquest past when laws against rape were strictly enforced. Although she argues that woman's consent looms larger as an issue in romance than statute law, the underlying concern with order and the protection of property rights (including the rights of fathers over daughters or husbands over wives) complements Menuge's reading of the same source. Neither Menuge nor Saunders choose to read their romances in isolation however. Rather, they read them alongside legal sources and in this way are more acutely sensitive to the ways in which the one echoes the other, or conversely offers a different emphasis.

Menuge and Saunders are not alone. The essays in this collection as a whole demonstrate the value of an interdisciplinary methodology. To examine individual sources in isolation is, as we have just seen, to encounter optical illusions. Only in conjunction with other sources can a more rounded understanding of the past emerge. Cordelia Beattie, for example, uses poll tax returns, wills, deeds, and records of matrimonial litigation (cause papers) in conjunction to suggest a more nuanced and complex picture of social relations than the neat packages suggested by individual sources. The distinction between historical sources and literature is, moreover, not necessarily helpful. The contributors here prefer instead to treat all written sources as texts: all are discursively constructed; none provides privileged access to a hidden 'truth'. Beattie is thus able to question certain orthodoxies about household structure and relationships by reading poll tax returns as legal discourses. She thus provides telling evidence that, to use her preferred phrase, women without husbands can be shown sometimes to have occupied non-standard household structures where notions of headship and dependence may have little meaning. Likewise she challenges Charles Donahue's objection that 'interesting' cause papers should be dismissed as inherently untruthful by showing that the evidence has a value that does not depend on such narrowly defined notions of truth.

We are confronted by optical illusion again in so far as apparent visibility or invisibility of women in certain sources may conceal as much as it reveals. Beattie observes that the frequency with which women in cause papers, wills, or poll tax returns are constructed as dependants reflects only the common concern of these sources with money. The actual emotional relationships that lie behind these constructs are almost entirely obscured. Emma Hawkes, likewise, in a study focused on the later fifteenth and earlier sixteenth centuries in England, shows that women (implicitly aristocratic women) were hardly visible in bringing cases before the common law courts of King's Bench and Common Pleas. They were only slightly more visible in making petitions to the Chancellor. The originality of her argument is not in presenting statistics for what is seen and recorded, however, but in offering those rare glimpses into what goes otherwise unrecorded. In particular she uses a letter by Agnes Plumpton from 1502, who writes knowledgeably of technical legal actions, to support her hypothesis that women were both informed about the law and engaged in matters of a legal nature up to the point of bringing action in the courts. 'Agnes' role,' she argues, 'was to gather information, to do the accounts, to encourage and urge her menfolk to go to court and to undertake the routine legal procedures which did not take her to court.' The legal record, consequently, is a very poor indicator of aristocratic women's actual participation in legal affairs.

What is demanded of the medievalist asking questions about women and the law, therefore, is a capacity to work sometimes exiguous sources very hard. This is well demonstrated by Victoria Thompson's study of aristocratic Anglo-Saxon women, which, like Smith's study, serves to undermine notions of the *bon vieux temps*. Whilst lamenting the largely lost genre of embroidery, and armed with but a dozen wills, she is still able to suggest something of women's concerns and priorities. She shows how the well-born lady might use public speech and the bestowal of treasure to buy herself protection. (Here again the literary figure of Wealhtheow complements the will-making personage of Ælfflæd.) She shows a concern with family and memorialisation, illustrated both by Ælfflæd's patronage of the monastery of 'Stoke where my ancestors rest', and, it may be suggested, by her bequest to Ely of a tapestry depicting the deeds of her husband. Thompson also reveals the gendered association between women and textiles and other household goods as reflected in wills. This last is strikingly similar to the testamentary patterns observed by Katherine Lewis using a sample of wills some four centuries later in date. Ælfflæd's bequest of the tapestry is akin to Margaret Chocke's bequest of a tapestry-work coverlet as an altar frontal for feast day use. In both instances these women were probably naming items worked by their own hands and were thus imbued with some personal and emotional significance.

Lewis's study in fact compares and contrasts in interesting ways with Thompson's. Both stress the oral nature of the will, though it is clear that the relationship between the utterance of the will and the recording of the same changed over time. Indeed it is tempting to suggest that the insistent repetition of 'I will' and 'I bequeath' in late medieval wills only highlights the documentary nature of extant texts. Whereas Thompson argues that women sometimes only *appear* to have exercised agency in their disposal of 'their' possessions, being in fact agents of male family members, Lewis implicitly argues for a much greater degree of autonomy, at least for the well-born widows who make up most of her sample. The most interesting aspect of Lewis's study, however, is her reading of the will as a literary genre and a form of autobiography. Women's wills, she shows, 'frequently comprise the reiteration of very personal, familial, and wider domestic preoccupations' and are characterised by large numbers of bequests of personal possessions, whereas men's wills tend to be concerned only with matters of particular import and to leave sums of money rather than individual possessions. These observations may be particularly sharply focused given the generally aristocratic nature of the probate source used. A concern with family is thus common to women's wills of both the later Anglo-Saxon and the late medieval eras.

Two other essays that especially complement one another are those by Saunders and Kim Phillips. As we have seen, Saunders makes particular use of romance literature to explore the problem of *raptus*, a term that conflates both rape and abduction and hence immediately signals that medieval and modern meanings of rape differ. Her study ranges chronologically from the romance of *Havelok* with its nostalgic looking back to an imagined pre-Conquest past, to the *Morte D'Arthur* of Sir Thomas Malory. Her analysis shows that *raptus* was seen primarily as a crime against property, although sexual violation is nevertheless recognised as a wrong. The knight who 'forces' ladies violates the chivalric code as much as his victim's body. Phillips's concern is more with the evidence of legal treatises, statute law, and the evidence of litigation, but as with Menuge's study, the symbiotic relationship Saunders uncovers between romance and legal narratives is often striking. Thus the description of alleged rapes as occurring in woods, parks, or moor land contained in legal records mirrors romance descriptions; Malory's Sir Perys de Forest Savage, a serial rapist, epitomises what Saunders describes as the 'heathen and hostile world beyond the court'. Where, however, Kathryn Gravdal sees rape narratives contained in legal records as in some way normalising rape, and Barbara Hanawalt as providing voyeuristic and salacious detail, Phillips suggests that the purpose was instead to draw attention to those crimes most deserving of penalty, such as the rape of girls.

Phillips's primary concern, however, is to show how the legal discourse on rape changed in significant ways between the time of *Glanvill* and the statutes of Westminster I and II. Characterising medieval rape law as focusing on the body rather than the will, she distinguishes a shift from first 'the bleeding body', subsequently 'the deflowered body', finally to the 'abducted' or 'absent body'. Phillips locates these changes in the context of the growing influence of the aristocracy first in the enforcement of the law and subsequently in the framing of the law. By the fifteenth century the conflation of rape and abduction described by Saunders was almost complete and the victim of rape was no longer primarily the wronged woman, but rather the (aristocratic) father, husband, or guardian who claimed authority over her.

Women, Power and Protection in Tenth- and Eleventh-Century England

VICTORIA THOMPSON

Introduction

THIS article explores a selection of late tenth- and eleventh-century texts in which women's voices are represented, with the aim of evaluating the nature of women's power and legal agency, and the extent to which that power was real or rhetorical. The first texts under consideration are the narratives commissioned by eleventh-century English queens, the *Encomium Emma Reginae* and the *Vita Eadwardi*, and the ways in which these were deployed to recreate personal and national history. The article then surveys the legal situation of women in tenth- and eleventh-century England, their access to land, moveable wealth and power, and their wills. It then moves on to consider the roles powerful women might play in the imagination of the period by examining the character of Queen Wealhtheow in *Beowulf* and her presentation as an articulate and confrontational figure with access to valuable goods which she uses to influence political reality. It concludes with a case study of the will of Ælfflæd, a noble widow who died at the beginning of the eleventh century.

Power is a complex concept; it is not used here in the sense of 'absolute power' but as a form of what Nelson terms 'room for manoeuvre'.[1] How could noble and royal women, the only ones visible at this period, use their voices, their relationships and their property to bring about the results they desired? Even aristocratic women's access to a public voice was constrained, and the dozen surviving women's wills are among the few contexts in which we can see them structuring the narrative of their lives, 'telling their stories', in effect.

---

1 J.L. Nelson, 'The wary widow', *Property and Power in the Early Middle Ages*, ed. W. Davies and P. Fouracre (Cambridge, 1995), pp. 82–113, p. 83. Roberta Frank and Jocelyn Wogan-Browne discuss powerful late-Anglo-Saxon women also: Roberta Frank, '*Quid Hinieldus Cum Feminis*: The Hero and Women at the End of the First Millennium', pp. 7–25; Jocelyn Wogan-Browne, 'The Hero in Christian Reception: Ælfric and Heroic Poetry', pp. 324–46; both in T. Paroli, *La Funzione dell'Eroe Germanico: Storicà Metafora, Paradigma* (Rome, 1995).

The sources and their limitations

Turning first to the question of the nature of female status and experience in the late Anglo-Saxon period, it is necessary to acknowledge the limitations of the sources. The available data, whether legal, poetic, epistolary or hagiographical, deal overwhelmingly with topics of apparently neutral or explicitly male concern. Even where women are discussed, the writer is often identifiable as male. Other than the wills, the corpus of writing in a female voice consists of two short poems, *Wulf and Eadwacer* and *The Wife's Lament*, preserved in a tenth-century context,[2] a ninth- to tenth-century prayer-book where 'sinner' occurs in the feminine form *peccatrice*,[3] and a few letters from nuns among the eighth-century correspondence of Boniface. Fell characterises these letters as 'vivid' but in fact they are conventional and formulaic; Rosenthal compares them with Alfred's *Laws* and concludes that '[i]ndividuality was predominantly a male preserve . . . a woman's private letter turns out to be less assertive than the preface to a law code'.[4] The one narrative genre which was dominated by women, embroidery, has almost entirely disappeared, with only the Bayeux Tapestry and the embroideries from the tomb of St Cuthbert standing witness to the loss.[5] As a result, the surviving women's wills, the majority of which are cast in the first person, are among the very few pieces of Anglo-Saxon writing where a woman's voice speaks directly to her audience.

The narrower question of female legal autonomy is little easier to elucidate. The main sources of evidence are the series of law codes and various related legal documents. These often explicitly refer only to men; in some cases the pronouns used are ambiguous and may refer to men only or to both men and women.[6] Women are usually only discussed as such where sexual crimes are concerned or where their marital or religious condition is relevant. Women are not perceived as having independent status; rather they are defined by the position and *wergild* (the sum of money at which a life was valued) of the man with whom they are associated. This said, there is evidence that women had some choice in whom they married: the Laws of Cnut

---

[2] Both are in the Exeter Book: G.P. Krapp and E.V.K. Dobbie, eds., *The Exeter Book* (New York, 1936), pp. 179–80, 210–11.

[3] C. Fell, *Women in Anglo-Saxon England* (Oxford, 1986), p. 127.

[4] Fell, *Women in Anglo-Saxon England*, pp. 111 ff.; J.T. Rosenthal, 'Anglo-Saxon Attitudes: Men's Sources, Women's History', *Medieval Women and the Sources of Medieval History*, ed. J.T. Rosenthal (London, 1990), pp. 259–84, 268–69.

[5] All contemporary references to embroiderers assume they are female: A. Christie, *English Medieval Embroidery* (Oxford, 1938), Appendix 1.

[6] M.P. Richards and B.J. Stanfield, 'Concepts of Anglo-Saxon Women in the Laws', *New Readings on Women in Old English Literature*, eds. H. Damico and A.H. Olsen (Indiana, 1990), pp. 89–99.

of 1020–1023 insist that no widow or maiden 'is ever to be forced to marry a man whom she herself dislikes'.[7] Furthermore, married women and widows had a degree of financial independence: one instance occurs in the marriage agreement between Wulfric and the un-named sister of Archbishop Wulfstan, drawn up around 1014–1016, in which she is given estates variously for her own lifetime, for three lifetimes, and 'to grant to whomsoever she pleased during her lifetime or after her death'.[8] The namelessness of the woman, however, defined only in relation to her male kin, undercuts the impression of autonomy. A degree of independence may also be demonstrated by the very fact that women made wills: if they had no say in the disposal of their property there would be no point in making the bequests. This argument could be countered, however, by pointing out that we do not know to what extent a woman might be only the mouthpiece of more powerful male interests controlling the woman's nominal property from behind the scenes. The argument for a limited autonomy within closely defined parameters is strengthened by the behaviour of the fictional Wealhtheow, who is shown using her power to persuade rather than to compel.

The Question of Female Autonomy

Women's access to land, treasure and the rhetoric of power

The highest-ranking women of the tenth and eleventh centuries are the only ones visible in the surviving sources, and even they are elusive. The only lay-women whose wills survive are the close relations of kings and ealdormen[9] and it is almost impossible to discover what access to land and property was available to them, let alone to women lower down the social scale. Even where the royal and noble women are concerned, the debate over the extent of their legal agency is also unresolved. Recent opinions range from arguing for their near-complete autonomy[10] to concluding that their choices were limited almost out of existence.[11] In the texts under examination here there are several examples of women apparently acting powerfully and independently. Even if women's power was rhetorical rather than actual, the wills, the

---

7 II Cnut 74, translated in D. Whitelock, ed. and tr., *English Historical Documents c. 500–1042* (London, 1968), p. 429.
8 Ibid., pp. 547–48.
9 D. Whitelock, *Anglo-Saxon Wills* (Cambridge, 1930), VIII, pp. 20–23; XIV, pp. 34–37; XV, pp. 38–43; XXXII, pp. 84–87.
10 Fell, *Women in Anglo-Saxon England*, p. 21.
11 A wide range of interpretations of the roles of Anglo-Saxon women is discussed by P. Stafford, 'Women and the Norman Conquest', *Transactions of the Royal Historical Society*, Ser. 6, vol. 4 (1994), pp. 221–49.

texts sponsored by Queen Emma and Queen Edith, and *Beowulf* share an understanding of that rhetoric.

The voices of powerful women

That women were capable of sophistication in manipulating language to influence their situations is evident in the two eleventh-century Latin texts commissioned by English queens, the *Encomium Emmae Reginae* and the *Vita Eadwardi*. These accounts of recent events were written, respectively, for Emma, queen of first Æthelræd and then Cnut, and her daughter-in-law Edith, queen of Edward the Confessor. They are highly partial accounts, presenting telling narratives of the overriding concerns of the two queens.

The *Encomium Emmae* was written in 1041-2, after Cnut's death, when Emma seemed secure as the mother of the newly-enthroned Harthacnut, Cnut's son, and Edward, Æthelræd's son, who had been recalled to England to share in his half-brother's reign. It glosses over the problems that Edward was the older brother of Harthacnut and that the succession had not gone smoothly by simply ignoring Emma's first marriage, to Æthelræd, and painting a picture of a united family.[12] By redrawing her family tree and its recent past in this way, Emma hoped to recreate it, although she was unsuccessful;[13] the accuracy of her depiction may be judged by the fact that, as soon as he succeeded in 1042, Edward confiscated all her land and treasure.[14] Emma's ambitious attempt to rewrite history is comparable to Wealhtheow, who also uses her eloquence to describe a harmonious royal family ruling a loyal land, hoping thereby to bring this happy state of affairs into being.

In the *Vita Eadwardi*, written over a period from 1065 to 1067, the intention of the work was originally the glorification of the house of Godwin, Edith's own family, and this is evident in Book One in which the often stormy relationship between Edward and Godwin is presented as one of harmony. The second book was written after the deaths of her brothers at Stamford Bridge and Hastings, and the focus of the work becomes instead a quasi-hagiographical treatment of her late husband, Edward.[15] By presenting Edward as saintly and celibate, Edith hoped to justify their childlessness and retain her status and property under Norman rule. Edith shines in the reflected glory of her father, brothers and husband in a narrative that inciden-

---

[12] A. Campbell, ed., *Encomium Emmae Reginae*, Camden Classic Reprints 4 (revised edn, Cambridge, 1998), p. 52.
[13] P. Stafford, *Queen Emma and Queen Edith: Queenship and Women's Power in Eleventh-Century England* (Oxford, 1997), p. 29.
[14] F. Barlow, *Edward the Confessor* (London, 1970), p. 76.
[15] F. Barlow, ed. and trans., *The Life of King Edward who rests at Westminster* (revised edn, Oxford, 1992), p. xvi.

tally also emphasizes the precarious state of a woman caught up in a feud between her own family and her husband's, a ubiquitous theme in *Beowulf*.[16]

These women are able to manipulate the writing of history to their own advantage. They are constructing a past, while in the wills and Wealhtheow's speech there is a comparable attempt to construct the future. In both genres we see objects and relationships manipulated with the aim of influencing events in a very specific way for many years to come.

Women, land and material culture

Having established that women could at least theoretically dispose of their property in law, it is time to look briefly at the nature of that property as it appears in the wills. It falls into two broad categories, land and treasure, which covers everything from gold to drinking-cups, horses and tapestries. By looking closely at the specific bequests, it may be possible to discover to what extent property could be used by the individual to further her or his own ends.

Land was held in two main ways, *bocland* and *folcland*.[17] *Folcland* was inalienable and therefore does not appear in the wills, whereas acquired land, that is, *bocland*, was alienable and heritable.[18] Land and its control were the basic sources of wealth and power in Anglo-Saxon England: as a result, bequests of land were more likely to be closely monitored by interested kin than were bequests of individual objects. There is evidence for this in the late tenth-century wills of Ealdorman Ælfgar of Essex and his daughters Æthelflæd and Ælfflæd, the only surviving group of wills to come identifiably from one family.[19] Read in isolation, the women's wills appear to bequeath land freely to kin, associates and religious foundations; reference to their father's will, however, makes it clear that in fact they are following his instructions with little deviation.[20] Stafford suggests that Ælfgar himself may have been fulfilling the king's wishes in steering the ownership of land from generation to generation in one particular course.[21] Mayer, in a study of the queen's

16 E. John, *Reassessing Anglo-Saxon England* (Manchester, 1996), p. xvi; the comparatively high level of violence among aristocrats in England at the period is discussed by J. Gillingham, '1066 and the Introduction of Chivalry into England', *Law and Government in Medieval England and Normandy*, ed. G. Garnett and J. Hudson (Cambridge, 1994), pp. 31–55, 38–39.

17 H.R. Loyn, *The Norman Conquest* (3rd edn, London, 1982), p. 76. For a discussion of the complexities of *bocland*, see M.T. Clanchy, *From Memory to Written Record, England 1066–1307* (2nd edn, Oxford, 1993), pp. 53–54.

18 J. Hudson, 'Anglo-Norman land law and the origins of property', Garnett and Hudson, *Law and Government*, pp. 198–222, p. 201.

19 P. Stafford, *Unification and Conquest: A Political and Social History of England in the Tenth and Eleventh Centuries* (London, 1989), p. 175.

20 K.A. Lowe, 'The Nature and Effect of the Anglo-Saxon Vernacular Will', *Legal History* 19 (1988), pp. 23–61, p. 41.

21 P. Stafford, 'Women and the Norman Conquest', pp. 231–32.

access to land, points out that even the country's most powerful women were constrained by and dependent on the will of their male kin.[22]

Land was not the only thing that people had to bequeath. Men of the rank of thegn or higher were obliged to leave horses, gold and war-gear[23] to the king as their *heriot* (from *here-geatu*, military equipment), as set out in II Cnut 71.[24] This statute makes no reference to payment by women, but the tax acted as a contractual *quid pro quo* guaranteeing that the king would honour the terms of the will, a guarantee equally necessary to both sexes. While the term *heriot* occurs only once in a woman's will,[25] several list extensive bequests to the king which should surely be understood as an equivalent payment,[26] perhaps indicating equivalent status.[27] The joint will of Ælfswith and her husband Brihtric first lists the gold, weaponry, horses, hawks and hounds due to the king, then leaves a gold armlet and a stallion 'to the queen . . . for her advocacy that the will might stand'.[28] Clearly the queen's voice was worth having: this is another indication of the expectation that women could plead their causes in public, although the queen here receives treasure rather than bestows it. The contractual nature of Anglo-Saxon wills is discussed more fully below, but should be noted here as an important element in the payment of *heriot*.

Valuable property also appears in the wills in the form of personal bequests: Wulfwaru leaves the women of her household 'a good, well-decorated chest';[29] Ælfgifu leaves her brother's wife Æthelflæd 'the headband which I have lent her'.[30] Although there is some overlap between the different kinds of material culture mentioned in men's and women's wills, goods for the most part are gender-specific. As one might expect from a culture that divided women and men into *wifmenn* and *wæpenmenn*, woven goods are more common in women's bequests and weapons in men's. A comparable instance is the language used by King Alfred in his will where he describes his grandfather bequeathing land 'on the spear-side not on the spindle-side' (*on þa sperehealfe næs on þa spinlhealfe*), in contrast to his own intention to

---

[22] M.A. Mayer, 'The Queen's "Demesne" in Later Anglo-Saxon England', *The Culture of Christendom: Essays in Medieval History in Commemoration of Denis L.T. Bethell*, ed. M.A. Mayer (London, 1993), pp. 75–104.

[23] For a discussion of the poetic and prose treatment of weapons and treasure, see E. Tyler, 'Treasure and Convention in Old English Verse', *Notes and Queries*, New Series vol. 43, no. 1 (1996), pp. 2–13.

[24] Whitelock, *English Historical Documents*, p. 429.

[25] Whitelock, *Wills*, XXXII, p. 84.

[26] Whitelock, *Wills*, VIII, pp. 20–23; XIV, pp. 34–37; XV, pp. 38–43; XXIX, pp. 76–77.

[27] P. Stafford, 'The King's Wife in Wessex, 800–1066', Damico and Olsen, *New Readings on Women*, pp. 58–78, p. 65.

[28] *Dære hlæfdian ... to forespræce. þæt se cwyde standan moste.* Whitelock, *Wills*, XI, p. 26.

[29] *Ic geann eallum minum hiredwifmannum to gemanum anes godres castenes wel gerenodes.* Whitelock, *Wills*, XXI, p. 64.

[30] *Æþælfledæ minæs broþur wifæ þæs bændes þæ ic hire alæneð hæfdæ.* Whitelock, *Wills*, VIII, 20.

bequeath it 'in the female line or the male line' (*swa wifhanda swa wæpned-handa*).[31] Fell suggests that the household textiles produced by women remained in some sense their property.[32] Ælfflæd gave the monastery at Ely a tapestry representing her husband's deeds, and this association between women and textiles also emerges in *Beowulf*, when Wealhtheow gives Beowulf a *hrægl* (cloak, 1217) in contrast to the weapons, horses and mail given by her husband Hrothgar (1020 ff.) Lengths of woven cloth might not be as important as woods and farms, but they had a significant place in the nexus of gift-giving.[33]

Wills

The surviving Anglo-Saxon wills, some sixty in number, date from the early ninth century onwards and are preserved as single sheet charters and in monastic cartularies where they record bequests to the religious houses, in particular to Abingdon (Oxon), Bury (Suffolk), Winchester (Hants) and Christchurch, Canterbury (Kent). They differ from modern wills in many respects, crucially in that while a modern will is a 'unilateral written disposition to take effect on the death of the testator',[34] its Anglo-Saxon predecessor was a bilateral, oral disposition, often containing elements that took effect within the lifetime of the testator. A modern will requires an executor; only occasionally do the Anglo-Saxon wills name a *forespræca* or advocate, though, as noted above, the king was expected to honour the will in return for *heriot* and the queen may also have had a particular role as protector of widows' claims.[35]

The oral nature of the will was also paramount: the written document was only a record of the witnessed oral performance and not a legal requirement: many, probably most, wills of the ninth to eleventh centuries were never recorded in writing. This is of course true in the later medieval period as well: Clanchy asserts that the will was primarily oral until the thirteenth century, even when it became the norm for it to be written down. By the thirteenth century a nuncupative will was presented by its witnesses to the probate officer, by whom it was written down, and written wills were not legally required until 1677.[36]

---

31 F.E. Harmer, *Select English Historical Documents of the Ninth and Tenth Centuries* (Cambridge, 1914), p. 19.
32 Fell, *Women in Anglo-Saxon England*, pp. 44–45.
33 Stafford, *Queen Emma and Queen Edith*, p. 157.
34 H.D. Hazeltine, 'General Preface: Comments on the Writings Known as Anglo-Saxon Wills', Whitelock, *Wills*, vii–xl, vii.
35 Stafford, *Queen Emma and Queen Edith*, p. 158.
36 Clanchy, *From Memory to Written Record, England*, p. 254; M.M. Sheehan, 'English wills and the records of the ecclesiastical and civil jurisdictions', *Journal of Medieval History* 14 (1988), pp.

The oral nature of the wills is reflected in their language: a will is often called a *cwyde*, literally 'speech', giving us the modern *bequeath*; to die intestate is to be *cwydeleas* – speechless. The language of the wills, English rather than Latin, may point to their being close transcriptions of the original speeches,[37] although it is possible that many of the texts have been edited in the copying process, with the bequests that later scribes considered irrelevant to the needs of their own day being omitted. The relationship between the oral ceremony and the production of legal documents is uncertain:[38] the language of some suggests that a document was first written to be read out in public,[39] whereas others may have been drawn up after the event.[40] Certainly, the phrasing of many of the wills assumes an audience: Æthelwold's will of the mid-tenth century emphasizes this, ending his will with 'then I wish that the things be shared out for my soul just as I now said to the friends with whom I spoke'.[41] The members of that original audience of the *cwyde* are sometimes mentioned: Ordnoth and his wife announced their will in the presence of the community of the Old Minster, Winchester, probably in the late tenth century.[42] At the reading of a modern will, the testator is safely buried; when an Anglo-Saxon will was made public the testator, or in this discussion testatrix, was at the centre of the action and expecting to live for some time to come.[43]

Difference between men's and women's wills

Two differences between men's and women's wills have already been touched on: men are far more likely to use the term *heriot* and women are more likely to bequeath sets of bed-clothes, tapestries and table linen, as well as other household effects.[44] Other differences derive more from context than

---

3–12, p. 4 and *The Will in Medieval England*, Pontifical Institute of Medieval Studies: Studies and Texts VI (1963), pp. 186–67; B. Danet and B. Bogoch, 'Orality, literacy and performativity in Anglo-Saxon wills', *Language and the Law*, ed. J. Gibbon (New York, 1994), 100–35, 106.

[37] Hazeltine in Whitelock, *Wills*, xv.

[38] For a discussion of the circumstances of charter production, see S. Kelly, 'Anglo-Saxon Lay Society and the Written Word', *The Uses of Literacy in Early Medieval Europe*, ed. R. McKitterick (Cambridge, 1990), pp. 37–62, p. 44.

[39] Danet and Bogoch, 'Orality, literacy and performativity in Anglo-Saxon wills', p. 105, citing the will of Æthelstan, which addresses *þe minne cwyde gehyron rædan* ([those] who hear my will read).

[40] Kelly, 'Anglo-Saxon Lay Society and the Written Word', p. 44.

[41] *þonne wylle ic þæt þæt sie gedeled fore mine sawle swa swa ic nu þam freondum sæde þæ ic to spræc.* Harmer, *Select English Historical Documents of the Ninth and Tenth Centuries*, p. 33.

[42] *Þis is seo gewitnes ðe Ordnod. Wile habban godæs 7 his hirede on ealdan mynstre. þæt is þæt he 7 is wif cwæden on heora gewitnesse* . . . Whitelock, *Wills*, V, p. 18.

[43] Lowe, 'The Anglo-Saxon Vernacular Will', p. 38.

[44] Stafford, *Unification and Conquest*, pp. 164–65.

content, the major difference being that women's status depended on their position as maidens, wives or widows, whereas men's marital status made no difference to their ability to own property or their visibility in the laws. As a result, the women who are discernible in the historical record as having disposable lands and possessions are overwhelmingly likely to be widows, whereas men's marital status goes unrecorded.

That widows could be married without their consent is inferred from the laws prohibiting the practice,[45] and there is a clear awareness among legislators of their vulnerability.[46] Protection was therefore a problem for them. Rich widows were useful to power-hungry men: Cnut married Emma, Æthelræd's widow, to strengthen his claim to the English throne, and Harold Godwinson married Alditha, widow of Gruffydd of Wales, although both men seem to have been married already.[47] The dangers of widowhood shape the experience of both the women who are the main focus of this study: Ælfflæd was the widow of Byrtnoth, the Ealdorman of Essex killed at the Battle of Maldon against the Vikings in 991; Wealhtheow is still a wife when she appears in *Beowulf*, but in her speech she anticipates her husband's death and her own ensuing vulnerability.

Two Case Studies: Wealtheow and Ælfflæd

It is now time to look in more detail at two particular examples of women's voices in action, one set in the imaginative context of Hrothgar's hall, the other rooted in the reality of Æthelræd's court. Looking first at *Beowulf*, I suggest that Wealhtheow's situation is a romanticised dramatisation of the concerns and challenges facing aristocratic women at the time that the poem as we have it was written down. There are notable similarities between the setting and the vocabulary of Ælfflæd's will (discussed fully below) and *Beowulf* 1175–1231: in the poem Wealhtheow dispenses treasure and makes a public speech with the aim of creating a reciprocal relationship that will gain her protection; in the legal text, Ælfflæd makes a public statement in which she also dispenses treasure with the aim of creating reciprocal relationships to gain herself protection. Although the two documents come from wholly different genres, they were both produced around the year 1000,[48] both are

---

45 V Æthelræd 21, II Cnut 73 and Stafford, ibid., pp. 146, 148.

46 Fell, *Women in Anglo-Saxon England*, pp. 61–62.

47 I.W. Walker, *Harold: The Last Anglo-Saxon King* (Stroud, 1997), pp. 129–31.

48 The *Beowulf* manuscript, British Library Cotton Vitellius A XV, is dated on palaeographical grounds to 'the end of the tenth century': F. Klaeber, ed., *Beowulf and the Fight at Finnsburh*, 3rd edn (Boston, 1950), p. xcvi (all references to *Beowulf* are to this edition); Ælfflæd's will must post-date the death of her husband in 991 and Dorothy Whitelock dates it to '1002 or a year or two earlier', Whitelock, *Anglo-Saxon Wills*, XV, pp. 38–43, 141.

written in English, and both are informative about the quality of women's power at the highest level of society.

Beowulf, while a work of fiction, has independently-attested historical events at its core, and Hrothgar, Wealhtheow's husband, is also remembered as a character in Icelandic sagas.[49] *Beowulf's* original audience may well have perceived the work as historical as much as fictional, with the poet recreating his traditional characters to meet contemporary expectations. Although Ælfflæd was not (as far as we know) commemorated in verse, the death of her husband in 991 at the hands of the Vikings is the theme of *The Battle of Maldon*,[50] characterized by its intentionally 'archaic, heroic' language,[51] suggesting that the tenth- and eleventh-century aristocracy self-consciously represented itself as the inheritors of a heroic past.

This is not the place to consider the late Anglo-Saxon understanding of what constituted history, or the nature of the audience of Old English poetry. Nor am I arguing that *Beowulf* gives us an accurate vignette of life at the court of Æthelræd the Unready or Cnut: the date of the original composition of *Beowulf* remains unknown and is probably unknowable.[52] However, the manuscript is exactly contemporary with Ælfflæd's will. The material culture of cups, weapons, horses, tapestries and arm-rings described in the wills and the poem is also similar. Most relevantly, as mentioned above, Wealhtheow gives Beowulf a cloak (1217) and gold-adorned tapestries decorated the walls of Heorot,[53] while textiles figure largely in women's wills and Ælfflæd gave Ely a tapestry in memory of her husband.[54] A comparison of the texts suggests that Ælfflæd would have recognised Wealhtheow's conduct, concerns and phraseology as those of a contemporary, as much as those of a distant, legendary figure. Wealhtheow, a challenging and articulate character, dramatises the range of rhetorical options open to women of Ælfflæd's background and generation.

The context of Wealhtheow's speech

Beowulf has dispatched the monster, Grendel, and a feast in his honour is being held in the royal hall. During the feast, Queen Wealhtheow makes a speech and rewards Beowulf for his valour. The gathering appears to be one of

49 Klaeber, *Beowulf*, p. xxxiv.
50 R. Hamer, *A Choice of Anglo-Saxon Verse* (London, 1970), pp. 48–70.
51 U. Schwab, 'The Battle of Maldon: A Memorial Poem', *The Battle of Maldon: Fiction and Fact*, ed. J. Cooper (London, 1993), pp. 63–85, p. 63.
52 For a broad range of opinion on dating *Beowulf*, see C. Chase, ed., *The Dating of Beowulf*, Toronto Old English Series, no. 6 (1981); A.J. Frantzen, *Desire for Origins: New Language, Old English, and Teaching the Tradition* (New Brunswick and London, 1990), p. 171.
53 *Goldfag scinon/ web æfter wagum.* (994b–995a)
54 *Liber Eliensis*, ed. E.O. Blake (Royal Historical Society, London, 1962), II, pp. 63, 136; C.R. Dodwell, *Anglo-Saxon Art: A New Perspective* (Manchester, 1982), pp. 133–35.

celebration, but it is beset with irony and foreboding; Wealhtheow, concerned to further the interests of her children, is faced with threats from two
directions at the feast.

The first threat comes from her husband. Before the feast begins, Hrothgar
welcomes Beowulf in a speech where he appears to offer to adopt the hero
(946–949a). Hrothgar has two sons of his own with Wealhtheow, but they are
still too young to be warriors; his speech implies that he is prepared to over-
ride their claims in the interest of the defence of Denmark.[55] He is also prepared to ignore the claims of his nephew Hrothulf. Neither Beowulf nor
anyone else responds to Hrothgar's offer at this point, but the poet hints at
the mood in the hall by referring to the treacherous deeds which some of the
warriors in the hall may already be plotting:

> Their kinsmen Hrothgar and Hrothulf, bold-minded, gladly drank
> many cups of mead in the high hall. Heorot was all filled with friends;
> for the time being none among the Scyldings performed any deeds of
> treachery.[56]

Hrothulf is the second threat to Wealhtheow: he is the already adult nephew
of her husband and will lay claim to the inheritance of her boys, Hrethric and
Hrothmund. The poet never says in so many words that Hrothulf will be a
traitor but it is strongly implied in this passage and explicit from other
sources.[57] Indeed, Heorot's destruction through fire and treachery has been
foretold from the start of the poem (82b–85).

The content of Wealhtheow's speech

Wealhtheow walks among this highly-charged group of men with her vessel
of mead. It has been argued that the role of women at these gatherings was to
promote harmony,[58] but Wealhtheow's aim here is publicly to challenge her

---

[55] J.M. Hill, 'Beowulf and the Danish Succession: Gift-giving as an Occasion for Complex
Gesture', *Medievalia et Humanistica* 11 (1982), pp. 177–97.

[56]   . . . *fægere geþægon*
medoful manig   magas þara
swiðhicgende   on sele þam hean,
Hroðgar ond Hroþulf.   Heorot innan wæs
freondum afylled;   nalles facenstafas
Þeod-Scyldingas   þenden fremedon.   (1014b–1019)

[57] F.C.Robinson, 'History, Religion, Culture: The Background Necessary for Teaching *Beowulf*',
ibid., '*The Tomb of Beowulf* and Other Essays on Old English (Oxford, 1993), pp. 36–51, p. 38.

[58] M.J. Enright, *Lady with a Mead Cup: Ritual, Prophecy and Lordship from La Tène to the Viking
Age* (Dublin and Portland, OR, 1996), p. 14; L. John Sklute, 'Freoðuwebbe in Old English Poetry',
New Readings on Women in Old English Poetry, ed. H. Damico and A.H. Olsen (Bloomington and
Indianapolis, 1990), pp. 204–10.

husband. She takes the cup to him first, bidding him to show his appreciation of Beowulf, but also to remember his priorities *sub specie aeternitatis*:

> 'I have been told that you wish to have this warrior for your son. Heorot is cleansed, the bright ring-hall; partake of its many rewards while you may, and leave the people and the kingdom to your sons, when you have to die, to face fate's decree.'[59]

She is in a quandary, trying to deduce whether Hrothulf or Beowulf presents the greater danger, and decides to endorse Hrothulf, describing him in glowing terms, then saying:

> 'I believe that he will repay our children with goodness, if he remembers everything that we two have done out of kindness for his pleasure and his honour, formerly, while he was growing up.'[60]

Wealhtheow is trying to create the emotional situation that she is describing but she can only hope that her words will have the intended result. She then takes the cup to Beowulf, giving him a cloak and armrings, and decides to try to hedge her bets, asking Beowulf to stand a mentor to her sons:

> 'Distinguish yourself with skill, and be kind in counsel to these young men. I shall remember your reward for this . . .
> May you be blessed henceforth, prince! I grant you treasures sincerely.
> May you be good to my sons in your deeds, being happy yourself!'[61]

Wealhtheow concludes her speech with a bravura piece of description, trying to bring about the peace and amity she desires by sheer effort of will:

> 'Here each earl is true to the other, mild in mood, loyal to his lord, the

59 Me man sægde,   þæt þu ðe for sunu wolde
    hererinc habban.   Heorot is gefælsod,
    beahsele beorhta;   bruc þenden þu mote
    manigra medo,   ond þinum magum læf
    folc ond rice,   þonne ðu forð scyle,
    metodsceaft seon.   (1175–1180a)
60 wene ic þæt he mid gode   gyldan wille
    uncran eaferan,   gif he þæt eal gemon,
    hwæt wit to willan   on to worðmyndum
    umborwesendum ær   arna gefremedon   (1184–1187)
61 cen þec mid cræfte,   ond þyssum cnyhtum wes
    lara liðe!   Ic þe þas lean geman . . . (1212–20)
                Wes þenden þu lifige
    æþeling, eadig!   Ic þe an tela
    sincgestreona.   Beo þu suna minum
    dædum gedefe,   dreamhealdende!   (1224b–1227)

thegns are united, the people are eager, the followers at their drink do as
I pray.'[62]

The audience is already aware that this is not true and Heorot is a dangerous
place, full of rivalry and treachery. This speech has been described as pro-
phetic,[63] but her forecast is faulty where her own family and folk are concerned. In Wealhtheow, the poet presents a picture of a strong-minded and
independent woman, with access to a particular range of valuable objects,
namely ornaments and textiles, which she can use to construct independent
networks of obligation. Denied the weapons, naked symbols of male power,
and described as 'the people's pledge of peace' (*friðusibb folca* 2017a), she must
use more subtle material gifts and verbal skills both to confront her husband
head on and to offer alternative solutions to the dangers which she and her
children will encounter. Although Wealhtheow is a fictional character, she
negotiates problems that were real and relevant to women in the late tenth
and eleventh centuries, providing a context for the consideration of the
voices of individual historical women.

The Will of Ælfflæd

Ælfflæd's will survives, together with the will of her older sister Æthelflæd,
in an early eleventh-century Bury charter (British Library, Harley Charter 43,
C.4). Ælfflæd's will is of particular interest, firstly because of the associated
family wills, and secondly because she had been a great heiress but had no
children of her own and seems to have had no close male kin to protect her
interests. As a result, her familial concerns differ from those of Wealhtheow:
it is her past rather than her future that she wants to safeguard, the graves of
her ancestors rather than the lives of her children. In her need to protect
those concerns, however, her situation parallels Wealhtheow's very closely. It
is possible to unpick Ælfflæd's will and identify the ways in which she uses
her limited freedom of manoeuvre to construct fictive kinship relationships
to protect herself and her blood relations who have predeceased her.

Like many of the wills, Ælfflæd's testament shifts between the first and
third person singular, beginning *Ælfflæd gæswytelaþ* (Ælfflæd declares) but
switching in the next sentence to *Ærest þæt ic an* (First that I grant) and continuing in the first person. This change of person may arise from the process
of committing speech to writing, the scribe being unsure whether he should

---

62   *Her is æghwylc eorl   oþrum getrywe,*
       modes milde,   mandrihtne hold,
       þegnas syndon geþwære, þeod ealgearo,
       druncne dryhtguman doð swa ic bidde. (1228–1231)
63 H. Damico, *Beowulf's Wealhtheow and the Valkyrie Tradition* (Madison, 1984), p. 97.

produce a transcription or a narrative,[64] or it may be intended to give an air of formality to the statement.

Her first bequest, *heriot de facto* if not *de jure*, is to King Æthelræd: she leaves him eight estates, two rings (*bæha*), two drinking cups (*sopcuppan*) and a silver vessel (*seolfran fæt*). In return, she requires the king's protection:

> And I humbly pray you, beloved lord, for the love of God, and for the love of my lord's soul, and for the love of my sister's soul, that you protect the holy place at Stoke where my ancestors rest, and the possessions that they gave thither forever as a free right of God.[65]

As the phrase *þæ leof æadmodlice bidde* (I humbly pray you, beloved lord) shows, the will is addressed directly to Æthelræd and may have been originally spoken in his presence.

She goes on to bequeath numerous estates of which she had the usufruct but which, as her father Ælfgar and sister Æthelflæd's wills had made clear, had long been promised to various religious houses on her death. These monasteries eventually got more property than Ælfgar had originally foreseen: he had repeatedly made it clear in his will that, should his daughters have children, those grandchildren could inherit,[66] but neither Ælfflæd nor Æthelflæd appears to have had surviving offspring. The Suffolk estates of Baythorn, Lavenham, Colne and Tey are all specified by Ælfgar as heritable, but the first one ends up going to the monastery at Barking and the rest to Stoke by Nayland, where many of their family were buried. Ælfflæd then leaves estates to Ely, 'where my lord's body lies buried',[67] although she does not indicate where she wishes to be buried herself, leaving open the question of whether she would join her blood-kin or her husband in death. She mentions that one of the estates left to Ely, Rettendon, had been her *morgengifu* (marriage gift) from Byrtnoth; another, Ditton, had already been left to Ely by Æthelflæd, and the third, Soham, had been left to Ely by Byrtnoth. Thus, very little of the property in Ælfflæd's will was hers to dispose of freely: she was already constrained by other people's earlier bequests.

Up to this point, Ælfflæd's will has been a conventional mixture of contracts with representatives of both the worldly and the heavenly kingdoms, *fore gode [and] fore worldæ*, disposing of her property *post mortem*. But, exceptionally, the closing section of the will changes focus and concentrates on her situation *ante mortem*. In this she bequeaths estates to two men, both named

---

[64] Danet and Bogoch, 'Orality, literacy and performativity in Anglo-Saxon wills', pp. 110–111.

[65] *7 þæ leof æadmodlice bidde for godes luuan. 7 for mines hlafordæs sawle lufan. 7 for minræ swystor sawlæ lufan þæt þu amundie þa halgan stowæ et Stocæ þæ mine yldran on restaþ. 7 þa are þæ hi þiderin sæeadon a to freogon godæs rihte.* Whitelock, *Wills*, XV, pp. 38–39.

[66] E.g. *And ouer aldreday ic an þat lond at Lavenham mine douhter childe gif þat god wille þat heo ani haueð.* Whitelock, *Wills*, II, pp. 6–7.

[67] *þer mines hlafordes lichoma rest*, Whitelock, *Wills*, XV, pp. 40–41.

Æthelmær, on condition that they assist her during her life as well as after her death. Although the coincidence of the name suggests there may be one rather than two legatees involved, the names are spelt differently in the manuscript and two different roles, *forespeca* and *mundiend*, are specified. The first clause reads:

> And I grant to Ealdorman Æthelmær the lands at Lelling after my day, with produce and people, exactly as it stands, on condition that he be, during my lifetime, my true friend and advocate and to my people also, and, after my death, be true friend and advocate to the holy foundation and property at Stoke, where my ancestors lie.[68]

The word for advocate, *forespeca*, can refer to people or documents. A godparent or a preface can equally be a *forespeca*, producing words before, or on behalf of, something else. As noted above, the queen could be the advocate of a will, pleading its cause on behalf of the deceased who could no longer speak for themselves.[69] The widowed Ælfflæd, however, clearly believes that her wishes need formal advocacy while she is still alive, since her own public voice is not strong enough.

This impression is reinforced by the second clause:

> And I grant the lands at Liston to Ethelmer my [. . . e] with the produce and the people exactly as it now stands, and humbly pray him that he will be my true friend and protector during my life, and after my death help that my will and those of my ancestors might stand.[70]

Unfortunately there is a hole in the manuscript, indicated by the square brackets, so the precise relationship between Ælfflæd and Ethelmer is unknown. She asks him to be her *mundiend*, protector, in the sole occurrence of this word in Old English. The estates she use to create these two relationships, Lelling and Litton, are not mentioned in the earlier wills of either Ælfgar or Æthelflæd and may therefore not have been family property, nor do they seem to have come from Ælfflæd's husband, Byrtnoth. They may thus have been her own property, free from the constraints imposed by obligation to family members, living or dead. Though we do not know the precise relationships of the two legatees to Ælfflæd, they were either not her kin, or not close enough to be identified as such.

---

[68] 7 Ic gean Æðelmære ældorman þe landes æt Lellinge ofer mine deg mid mete. 7 mid mannum, ælswa hit stent on þet gerad þæt he beo on minum life min fulla freod. 7 forespreca. 7 mira manna. 7 efter minum dege beo þara halgan stowe. 7 þeræ are ful freod. 7 forespeca æt Stocæ þe mine yldran on restaþ.

[69] Whitelock, *Wills*, XI, p. 26.

[70] 7 ic gean Þes landes æt Lissingtune Eðelmere mines ....e mid mete. 7 mid mannum ealswa hit stent, 7 hine eadmodlice bidde þæt he min fulla freod. 7 mundiend beo on minum dege. 7 efter minum dege gefelste þæt min cwide 7 mira yldran standan mote.

15

In these two clauses, Ælfflæd is using what freedom she has to construct or consolidate new relationships in order to preserve the identity of her family, even after its death and burial. The family monastery has literally become the embodiment of the family. We do not know whether her wishes were respected in the short term, but within three generations Ælfflæd's attempts to influence events had proved in vain: by 1066 the estates she had left to Stoke were in a variety of private hands and no-one remembered that the religious house had ever existed.[71]

The vocabulary of gift-giving

There are many parallels between the situations in which Wealhtheow and Ælfflæd find themselves; there are also similarities in the range of vocabulary that they employ. One of the verbs that Wealhtheow uses, *an* (from *ge-unnan*, to grant, *Beowulf* 1225) is also one of the commonest words used in the wills to describe bequeathing; Ælfflæd uses it ten times whereas she uses a form of *giefan* (give) four times, *becwædon* (bequeath) twice and *sædon* (say) once. This underlines the fact that Wealhtheow is not only giving Beowulf her blessing but also offering him a formal contract: concrete rewards in return for his good will and protection. In the next passage, she uses the word *bidde* (*Beowulf* 1231), also familiar from the wills: *Þæ leof æadmodlice bidde* (I humbly pray you, beloved lord) are the words with which Ælfflæd addresses Æthelræd when she beseeches him to protect Stoke by Nayland. This coincidence of vocabulary reinforces the impression that the relationships and social structures of *Beowulf* would have been familiar to a late tenth-century audience.

Conclusions

A comparison of these disparate texts suggests that the idea of a woman using rhetoric and property to take control of her situation was not unfamiliar in the late Anglo-Saxon period. Whether in the person of the fictional Wealhtheow, or the historical Emma, Edith and the producers of the wills, women are represented as able to construct and reconstruct their life stories, giving priority to certain places, people and events, and attempting, through wills, gifts and reciprocal relationships, to extend their power forward to control future events. What is less certain is whether this idea bore any relationship to reality. It is worth noting that these attempts to gain control failed: Ælfflæd's family monastery at Stoke is not mentioned in Domesday; Emma's property was confiscated by her son Edward on his accession in 1042.

---

71 Whitelock, *Wills*, p. 105, n.19. See also will XV, pp. 40–41.

The poet's depiction of Wealhtheow as a figure of tragic irony is coloured by the knowledge that her sons disappear out of legend. Furthermore, even where the texts under discussion were sponsored by women or claim to record their voices, they were almost certainly written by men: the *Beowulf* poet, the authors of the *Encomium Emmae* and the *Vita Eadwardi*, the scribe who copied Ælfflæd's will. Thus the women's own voices disappear under closer examination. In the end, what little survives of our evidence for the power of individual women is as insubstantial as a thread from one of their vanished tapestries.

Unfamiliar Territory: Women, Land and Law in Occitania, 1130–1250

JENNIFER SMITH

CRITICAL opinion on the experience and position of Occitan women has long taken as its basis the notion that Occitan legal and customary practices favoured women, as opposed to the systems in operation north of the Loire. The idea that the twelfth and thirteenth centuries in Occitania represented a moment of heightened prestige and power for women is widely accepted, and often unquestioned. For example, Philippe Wolff in his *Histoire du Languedoc* makes mention of the high position held by women in Occitania in the ninth and tenth centuries – for which, he notes, there is no contemporaneous northern equivalent – which leads him to ask whether there might be some indication of the position that would be afforded to Occitan women in the course of the twelfth century.[1] He does not go on to discuss what the position held by women in the twelfth century was; presumably he felt no need. The so-called 'golden interlude' articulated by Marti Aurell i Cardona[2] of the period between 1180 and 1230 in Occitania has been taken up with fervour by historians and literary critics to the point that it has become an unquestioned 'fact'. In this article I seek to question this 'fact' and to consider the role of women in Occitania, in particular the poetic *domna*, to ascertain to what level the Occitan woman was 'free', and how she was understood in contemporary authoritative discourses. I will suggest that far from reflecting a sanctioned position of high status for women, the title *domna* reflects a movement between poetic and administrative discourses which seeks to define women, and by defining, to contain them.

The problem of the simple view of the position of women in twelfth- and thirteenth-century Occitania so often advanced has been occasioned by the assumption of an easy relationship between literature and society. In this

---

1 Philippe Wolff, *Histoire du Languedoc* (Toulouse, 1967), pp. 136–37.
2 Marti Aurell i Cardona, 'La détérioration du statut de la femme aristocratique en Provence (Xe–XIIIe siècles)', *Le Moyen Age* 91 (1985), pp. 5–32, p. 22. Cardona postulates that there was a 'parenthèse dorée' between 1180 and 1230.

assumption, the apparently elevated position given to the *domna*[3] in the Occitan lyric – made even more certain by the presence of lyrics produced by women themselves – is seen to reflect the similarly high status of women in Occitan society generally. Joan Kelly made this connection in her influential article 'Did Women have a Renaissance?' when she suggested that 'courtly love' represented an 'ideological liberation of their [women's] sexual and affective powers'.[4] She drew this notion out into society by suggesting that such ideological liberation must necessarily have derived from a 'social ideal' that allowed, or even idealised, the transgression and even reversal of traditional gender roles in marriage, and that an examination of the society that produced this ideal would reveal as much.[5] In her examination Kelly sets up Occitania as a land where women ruled, owned land, and basically performed all of the same functions as did their men. Kelly sees women as a driving force behind the courtly lyric as a direct result of the strong positions they already held in their society.[6]

This kind of reading, or rather misreading, of both the lyric and the social dynamics as represented by the genre has in some circumstances led to an elision of the effects of other social factors on the position of women, leaving Occitan women seemingly entirely determined by the genre alone.[7] The majority of historical and literary study of women in this time period works from undemonstrable assumptions about the high status of women. Exactly to what extent women held superior positions, and in particular *why*, is never made very clear. Cardona postulates that women's status in Occitania underwent several ups and downs between the late tenth and early thirteenth centuries, finally plummeting after the acceptance of changes to marriage

---

[3] For the purposes of the article *domna* is the title given to the notionally 'beloved' in the lyrics of the troubadours. It is the vernacular form of *domina*, the feminine equivalent of the masculine *dominus*, though whether this implies individual power for the woman bearing the title, or merely represents the status of her husband is by no means certain. Glynnis Cropp has suggested that the use of the title *domna* in the troubadour lyric is specific to the troubadour lyric, and not part of a more general poetic tradition, and thus derived from within the society in which the poets composed. She sees it as an honorific bestowed on a very high rank of woman, particularly the wife of a nobleman. See *Le Vocabulaire Courtois des Troubadours de l'Epoque Classique* (Genève, 1975), pp. 26–28. For Mundy, *domna* is simply a title assumed by all adult women participating in recorded transactions, and even, he suggests, in ordinary speech, regardless of social station: John Hine Mundy, *Men and Women at Toulouse in the Age of the Cathars* (Toronto, 1990), p. 37.

[4] Joan Kelly, 'Did Women Have a Renaissance?', in *Women, History and Theory* (Chicago, 1984), p. 26.

[5] Ibid., p. 26.

[6] Ibid., p. 30.

[7] See for example Anne Callahan, 'The Trobairitz', in *French Women Writers: a Bio-bibliographical source book*, eds. Eva Martin Sartori and Dorothy Wynne Zimmerman (Westport, 1991), pp. 495–502. Callahan suggests that 'the privileged status of aristocratic women in Occitania was due in part to the sexual power given by the twelfth-century philosophy of love, *fin'amors* . . . .': pp. 495–6, but does not suggest what other factors might have been at least partially involved in elevating Occitan women's status.

practices and the reintroduction of Roman Law on a large scale in the period following 1230. He demonstrates this 'golden interlude' using the evidence left from one woman, Guilhema Garcin, whose experience of inheritance and landholding argues for women's rights to own and administer property being strongly upheld in this period. Far from being an unexceptional woman, however, Guilhema was the daughter of a knightly urban family whose brother (Cardona does not tell us if she had any others) joined the Hospitallers when young thus leaving her to inherit a significant amount of land from her father, and whose husband left her his property freely rather than in usufruct and had no children to interfere with the possession thereof (Cardona notes her 'good luck' in this instance). As such, therefore, Guilhema seems an inappropriate subject for such generalised claims. Unfortunately, Cardona never demonstrates exactly why he believes this change occurs. He does, however, suggest a correspondence between Guilhema's privileged status and the high status afforded women in the songs of the troubadours.[8]

The reasoning here is circular. That is, the high position of Guilhema both confirms, and is in turn confirmed by, the elevated woman of the troubadours, whose position, like that of Guilhema, remains unquestioned. The politics of landholding and inheritance practices that allowed Guilhema to possess the land she did are unquestioningly linked to the politics of the troubadour lyric, which 'elevate' – though this is by no means agreed to be a liberating impulse – the *domna*, to support the theory of a 'golden age' for which no other reason nor analysis is offered. R. Howard Bloch has also tried to explain the rise of the poetic *domna* in social terms, but suggests that while the elevation of women to the level of *domna* in some degree indicates the power of women, it is an attempt to contain rather than to celebrate this power.[9] This approach nonetheless still relies on a direct correlation between the social and the poetic. This explanation, where powerful social *domna* = powerful poetic *domna*, is too simplistic, as it assumes an easy relationship between literature and society, where, somehow, literature mirrors life and vice versa. This relationship also assumes that life for women in Occitania in this period was not affected by the constraints placed on women throughout the history of western European society. It begs the questions of what power and freedom actually mean. Were women in Occitania on an equal footing with men, or just relatively 'freer' and 'more powerful' than their northern sisters? It also

---

8 Cardona, 'La détérioration', p. 22:
    Son statut privilegié correspond-il a une parenthèse dorée pour la femme provençale des anneés 1180–1230? A cette époque, en effet, les chants des troubadours, qui universent les rapports de fidelité en faveur de la dame, battent leur plain dans les cours du comté.
9 R. Howard Bloch, *Medieval Misogyny and the Invention of Western Romantic Love* (Chicago, 1991), p. 196.

raises the questions of exactly how 'free' is the *domna* of the lyrics, what is her power, and on what is it based? This is not to say there is no connection between literature and society, indeed there cannot but be, only that the connection is no simple matter of undistorted reflection between the two, and that the connection can only be understood in terms of the political purposes of the poetry, and how it relates to the society which it purports to describe.

An examination of the legal customs and statutes of Occitan cities and a consideration of the construction of the poetic *domna* will reveal both that the position of women in Occitania in this period, and that of the *domna* in particular, is by no means a clear or simple matter and that, in fact, the society exhibited a pronounced anxiety about powerful women, and about powerful landholding women in particular. In this paper I will examine the poetic *domna* in terms of her notionally 'real' social correlatives, that is in terms of how the *domna* is represented as a legal entity and as a participant in trans-actions recorded in charters, through a comparison of their agency and role as constructed in terms of the ability to hold and transfer property. I will focus on the area of the disposal and acquisition of property for a number of reasons. Firstly, in any study of power in this period, the consideration of land – the most important of possessions and arguably the greatest route to the attainment of power – seems absolutely imperative. Secondly, Occitania as an area produced comparatively few textual records in this period, but what we do have consists largely of charters recording varying legal transactions, the majority of which record some transfer of property, or of rights over property. Thirdly, the legal records that come down to us from this period likewise evi-dence an interest in regulations governing the exchange of land. Lastly, the poetry of the troubadours, in which the poetic *domna*, notionally at least, holds pride of place, is also focused on ideas of land, albeit a romanticised landscape of love. I will consider the idea of woman as constituted in the legal discourse of the time to discern what rights were afforded to women and in what public roles women were imagined. I will also consider the *domna* as an agent in the transfer of property, as evidenced through the charters arising from this time and place to determine how and in what roles 'real' women did access the power to hold and dispose of land.

The *domna* of the lyric has been the focus of much scholarly attention. Originally held up as a beacon in the otherwise black expanse of historical constructions of women, the *domna* of the Occitan lyric has been seen as a liberating, empowering idea of woman, constructed along the lines of a feudal lord, and possessing power and influence over her male vassals.[10] More recent critical opinion has identified the misogyny in the construction of the *domna*, seeing her as a woman on a pedestal, an object of male sexual desire, but ulti-

---

[10] See, for example, Alfred Jeanroy, *La poésie lyrique des troubadours* (Paris, 1934); Meg Bogin, *The women troubadours* (New York, 1976).

mately an object, possessing no power or agency of her own.[11] For my purposes here, the question must be asked as to how the poetic *domna* relates to
the social *domna*, or how the desired 'ideal' woman of the lover/poet, as she is
so often assumed to be, relates to the 'ideal' woman in Occitan society. The
poetic *domna* has often been equated by critics[12] with the wife of the
poet/lover's Lord, a woman through whom the lover can forge a relationship
with the real object of desire, the Lord himself. This theory posits the heterosexual love of the poet for the *domna* as merely a mask for his homosocial
desire for community with another man.

If we investigate the equation of the poetic *domna* with the Lord's wife,
however, it becomes clear that there are a number of important divergences
between them which revolve around the relationship of the woman in question to her husband, his property and his power. The ideal wife, as many
medieval commentators and critics will tell you, is, after the model of Eve, a
helpmate to her husband, an inferior in relation to his superior position as
'Lord and Master', and the bearer of his children. In her passive role of wife
and mother she is fundamental to the continuity of society. She is the conduit
through which her husband's seed passes on its way to becoming his heirs, the
parts of him who will ultimately possess his property. Like his land she is the
possession of her husband, and does not herself possess. She is, in many ways,
the antithesis of the poetic *domna*. Unlike the ideal wife, who is always
present, available and reproductive, the *domna* is characterised by her
absence, unattainability and sterility.[13] When the troubadour sings of his
domna, it is in terms of a distant woman,[14] often inhabiting,[15] if not actually

---

11 See, for example, Linda Paterson, *The world of the troubadours: medieval Occitan society, c. 1100
–c. 1300* (New York, 1993); R. Howard Bloch, *Medieval Misogyny*; Sarah Kay, *Subjectivity in troubadour poetry* (Cambridge, 1990).

12 Amongst the most influential of these are Georges Duby, *The chivalrous society*, translated by
Cynthia Postan (London, 1977); Erich Köhler, 'Observations historiques et sociologiques sur la
poésie des troubadours', *Cahiers de Civilisation medieval Xe–XIIe siècles* 7 (1964), pp. 27–51.

13 Paul Zumthor, indeed, sees the dominant motif of the love relationship espoused by the troubadours as being the absence of the *domna*. See chapter one, 'An Overview: Why the Troubadours?', in *A Handbook of the Troubadours*, ed. F.R.P. Akehurst and Judith M. Davis (Berkeley,
1995), p. 15.

14 See for example Arnaut Daniel's *Chansson do·il mot son plan e prim* in which the *domna* is
clearly both absent and distant.

> Si be'm vau per tot a es[t] daill,/mos pessament lai vos assaill
>
> (Although I move through all this in [backward] fashion, My thought leaps out to you
> over there).

Translation from *The Poetry of Arnaut Daniel*, ed. and tr. James J. Wilhelm (New York, 1981), p. 7.

15 See for example Giraut de Borneil's *Ar ai gran ioi* in which the *domna* is in another 'land' alto-
gether.

> Qu'ieu non consir s'er en un gran merchat/Mas quant de lieis on mos cors s'es assis,/E
> tenc los oillz viratz vas cel pais/On il estai, e parl'en mon coratge/Ades de lleis on mos
> fins cors s'aten

herself becoming, a distant land[16] with whom the poet/lover can never consummate his love.[17] She is presented as existing in a space outside that of the poet, and often a non-space, as it were, which cannot be named or described.[18] This spatial dislocation of the *domna*, the 'powerful' and inaccessible woman, can be seen as indicative of a social anxiety about women's relationship to, and potential power over, land.

The location of the *domna* in distinction to the Lord's lady can be briefly but well demonstrated by considering the *tornadas* of several lyrics.[19] It is a common trait for the *tornada* of a *canso* to change direction or address from the *domna* to a geographically located person, usually a male lord, who then

(For in a great market-place I think only of her in whom my heart has taken up abode, and I keep my eyes turned towards the land where she dwells, and in my mind I speak constantly of her on whom my faithful heart is fixed).

Text and translation from Ruth Verity Sharman, *The cansos and sirventes of the troubadour Giraut de Borneil: a critical edition* (Cambridge, 1989), p. 97.

16 See for example Peire Vidal's *Per miehls sofrir lo maltrait e l'afan*, in which the *domna*'s location seems, symbolically at least, to conflate with her own body, as her location becomes her 'soft country':

qu'ades planh e sospire,/quar no vei lei, don mos cors non s'ahire,/quar tant m'es luenh la terre'l dous pais/on es selha vas cui ieu sui aclis

(je pousse plaintes et soupirs en ne voyant pas celle qui rejouit mon coeur, car ils sont si loin de moi la terre et le doux pays ou vit celle a qui vont tous mes desirs).

Text and modern French translation from Joseph Anglade, ed., *Les Poesies de Peire Vidal* (Paris, 1923), p. 159.

17 See for example Raimon de Miraval's *Aissi cum es genser pascors*, where it seems that for the lover to be worthy and true, it is a necessary condition that the lady be absent and distant, since those lovers who do get close are the least worthy. The audience then in the act of identifying, must, like the poet, find themselves at a safe distance from the lady or be considered 'fals'.

Un plait fan domnas q'es follors;/Qant trobon amic qe's mercei,/Per assai limovon esfrei/E-l destreignon tro-s vir'aillors;/E, qant an loingat los meillors,/Fals entendedor menut/Son per cabal receubut

(Il y a une façon d'agir chez les dames qui est folie: Quand elles trouvent un amant qui crie merci, pour l'éprouver elles lui inspirent la crainte et le contraignent à tel point qu'il se tourne d'un autre côté; et apres qu'elles ont eloigné les meilleurs, les faux et chetifs adoratuers sont ténus pour excellents).

Text and modern French translation from Leslie Topsfield, ed., *Les Poesies du troubadour Raimon de Miraval* (Paris, 1971), p. 285.

18 See for example in Giraut de Borneil's *Quar non ai*, in which there seems a necessary precondition to keep the lady in an unstated location, and the location of the lady cannot be named.

E dirai/Qui es ni don?/Non eu, qe/Leugieramen/Fail e mespren/Qui's fai ianglos/A sazos;/Per que s'ieu dizia/Cui am e dezir,/Perc si no'n consir . . .

(And shall I say who she is and where she is from? Not I, for the man who is apt to chatter falls swiftly into sin and error, so that it is my loss if I were to speak, without thinking, the name of her whom I love and desire . . . .)

Text and translation from Sharman, *The cansos and sirventes of the troubadour*, p. 206.

19 The *tornada* is usually several stanzas at the conclusion of a lyric where the rhyme and meter often change, in which the poet leaves off 'composing' as it were, to address the lyric to a recipient directly.

appears as the 'real' recipient of the lyric.[20] When the poet sends the lyric to his *domna*, it is not to a specific location, but to an undefined land where the *domna* resides. Generally, songs which retain the *domna* as their focus do not have a concrete location to which to progress in the *tornada*, but are rather transmitted to an undefined 'there'.[21] This enforced distance between lover and the *domna* is a constant of the troubadour lyric, although the exact meaning of placing the lady in such a location has been debated. For Simon Gaunt, the purpose is containment, the poet remains *sai* (here) while the *domna* is contained *lai* (there) in 'that faraway landscape of the poetic imagination which is the conquered territory of desire'.[22] The spatial differentiation between here and distant and undefined there, and its concomitant distinction between masculine Lord and *domna*, is well illustrated in Arnaut de Marueil's *L'ensenham ens e·l pretz e la valors*:

> Chansoneta, cel cui es Monpesliers,
> qu'es gais e pros, volgra ben que t'auzis;
> mas enans vai lai a mon Gen Conquis.[23]

The lyric is sent in two directions, one the 'real' located in Occitania, the other an unspecified non-place that the lady inhabits. The power over land, and in particular over concrete, named land associated with power and prestige, remains firmly fixed with a male recipient, while the address to the *domna* seems rather to disappear into a non-space which only confirms the presence and power of the named, male Lord.

The *domna* of the lyric is likewise often sharply differentiated from the stereotypical Lord's wife within the *tornada*. What the female addressees tend

---

[20] Reuben Cholakian has commented on this use of 'real' men in 'real' locations in the lyric, and seen them as much more desired, and afforded more individuality, than the *domna*: *The troubadour lyric: a psychocritical reading* (Manchester, 1990), p. 101.

[21] An example is in Arnaut Daniel's *Er vei vermeills, vertz, vlaus, blancs, gruocs*, where the location of the lady is no more specific than the place where she is.

> A lieis cui son, vai, chanssos, derenan,/c'Arnautz non sap comtar sas grans ricors,/que d'aussor sen li auria ops espandres!

> (To her to whom I belong, go, my song, from now on,/Since Arnaut doesn't know how to count up her great riches,/For he'd need the expanses of a greater mind!)

Translation from Wilhelm, *The Poetry of Arnaut Daniel*, p. 55. Also, in Bernard de Ventadorn's *Non es meravelha s'eu chan*, the *domna* is simply 'there'.

> A Mo Cortes, lai on ilh es, /tramet lo vers, e ja no·h pes/ car n'ai estat tan lonjamen.

> (I send the verse to my Cortes, where she is, and may it not grieve her that I have been away so long.)

Text and translation from Stephen G. Nichols Jr., ed., *The Songs of Bernart de Ventadorn* (Chapel Hill, 1962), p. 132.

[22] Cholakian, *The troubadour lyric*, p. 106

[23] 'Chansonette, je voudrais que le seigneur de Montpellier, qui est gai et preux, t'entende; mais auparavant [en avant] va la-bas chez mon Gen Conquis'. Text and modern French translation from R.C. Johnston, ed., *Les poesies lyriques du troubadour Arnaut de Mareuil* (Paris, 1935), p. 70.

to have in common, and which differentiates them from the *domna*, is not
that they exhibit a connection to particular land, but rather, that they hold a
connection to a particular man, again often powerful, in a real Occitan location. An example of this is the Lady Beatrice de Montferrat in Raimbaut de
Vaquieras' *Eissamen ai gerreiat ab amor*:

> Na Biatritz, las melhors an enveya
> de vostre pretz e de vostra beutat,
> que gensa vos e l don de Monferrat.[24]

The female addressee then shares some values with the *domna*, her 'pretz'
and 'beutat', yet the meaning and function of these values are entirely different. Beatrice's qualities are not her own preserve, but serve also to bring lustre
to the Lord of Montferrat, her husband. Fred Cheyette has drawn similar conclusions about the function of the *domna* as a way of flattering the troubadour's patron through implicit comparison.[25] In these terms the lyrics
continue to assert a desire for homosociality, and the *domna* appears to be not
the focus of the poet's desire, but the absent and distant body who incorpo-
rates undesirable qualities, and in this way becomes a foil for those with
whom the poet desires presence and community. The lyrics demonstrate well
the intersection between the discourses of poetry and politics; the absent
woman confirms the presence of the poet himself, and of the powerful lords
he seeks to praise. While the accepted aim of poetry is to elevate the *domna*,
the *domna* is, as has been remarked on, more often than not simply not there,
and the return to specific locations is the return to specific lords, whom the
poetry actually serves.

Poets then work between landscapes, a fictive landscape of love – where
the *domna* may or may not exist – and a 'real' landscape, where the lover
resides, as do the 'real' men with whom he desires community and in whom
are invested the courtly qualities the poet seeks to emulate.[26] The *domna* is
located not in the landscape in which the poet resides, a landscape so often
associated with real land, which, in the societies of the High Middle Ages was
almost certainly connected with real power; but in the fictive landscape, distanced from the arena of power, land and politics. The unrequited nature of
love in the genre – that the poet and the *domna* will never unite – leaves the
domna trapped, as it were, in the landscape of love. She is the possession
rather than the possessor of land, denied any agency to alter her position, or

---

[24] 'Lady Beatrice, the most excellent ladies envy your merit and your beauty, which give lustre to
you and to the lord of Montferrat.' Text and translation from Joseph Linskill, ed., *The Poems of the
Troubadour Raimbaut de Vaqueiras* (The Hague, 1964), p. 159.
[25] Fred Cheyette, 'Women, Poets and Politics in Occitania', unpublished conference paper,
Medieval Literature and Culture, Harvard University, March 15, 1993. Shortly forthcoming.
[26] The 'code' of courtliness advanced by the troubadours relies on the attainment and/or exhibi-
tion of certain qualities, such as *joi*, *joven* and *corteza*. For further explanation see Glynnis M.
Cropp, *Le vocabulaire courtois des troubadours a l'époque classique* (Genève, 1975).

to move between landscapes. The construction of the *domna* may well represent a powerful woman who holds land and authority, but it also denies the possibility of such a woman existing within the poet's immediate area of interest and influence, where land and power remain firmly in the hands of men, and women firmly under their control. This removal of a powerful, landowning woman from the Occitan landscape reveals an anxiety about powerful women, or at least unattached women with power over land, which is likewise present in the customs.

The legal statutes of the Occitan cities express anxiety about the ability of women to possess, and more importantly, to dispose of, land. The customs I have examined come from the cities of Saint-Antonin (1144), Saint-Gaudens (1203), Saint-Gilles (c.1140–1214), Carcassonne (1204), Montpellier (1204–1205), Toulouse (1150–1250) and Barcelona (1154), thus reflecting the legal systems of some of the largest and most powerful cities in Occitania, and in the case of Toulouse and Barcelona, centres which had power over much larger regions within the Midi generally. The customs demonstrate roughly two different kinds of law, which I have termed 'civic' and 'feudal'. I have used 'civic' to qualify those cities where the law is established as deriving from a legal body governed by elected officials of 'good men'; this is the case with Saint-Antonin, Carcassonne, Montpellier and Toulouse. I have used 'feudal' to apply to those customs which are given authority by a ruling Lord, either secular or ecclesiastical, as is the case in the records coming from Saint-Gaudens, Saint-Gilles and Barcelona. While the *domna* has been seen in the past as the construction of a predominantly 'feudal' society, given the attention devoted to Occitan 'difference' due to the presence of an urban aristocracy, it seems important also to consider the position of women within the civic customs, to investigate whether it is these that might provide some augmentation in women's rights. How do these customs construct the female legal experience, and in what roles and areas of activity are women considered within them? More significantly perhaps for the purposes of this paper, we must ask in what way the legal identity of the *domna* is constituted.

The first thing one might notice about the customs is the infrequent appearance of women within them. The customs of the Occitan cities, as we can presume do many other medieval law books, define and legitimate a system of male power structures, where laws concerning men are directed by men at men, and wherein women are truly exceptional. The customs generally direct themselves to the population of their cities, the *populi, habitancium* or *homines* of the town, and the majority of the articles apply themselves to such a general population. In the instance of articles directed at women, however, it is easier to see the different ways in which Occitan women were imagined as participating in legal experiences. The customs of Carcassonne include or differentiate women in 6 of their 113 articles, those of Montpellier in 7 of 122. In these instances they are identified as *mulier, uxor, filia, filia maritata, vidua,* and *puella*[27] in both sets of customs. In the customs of Saint-Gaudens, women are differentiated in only 4 of the 77 articles, as married women (*molher maridada*), and as *femnas* in the article giving protection to people entering the city at the time of the fair. Women in the customs of Saint-Gilles are even less noticeable, appearing only as female children (*infantes femine*) in the article concerning the property of orphans or wards, and as dowered daughters (*filia dotata*) in that concerning the regulation of dowries. Women are, therefore, clearly identified in the circumstances where the legislator saw it necessary to define them, and show a multitude of possible definitions beyond the simple *femina* and *mulier*, and indeed beyond the general *homo* and *vir* by which men are named. This multiplicity, however, reveals the way in which women are often subject to definition to create a legal identity, when a 'man' is defined as a legal agent by virtue of his gender alone. Where women are identified or directly acknowledged, it is in their roles which derive from and rely on relationships with men: wife, daughter, widow.[28]

This derivative status of women can be compared to the 'feudal' *Usatges* of Barcelona. The *Usatges* are less concerned with civil law than criminal, and so they give little detail on such matters as marriage and inheritance practices, areas most commonly associated with women in the other customs. What they do make clear, however, like the civic customs, is that the status of a woman is dependent on the position of her nearest associated male. Women are little considered in this system which orders itself around male 'feudal' roles, such as viscount, comitor and vavassour.[29] Women appear in the *Usatges* in 12 of the 125 articles, variously listed as *fembra, exorc* or *cuguç, muler, fembra verge/fembra que no sia verge, fila* and *neta*.[30]

The positions that the customs offer women as agents are very limited. Generally, their inclusion in the customs is not as agents in themselves, but as the objects of male agency, either as brides to be given away and daughters to be dowered, wives to be supervised in the construction of their wills, or adulteresses. Beyond these more general roles there are other possibilities which receive the odd mention, such as the innkeepers and jongleurs at Toulouse, household women or servants (*domestica*), and, of course, prostitutes. Any women who are portrayed as having some legal capacity or agency are represented in familial roles, that is, roles which rely on the presence and defining power of men. Entry into public and into the legal arena is thus through

---

[27] Wife, daughter, married daughter, widow and girl (usually unmarried).

[28] The only exception to this comes in the customary documents of Toulouse, where the presence of female innkeepers (*alberguatrices*) and jongleurs (*ioculatrices*) is acknowledged.

[29] For example, see Joan Bastardas, *Usatges de Barcelona, el codi a mitjan segle XII* (Barcelona, 1991), article 4, p. 65.

[30] Woman, adulteress, wife, virgin, non-virgin, daughter and granddaughter.

assumption of a sanctioned role determined by a relationship to a more powerful man. In terms of their landholding capacities, acquisition and disposal of
land by women are imagined in only a very limited number of areas, in the
possibility of their direct inheritance, legacy or exchange of property at the
time of, or following, marriage.

An area in which we may find women displaying some legal agency is that
of the testament. The customs are almost unanimous (the exceptions are
those of Saint-Gilles and Saint-Gaudens) in asserting the importance of and
preference for wills, and the rights of all to make them. The customs of Saint-
Antonin make this explicit in terms of both men and women by directing the
article to *homines vel femines manentes in villa supradicta.*[31] Likewise the
customs of Carcassonne make explicit women's right to make wills being
directed to *omnis homo vel femina permanens Carcassone.*[32] The customs of
Montpellier do not use any gendered terms in reference to the testator, but
refer to the procedures guaranteeing the legitimacy of the wills.[33] The
customs of Montpellier and Carcassonne share the same phrase which asserts
the right of all to make a will – *tamen unaqueque persona potest facere testamen-
tum seu dispositionem de jure suo*[34] – after the provisions for intestate partible
inheritance, but like the *Usatges* of Barcelona do not specifically gender these
will-makers female. Indeed, the final sentence in the relevant article of the
Usatges, genders the testator as male and as a father; thus while not necessarily limiting the rights of women as testators, it certainly does not imagine
them as legal agents in this capacity.[35]

Explicit restrictions are, however, placed on women's testamentary abilities in later articles of the customs of the Occitan cities. For example, married
daughters are considered, and therefore written outside the general populace
– that is those whom the statute perceives as able to make wills – as the
customs of Saint-Antonin, Montpellier and Carcassonne all limit the ability
of married women to make wills without parental consent. The customs of

---

[31] 'Every man or woman dwelling in Saint Antonin': 'Libertates et consuetudines villae S.
antonini Ruthensis' (J335, Carcassonne, no. 9, Copie ancienne), in Alexandre Teulet, *Layettes de
Trésor des Chartes* (Nendeln, 1977), vol. 1, p. 56.

[32] 'Every man or woman dwelling in Carcassonne': 'Libertates et consuetudines Carcassonensis
civitatis' (J335, Carcassonne, no. 9, Copie ancienne), in Teulet, *Layettes de Trésor des Chartes*, vol.
1, p. 279, article 94.

[33] J339, Montpellier et Maguelone, no. 23, in Teulet, *Layettes de Trésor des Chartes*, vol. 1, p. 260,
article 52.

[34] 'however, any person whatsoever may make will or assignment of his/her right': Carcassonne,
p. 273, article 10. See also Montpellier, p. 256, article 12.

[35] 'en aquesta guisa e en aquesta order pusque lo pare or l'avi milorar son fil o sa fila, son
net ho sa neta'

('In this way and manner, a father and grandfather can endow his son or daughter or
even his nephew or niece').

Bastardas, *Usatges de Barcelona*, pp. 151–2, article 118. Translation from Donald Kagay, *The
Usatges of Barcelona* (Philadelphia, 1994), p. 94, article 118.

Saint-Antonin are not very expansive on this topic, but place limitations on childless women – *filia maritata non habens infantes* – requiring parental consent or that of the closest relatives if the parents are absent.[36]

Although this article only applies itself to childless women, there are implications here for the unmentioned woman with children, in that the expectation of inheritance by her children effectively denies her any legal rights of disposal at all. The concern here is with the knowledge that inheritance will be passed properly on to heirs, and that there are indeed heirs to receive it. This is again reflected in an article from the 1205 customs of Montpellier which allows a woman to provide all of her goods in dowry to any subsequent husbands provided that she has no children.[37] Presumably childless women marrying for a second time presented a greater risk of losing property to their husbands, since they had not proven themselves capable of even producing heirs to whom the property should rightfully pass.

The customs generally reflect an anxiety over the power of women to dispose of property, and most particularly, to dispose of it outside of its family of origin: an image which is compatible with the construction of the *domna* as a powerful woman able to endow, and thus empower, the poet with land. In particular we may note that the customs of Montpellier and Carcassonne clearly reveal families' fears of losing property through their daughters' marriages, apparent in their prohibitions as to how much any married daughter can leave to any one man.[38]

Similar anxieties can also be perceived in the articles relating to intestate death, where married or dowered daughters cannot claim against the deceased parent's estate and the estate will be divided equally – *in equis portionibus* – between unmarried children.[39] While the provisions look to some

---

36 'Filia maritata non habens infantes, quando vult facere ultimam dipositionem suam, debet vocare patrem vel matrem suam. Et, si non habet patrem vel matrem, vocet aliquem de proximoribus parentibus suis'

('a married daughter without children, when she wants to make her will, ought to call upon her father and mother. And, if she has not father or mother, call upon some of her nearest relatives.')

Teulet, *Layettes de Trésor des Chartes*, vol. 1, p. 59.

37 'Omnis mulier, puella seu vidua, potest omnia sua dare in dotem tam primo quam secundo viro, licet infantes habuerit'

('Every woman, maiden or widow, may give all of her goods in dowry to her first husband or to her second husband, granted that she has no children.')

'Consuetudines ville Montispessulani, Montpellier 1205, 13 juin' (J339, – Montpellier et Maguelone, I, no. 23, Copie Ancienne), article 14, Teulet, *Layettes de Trésor des Chartes*, vol. 1, p. 289.

38 'quartam partem bonorum suorum, et non aliquid plus'

('a quarter part of her goods, and not anything more').

Carcassone, article 40, Teulet, *Layettes de Trésor des Chartes*, vol. 1, p. 276. For Montpellier see article 54, Teulet, *Layettes de Trésor des Chartes*, vol. 1, p. 260.

39 'in equal parts': Teulet, *Layettes de Trésor des Chartes*, vol. 1, p. 58. I have included here only those for Saint-Antonin, to which those for Montpellier and Carcassonne accord almost exactly.

extent equitable, in that property of an intestate father – again the will is conceived of as being made by a man and a father – will be divided between unmarried daughters and sons, it is nevertheless important to note that the customs do not preclude married sons from claiming from the estate in the same way that they do married daughters. The daughters' 'rightful' inheritance therefore comprises her dowry, that is, her endowment comprises the ability to be married rather than to hold any of the family property as an individual. There is of course the possibility of legacies left by the father to his daughters, but this is by no means 'customary' and remains an exception. The other important point about these customs is that they are laid down only as a provision for intestate death, that is, as a default option, rather than the norm. The customs of Montpellier and Carcassonne differ slightly in transferring the land left by intestate childless sisters to the brothers only – *Et si moritur aliqua de maritatis filiabus et heredatis a patre sine gadio et heredibus, bona ejus revertuntur communiter omnibus fratribus superstitibus, pater jam mortuo.*[40] They also, however, include a final phrase indicating the possibility of the mother's will – *et eodem modo dicimus de bonis matris.*[41]

The provision for intestate inheritance in the *Usatges* is more concerned with the rights of the lord – who will gain at least between one half and one third of the deceased's estate – than those of the heir or wife, who will divide the remainder with the deceased's relatives.[42] The experience presented in the *Usatges* is notionally male and the likely heirs of the deceased are defined explicitly as sons and wives – *qui passen sens testament . . . si gaquiran fils e no mulers . . . mulers e no fils.*[43] The possibility of a woman in the role of testator is exceptional, an afterthought – *atresi sia de les mulers qui moren entestades com és dels marits.*[44]

The other regulations governing testamentary practices set down by the *Usatges* deal with disinheritance, and the circumstances under which this may be carried out. We are told that sons, nephews or nieces (*fils o els nets o les netes*) can be disinherited for striking or dishonouring their relatives or accusing them of crimes. Sons and daughters in particular, however, face the possibility of losing their inheritance – for sons through treason or conversion to Islam, and, in the case of daughters, for refusing to marry and living shame-

---

[40] 'And if any married daughter or heiress die without heirs, their goods revert in common to her surviving brothers, if her father is already dead': Teulet, *Layettes de Tréor des Chartes*, vol. 1, p. 256, article 12. For Carcassonne see p. 273, article 10.
[41] 'and in the same way we say [it shall be] for the goods of the mother': Teulet, *Layettes de Tréor des Chartes*, p. 273, article 10.
[42] Bastardas, *Usatges de Barcelona*, p. 151, article 117.
[43] 'those who die without a will . . . if they leave sons and no wives . . . wives and no sons': Bastardas, *Usatges de Barcelona*, p. 151, article 117.
[44] Bastardas, *Usatges de Barcelona*, p. 151, article 117. Translation from Kagay, *The Usatges de Barcelona*, p. 94, article 117 – 'Thus exactly what is proclaimed above for men shall be in effect concerning intestate wives.'

lessly (*viure malament*).[45] Although the question of what, precisely, daughters can inherit is not made clear elsewhere in the *Usatges*, since the reasons behind disinheriting a daughter pertain exclusively to her refusing marriage, it does not seem unwarranted to assume that the daughter's inheritance constituted her dowry, as is made clear in the articles relating to partible inheritance in the customs of the Occitan cities.

What stands out most, though, after close reading of these articles, is that they are not concerned with ensuring equitable division of family property so much as they are concerned with maintaining property within the family of its origins. Women, who will neccessarily marry outside of this family, are therefore represented as an implicit threat to the patrimony, and are thus considered as potential heirs only when they remain firmly within it, that is, when unmarried. Within this legal discourse women are hence constructed in terms of minority and limited agency, and are distanced from any land to which they might claim some right.

Because marriage represented a potentially threatening exchange of property we find further anxieties about the misdirection of land through women within articles concerning marriage and the division of property it entailed. This is both in terms of the size of dowry and brideprice, and in the restriction of the choice of groom to the woman's parents rather than the woman herself. Several customs prohibit women marrying without parental consent.[46] The only time when a woman appears to have had any say over her marriage partner is when compelled to marry against her will – or that of her family – by her lord. In such an event the customs of Montpellier and Carcassonne actually place the consent firmly with the woman herself, *sine voluntate mulieris*.[47] While this regulation does notionally give the individual widow[48] some freedom over the choice of a second husband, it should be noted that the prohibition is directed towards the lord, and not towards the family of the woman. The control of the family over her first marriage is not reasserted, but neither is it denied. The regulation is thus a safeguard to prevent the lord's use of a woman for his political purposes, and thus the use of the dowry origi-

---

[45] Bastardas, *Usatges de Barcelona*, p. 155, article 119. Translation from Kagay, *The Usatges de Barcelona*, p. 95, article 119.

[46] The customs of Montpellier and Carcassonne both prohibit an unmarried daughter (*puella*) from marrying without parental consent. Teulet, *Layettes de Trésor des Chartes*, vol. 1, p. 262, article 85. For Carcassonne see Teulet, *Layettes de Trésor des Chartes*, vol. 1, p. 278, article 62. It is interesting to note that here, although the prohibition is on the daughter, the active member – and he who will be punished – is the man. The female here assumes the position of an object by which a man will commit a crime, rather than the criminal herself.

[47] Teulet, *Layettes de Trésor des Chartes*, vol. 1, p. 278, article 61. For Montpellier see p. 262, article 84.

[48] It should be noted that the 'freedom' provided by this stipulation to unmarried women is, however, cancelled out by the regulations that retain their parents' rights over the choice of the first marriage partner at least.

nally provided by the family for his own ends. Ultimately, the protection mechanism is set in place not for the individual woman, but for the family who dowered her.

Regulations governing marriage practices reveal further problems to do with landholding and the potential transfer of property at the time of either partner's death, and the possibility that one partner might gain at the other family's expense. The customs of Montpellier and Carcassonne show the influence of Roman law in stipulating that the donation given by both sides should be equal.[49] This equality of gifts is not stipulated in the customs of Saint-Antonin where emphasis is placed on the principle of equal treatment should one partner outlive the other, supporting the custom of usufruct for life in any remaining property unless this right has been denied by prior arrangement.[50] This clause is similar to that in the customs of Montpellier which retains the same rights, but only for the husband, over the land which the woman brought to the marriage.[51] This need to protect the rights of the husband perhaps indicates the anxiety on the part of the woman's family in seeking to regain her dowry following her death, at the expense of her husband's legal rights.

One final image of women common to all the customs, and indeed relevant to the issue of property, particularly in terms of its misdirection, is the adulteress. As a role that often entails the renunciation of all property rights[52] it did not seem appropriate for lengthy examination in this place, although we may perhaps link it with the image of the *domna* as the wife of the poet/lover's lord.[53] Suffice it to say here though that even within this area of potential female agency, women appear, particularly in the customs of Saint-Antonin and the *Usatges*, not so much as women actively committing the crime of adultery, but as being the object through which men commit crimes against, or form relationships with, other men.[54]

As these examples demonstrate, the customs seek to define women in those circumstances in which they might act to dispose of property, as *vidua*, *mulier*, *puella* and *filia/maritata*, and, having once defined them, seek to limit that potential by restricting the activities of these groups. In these instances, most particularly those of inheritance, the position of women is demarcated very clearly as subordinate to both the men by whom they are defined, and the maintenance of the family, and patrimony.

The important thing to notice overall, however, is that while female

49 Teulet, *Layettes de Trésor des Chartes*, vol. 1, p. 263, article 95. For Carcassonne see p. 278, article 69.
50 Teulet, *Layettes de Trésor des Chartes*, vol. 1, p. 59.
51 Teulet, *Layettes de Trésor des Chartes*, vol. 1, p. 264, article, 118.
52 See Bastardas, *Usatges de Barcelona*, p. 125, article 87.
53 See p. 23, above.
54 Again, see p. 23 above, where it is posited that the poet/lover may use his heterosexual relationship with the *domna* to indulge his homosocial desire for contact with her husband.

agency is constantly limited, it is never denied outright. Both the legal statutes and the troubadour lyric represent a social ideal, an image that distorts rather than reflects the society from which it comes, and skews it towards the desires of the jurist or poet by whom it was composed.

In general, the Occitan customs do not display a significant difference or improvement for women from the legal positions of their northern sisters. Women appear to be little understood as individuals within the law, and function only within limited areas in which they are secondary to a more powerful man. Examination of the customs reveals, or rather does not reveal, that the *domna* is not a role that figures in legal discourses at all. In both the legal records and the lyrics, the *domna* represents what might be called 'unfamiliar territory', a marginal figure whose agency lies outside the desirable limits established by the discourses.

There remains a world of female experience to be considered which, while not unaffected by such structures, can be seen occurring outside the discourses of law and the troubadour lyric. Thus, the idea of women as landholders is perhaps most correctly identified as being undefined, that is, there exists a large area of experience and opportunity not recognised within the law, but not prohibited by it either. For example, women could, and did, obtain land simply by legacy not concerning their marriage, or as gifts from parents or other family members. Land could be accrued through purchase or mortgage, articles relating to neither of which address themselves to women in the documents. The representation of women in the customs, is, I would argue, ambiguous. The areas of definition are limited, but not exclusive, and allow for possible agency which is not even considered. An examination of the charters will allow for consideration of the roles women do adopt in public settings, and how they behave in accordance with, against, or in ways unconsidered by, the customs.

In my examination of some 900 charters from the Languedoc region in which 1448 women are involved in some capacity, which I have based on the woman involved actually being named, only 291 women (or 20%) are described as *domina* or *domna*.[55] This first figure would imply that rather than being the ordinary form of address, *domna* was a title used only in certain circumstances. The assumption of high status for *domnas* in relation to land is, however, brought into question by the much greater proportion of women who do not share the title, yet participate actively in land transactions thereby suggesting that the title did not necessarily reflect a higher status in relation to land than that enjoyed by many other women. So who are these women, and how do they compare to the *domnas* of the lyric?

---

[55] The difference between the terms is effectively only one of language, *domina* being used in Latin charters, *domna* in those written in the vernacular. For the purposes of this article the terms will be used interchangeably.

Table 1. Total numbers of *Domnas* in
charters by transactional status.

Married	– primary agent	19		
	– secondary agent	79		
	– non-agent	<u>14</u>		
		112	(38.49%)	
			(44.96%)	
Widowed	– primary agent	23		
	– secondary agent	3		
	– non-agent	<u>3</u>		
		29	(9.96%)	
			(18.99%)	
Unspecified marital status				
	– primary agent	58		
	– secondary agent	29		
	– non-agent	<u>43</u>		
		130	(44.67%)	
			(44.31%)	
Unmarried	– primary agent	1		
	– secondary agent	1		
	– non-agent	<u>3</u>		
		5	(1.72%)	
			(2.35%)	
Bride	– primary agent	1		
	– secondary agent	0		
	– non-agent	<u>1</u>		
		2	(0.69%)	
Matronymic – non-agent		<u>13</u>	(4.47%)	
		291		

Primary Agents   102 (35.05%) av = 33.63%

Secondary Agents   112 (38.49%) av = 43.57

Non-Agents   77 (26.46%) av = 22.7

Note: primary agent = women acting for themselves, secondary
agent = women using men to act on their behalf, and where non-
agent = women's transactional connection to the land is negligible
or indiscernible.

I have divided the women into groups, dependent on the way in which
they participate in the charters, and whether this participation is mediated by
a man. Women can be involved as the primary agent in the charter, where
they act for themselves concerning their own land, or as a secondary agent,

where a male relative intervenes to act on their behalf, but where the land in question is still discernibly, in part at least, the property of the woman as indicated by the recognition of their co-action in, or consent to, the transaction. There are also a number of smaller groups in which the women's status in connection to the land could not be discerned; where it was not material to the transaction being recorded; or where their presence in the charter was a case of further definition rather than action, as in the case of matronymics. In these instances the women have been recorded as 'non-agents', although it is important to acknowledge that many such women still bear significance to such a study as they often appear as landholders or owners whose presence clarifies past possession or the current position of land under consideration. I have also broken the women into groups of married, widowed, or of uncertain marital status. The idea that the title *domna* might indicate the status of the woman's husband, rather than any power of her own, suggested the need to determine the marital status of the *domnas* in order to discern whether such a theory was indeed supported by the records. The figures for the *domnas* appear in Table 1, above.

The figures calculate the number of women in each category of agency according to their marital status. Totals and percentages of the group *domna* are indicated. The emboldened percentage indicates the percentage of each marital group across the total population. The greatest proportion, about 73%, of women called *domna* are acting, or being acted on behalf of, for land which they either own or to which they have claim. They also demonstrate a slightly higher figure for primary involvement in transactions. This is perhaps most important in contrasting the way in which *domnas* are depicted in the lyrics and the way in which they behave in 'real life'. Troubadour poetry functions, as mentioned above, is to contain the *domna*, and to distance her from the site of what could be seen as real political power, by locating her in a distant, fictive landscape. The *domnas* of the charters by comparison provide evidence of an immediate and close connection with land and the transfer of land, the most potent symbol of political power in the Occitania in this period. It would seem, therefore, that the 'ideal' domna of the troubadour lyric does indeed have a 'real' referent in the social composition of Occitania, and one who appears to manifest just those qualities about which the lyric and the legal discourse are most concerned. A closer examination of the types of women who hold this title power reflects interesting trends which suggest that this connection is indeed justified.

The groups of married women and widows – both *domnas* and in the population generally – participate in ways which we might predict, that is, married women are involved much less often in transactions by themselves but generally participate with, and after their husbands. The figure for participation of married domnas is, interestingly, slightly lower than that for the total population. Married *domnas*, it would appear, did not necessarily have greater rights over land than other women. Widows, again as one might expect, drop to a

Table 2. Marital status of women
participating in land transactions

Possible *domnas* due to rank of husband

Married	– primary agent	6
	– secondary agent	19
	– non-agent	3
		28
Widowed	– primary agent	11
	– secondary agent	2
	– non-agent	1
		14
Unspecified marital status		
	– primary agent	6
	– secondary agent	1
	– non-agent	1
		8
Bride	– primary agent	0
	– secondary agent	0
	– non-agent	1
		1
Total		51

smaller percentage of the total, but within their own group display a greater capacity for primary agency, in line with the greater freedom from control of both parents and husbands. The number of *domnas* identified as widows is significantly lower – almost by one half – than in the total population (see Table 2).

The largest group evidenced in connection with land transactions, and also that containing the most primary agents is the group whose marital status cannot be discerned, or is not made clear, through the charters. This figure is not isolated to the *domnas* but is seen throughout the population. The women controlling land appear, therefore, to be those who are not defined in the social roles advocated by the legal discourse, and, in this sense, conform still further to the 'undesirable' *domna* of the lyric. This trend would also suggest that *domna* is not a title closely connected with the status of a woman's husband, as the calculations for *domnas* due to the rank of husband confirm.

Of the *domnas* recorded 51 (17.5%) could be titled as such as a result of the high rank of their husband. Although not impossible, the idea that these women are simply *domnas* due to their husbands' status would seem improbable, due to the number of women acting as *domnas* (the other 82.5%), whose husbands are not called *dominus*, or who do have a title that would suggest that they rank amongst the aristocracy, or even the nobility (e.g. *comes, viscomes*). This would suggest that rather than revealing the social 'ideal' of a woman's status derived from her husband's, the title *domna* might function in some way as a mark of independence. One case of a widow in particular would seem to confirm this view, and to suggest that *domna* is a role into which a woman might move when she moves out of marriage upon the death of her husband. The role assumed by this widow appears to be directly concerned with landholding, and many of the *domnas* swear allegiance for land which has come to them from their dead husband's estate:

> Ego Aiglina, uxor quondam domini Poncii Petri de Agantico, tenens villam de Agantico et jurisdictionem ad eandem villam pertinentem, domina ex testamento seu ex ultima voluntate domini Poncii Petri, quondam mariti mei.[56]

Here Aiglina's position as *domna* seems explicitly connected with the death of her husband. Thus being a *domna* is linked effectively to both the possession of land, and the absence of a male to mediate such possession. *Domina* could in this context be seen as a role more determined by life cycle, the transition from a wife to a widow and hence to a *domina*, than by the social status of the woman, or of her husband. This idea of the role of *domina* as being taken on without the mediation of men, and the fact that few identified widows act in a secondary capacity, must bring into question the number of women of uncertain marital status acting as primary agents – to suggest that they in all likelihood could be widows also. The idea that being a *domna* is connected to possession of property unmediated by a male is also expressed by Poncia del Elzeria, who links her role as *domna* to inheritance gained from her family in spite of her already being married:

> ego Poncia del Elzeria, filia Rayjmondi Hugonis, consilio fratris mei Petri Raymundi, domina et habens potestatem tocius hereditatis quam dedit michi pater meus et mater mea in die desponsacionis mee, dono et trado ad alodum . . .[57]

The *domnas* of the lyric and legal records thus display important differences to those of the charters. The women in the charters, in contrast to those in the lyrics, display a wide range of activity and stages of life. In the lyric, the *domna* is fundamentally passive, and distanced from the land; in the

---

56 J. Rouquette and A. Villemagne, *Cartularie de Maguelone* (Montpellier, 1913), vol. II, pp. 218–21, no. CCCLXXXV (1222): 'I Aiglina, formerly wife of Lord Poncius Petrus of Angantico, holding the town of Agantico and the legal rights over it, domina from the testament and last wishes of Lord Poncius Petrus, who was my husband . . .' (my translation).

57 Rouquette and Villemagne, *Cartulaire de Maguelone*, vol. I, p. 119, no. LX (1134): 'I Poncia de

Table 3. Number of *domnas* present in charters
over different time scales

Domnas				
	pre 1100	1100–1149	1150–1199	1200–291
	0	6	123	163
Total	11	212	866	359
%	0	2.83	14.09	45.40
	pre 1129	1130–1179	1180–1229	1230–291
	1	60	134	97
Total	115	580	590	163
%	0.87	10.17	22.71	59.51

charters she is predominantly active, particularly in terms of land to which she herself often lays claim.

The independence suggested by the title *domna* is made more interesting still when one considers the time frame in which *domnas* occur. Bearing Cardona's 'golden age' in mind, I calculated the numbers of *domnas* present across two different time periods in an attempt to see whether their numbers changed significantly (see Table 3).

Here 291 indicates the total number of *domnas*. The figures following the total indicate the number of women in each time period recorded, and the percentage is that of *domnas* per time period. The figures indicate a steep rise in the number of *domnas* recorded in the charters with the progress of time. While it must be remembered that the charters in themselves represent another form of textuality and construction of women in texts and thus may not necessarily represent trends in 'real' life, it does not seem unwarranted to assume that the use of the title *domna* became more widespread following 1200, and particularly after 1230. This would locate the social *domna* as predominant at some stage later than Cardona's 'golden age', but also more importantly for this study, following rather than predating the use of *domna* as a term in the lyrics of the troubadours. The idea of a reflection of the society in the lyrics, so often assumed by critics, is therefore up-ended, to suggest rather a translation from literary terms into social discourse. This increase is even more interesting when one considers the distribution of women whom I have termed 'undefined' – that is, they are not defined by any familial or status titles. Unlike, and one might even suggest in direct contrast to, the

l'Elzeria, daughter of Raymond Hugo, with the counsel of my brother Petrus Raymundus, domina and possessing the power of all the heredity that my father and mother gave me on the day of my marriage, give and relinquish to you as allodial . . .' (my translation). This is not an uncommon situation, and many *domnas* appearing as primary agents with their husbands do so for land that is their own inheritance.

Table 4. Distribution of women in charters
undefined by status or title

Undefined

	pre 1100	1100–1149	1150–1199	1200–1273
	1	21	126	23
Total	11	212	866	359
%	9.09	9.91	14.78	6.41
	pre 1129	1130–1179	1180–1229	1230–1273
	13	65	86	7
Total	115	580	590	163
%	11.3	11.55	14.58	4.29

domnas, these women show a tendency to increase marginally for extended periods, but then decline sharply in the period following 1230 (see Table 4).

What these figures show is not so much a change in the status of women over time – and indeed in my work I have found little to suggest much change – but rather a change in terminology. The undefined woman of the early charters is gradually replaced as a new term enters social discourse through literature, a term that describes not the 'ideal' woman, but she whom the poets would locate outside their own landscape in 'unfamiliar territory'.

The proliferation of the title *domna* in charters can, therefore, be seen not only in terms of indicating some level of independence for women – a level, I hasten to add, which was sustained on a continuum rather than a sudden alteration – but also of explaining something of the social reaction to that independence. The increase in the application of *domna* would suggest that the term was used to familiarise, to give name and definition, and hence thereafter to have some measure of control over, the 'unfamiliar', the woman who could act without male mediation.

A Room of One's Own? The Legal Evidence for the Residential Arrangements of Women Without Husbands in Late Fourteenth- and Early Fifteenth-Century York

CORDELIA BEATTIE

A RECENT conversation with a council tax official brought home to me the contradiction between what the enforcers of particular laws view as a household and people's own perceptions of their living arrangements. For council tax purposes, whether I think of myself as part of a domestic unit is not considered important, whereas whether I share more than a kitchen and bathroom with another person is.[1] Such functional rather than emotional definitions pervade the sources that we have for the late medieval English household. They have been written from specific standpoints which require the household to be thought of in a certain way. Poll tax returns, lists of tax-payers compiled by local assessors to aid collection, have been used by modern scholars as key sources for the size and structure of households. However, such returns contain evidence of how assessors decided to classify people, which is no more 'true' than, for example, a depiction of a household in a fabliau. When questions are asked about the residential arrangements of women without husbands, it becomes apparent that both the models imposed

[1] Hareven and Tilly argue that the differences found in the number of women designated as living alone in the American and French censuses of c.1900 in part reflected different concepts of privacy. In France a small separate room, in a small house inhabited by other individuals, was conceptually equivalent to a separate house or apartment with a private entrance: Tamara K. Hareven and Louise A. Tilly, 'Solitary Women and Family Mediation in America [sic] and French Textile Cities', *Annales de Démographie Historique* (Paris, 1981), pp. 253–71, p. 257, n.7. The current essay is partly based on material from my unpublished MA dissertation: C. Beattie, 'Women Without Husbands in Late Fourteenth and Early Fifteenth-Century York' (Centre for Medieval Studies, University of York, 1996). I am grateful to Jeremy Goldberg and Felicity Riddy for all their comments.

by medieval authorities and those used by modern scholars concentrate on the male-headed, conjugal unit. The result of this is that women without husbands look like either women who have taken over such units as heads, or dependants. However, if these categories, household 'heads' and 'dependants', are treated as the constructs that they are, it might be possible to get closer to what women without husbands, for example, might have thought about their living arrangements.

The category 'women without husbands' encompasses both the never married and the widowed.[2] Studies of such umbrella groups have been criticised for letting the experiences of widows stand for the experiences of the never married too.[3] However, Judith Bennett's book *Ale, Beer, and Brewsters* shows that an umbrella grouping can work if scholars are cautious. Her chapter three, which advances the thesis of 'single women and widows as harbingers of change', both groups them together under the term 'not-married women' and distinguishes between the sometimes different circumstances of 'singlewomen' and widows.[4] Many medieval sources do not distinguish between the widowed and the never married so, pragmatically, it makes sense to use such a group and draw attention to any differences that can be shown. Another advantage of such an approach is that more can be said about the specificity of never-married women if widows are there for comparison.

The literature on both never-married women and women without husbands is small but growing.[5] Household structures are often given prominence but most of these studies take a quantitative approach and document, for example, how many women headed households and how many lived with kin.[6] Although this article is a case study of a particular time and place, York

---

[2] I use this term to avoid confusion because 'single women' has been used as both an umbrella term and to denote the never married only. For example, one article uses 'Single Women' as the opposite term to 'Wives', apparently including never-married women and widows, but also refers to 'widows and single women', thus marking out 'single women' as the never married only: Maryanne Kowaleski, 'Women's Work in a Market Town: Exeter in the Late Fourteenth Century', *Women and Work in Preindustrial Europe*, ed. Barbara A. Hanawalt (Bloomington, 1986), pp. 145–64, table 3, p. 150 and p. 156.

[3] Amy M. Froide, 'Marital Status as a Category of Difference: Singlewomen and Widows in Early Modern England', *Singlewomen in the European Past 1250–1800*, ed. Judith M. Bennett and Amy M. Froide (Philadelphia, 1999), pp. 236–69, pp. 260 ff. I am grateful to Amy Froide for allowing me to see a copy of this in advance of its publication.

[4] Judith M. Bennett, *Ale, Beer, and Brewsters in England: Women's Work in a Changing World, 1300–1600* (Oxford, 1996), especially p. 57. However, Bennett is currently working on a survey book on single women in late medieval England which only includes the never-married: personal communication. An article that discusses both groups while distinguishing between the two is Maura Palazzi, 'Female Solitude and Patrilineage: Unmarried Women and Widows During the Eighteenth and Nineteenth Centuries', *Journal of Family History* 15 (1990), pp. 443–59.

[5] For a helpful survey of the scholarship see the Introduction to Bennett and Froide, *Singlewomen in the European Past*. I am indebted to Judith Bennett for sending me a draft of this.

[6] On households see Palazzi, 'Female Solitude', especially pp. 453–55; Olwen Hufton, 'Women Without Men: Widows and Spinsters in Britain and France in the Eighteenth Century', *Journal of*

in the late fourteenth and early fifteenth centuries, it will instead discuss a few cases in detail to make some general but important points. At this early stage of research into the lives of medieval never-married women or women without husbands, this is arguably more helpful than another quantitative study.

A more critical approach to the sources used as evidence for medieval household size and structures needs to be taken. The first section will discuss poll tax returns, previously used as key sources, and suggest alternative ways of approaching them. Since categories such as household 'head' and 'dependant' tend to reinforce the norm of the male-headed conjugal unit, the second section will examine the case studies of two women who do not readily fit such constructs. Thirdly, the issue of whether obvious differences between the residential arrangements of the never married and the widowed can be deduced will be considered, again by way of two case studies.

I. The Evidence: Late Fourteenth-Century Poll Tax Returns

The medieval household has been studied largely from the perspective of the married.[7] This owes something to John Hajnal's theory that in much of pre-industrial, north-west Europe, marriage coincided with household formation. Newly married couples set up their own households rather than living with in-laws.[8] There is now fairly widespread agreement that this model applies to medieval England from at least the later fourteenth century onwards. It seems

---

Family History 9 (1984), pp. 355–76, especially pp. 357–62; Amy Louise Erickson, *Women and Property in Early Modern England* (London, 1993), ch. 11; Froide, 'Marital Status', especially pp. 238–43. For use of quantitative methods see, for example, Hareven and Tilly, 'Solitary Women'; Richard Wall, 'Woman Alone in English Society', *Annales de Démographie Historique* (Paris, 1981), pp. 303–17; Marilyn Cohen, 'Survival Strategies in Female-headed Households: Linen Workers in Tullyish, County Down, 1901', *Journal of Family History* 17 (1992), pp. 303–18, especially pp. 309 ff.; P.J.P. Goldberg, *Women, Work, and Life Cycle in a Medieval Economy: Women in York and Yorkshire c.1300–1520* (Oxford, 1992), pp. 305–18; Michael Anderson, 'The Social Position of Spinsters in Mid-Victorian Britain', *Journal of Family History* 9 (1984), pp. 377–93, pp. 388–90. A notable exception is John Cashmere, 'Sisters Together: Women Without Men in Seventeenth-Century French Village Culture', *Journal of Family History* 21 (1996), pp. 44–62, which discusses the existence of sisters cohabiting by focussing on one legal dispute.

7   Two historians, working on seventeenth-century France and Ireland c. 1900 respectively, have commented on how the ideology of a male centred and patriarchal household has deflected historians' attentions from alternative household formations: Cashmere, 'Sisters Together', p. 53; Cohen, 'Survival Strategies', p. 315.

8   J. Hajnal, 'Two Kinds of Pre-industrial Household Formation', in *Family Forms in Historic Europe*, ed. Richard Wall et al. (Cambridge, 1983), pp. 65–104, especially p. 69. Cf. R. Burr Litchfield, 'Single People in the Nineteenth-Century City: A Comparative Perspective on Occupations and Living Situations', *Continuity and Change* 3 (1988), pp. 83–100, p. 83, which credits Hajnal's work with leading to the recognition that single people have 'a significant place in European demographic and family history'.

that the norm in both rural and urban areas was a small and nuclear household, with the conjugal family as the basic core.[9] The key sources held to back up this view are the nominative poll tax returns of 1377, 1379 and 1381, which offer details about the majority of an area's population.[10] Poll tax listings are undoubtedly an important source, but they need to be understood as operating within a legal discourse with specific concerns, rather than as unproblematic sources for household size and structure. We need to consider how the ordering of the material reflects the assessors' concerns, rather than presume that it matches the scholar's. A more critical reading of the poll tax returns reveals a wider variety of household structures and positions. It is within such variations from the supposed nuclear family norm that women without husbands occupy positions other than that of household 'head' or 'dependant'.

Barbara Hanawalt's only criticism of poll taxes as evidence for household size was that they do not list all household members. Only those over the minimum ages of fourteen in 1377, sixteen in 1379 and fifteen in 1381 were assessed, and therefore a multiplier must be derived from other sources in order to arrive at a truer figure.[11] Jeremy Goldberg's more detailed work on this area considered the problem of high levels of under enumeration, especially in 1379 and 1381, and therefore focused on the 1377 nominative listings for calculations of mean urban household size. His multiplier of 1.65 was to compensate for a degree of exemption or evasion as well as the population under the age of fourteen.[12] However, I would like to problematise this source further and ask, how can we extricate households from what are essentially long lists of taxpayers' names? While Richard Smith states unequivocally that 'poll tax returns identify households', Goldberg notes that 'There are problems in distinguishing individual households from this material.' Nevertheless, he goes on to say that 'these are not sufficient to detract from the derived data', and produces tables listing the number of households in

---

9   E.g. Judith M. Bennett, *Women in the Medieval English Countryside: Gender and Household in Brigstock Before the Plague* (Oxford, 1987), passim but especially p. 48, pushes the dating back to the early fourteenth century; Barbara A. Hanawalt, *The Ties that Bound: Peasant Families in Medieval England* (Oxford, 1986), pp. 90–104, especially p. 94; Goldberg, *Women, Work, and Life Cycle*, pp. 305–9, 325; L.R. Poos, *A Rural Society After the Black Death: Essex 1350–1525* (Cambridge, 1991), p. 145; Richard M. Smith, 'Geographical Diversity in the Resort to Marriage in Late Medieval Europe', *Woman is a Worthy Wight: Women in English Society c.1200–1500*, ed. P.J.P. Goldberg (Stroud, 1992), pp. 16–59, passim but on p. 25 he suggests it might date back to 1250. Cf. David Herlihy, *Medieval Households* (Cambridge, Mass., 1985), who treated all of medieval Europe as if it was the same (see critique in Smith, 'Geographical Diversity', pp. 22–46).

10   Hanawalt, *Ties That Bound*, p. 92; Goldberg, *Women, Work, and Life Cycle*, p. 325; Smith, 'Geographical Diversity', especially p. 40.

11   Hanawalt, *Ties That Bound*, p. 90.

12   Goldberg, *Women, Work, and Life Cycle*, p. 305; also see P.J.P. Goldberg, 'Urban Identity and the Poll Taxes of 1377, 1379, and 1381', *Economic History Review* 43 (1988), pp. 194–216, for more detail on the problems of poll tax returns as a source.

various places with no comment on his criteria or methodology.[13] The neat extractions of households from the poll taxes have been partly based on the assumptions that when a group of people are listed together on one line, this line is equivalent to a household unit, or that when people are listed sequentially relationships are given, such as 'his wife' or 'his servant', which allow household groupings to be recreated.[14] Both assumptions are problematic.

Poll tax assessors were not interested in household units, or relationships, *per se*. However, it would have been easier to collect the taxes of a group of related individuals from one person, rather than from each person in turn.[15] The anthropologist Olivia Harris's comment on census taking is perhaps also applicable to the compiling of a tax return: 'The very *activity* . . . normally organises and defines households . . . around the identification of a single person.'[16] The household head is a useful construct and its authority derives in part from the responsibilities allotted them by other social structures. Heads are made answerable for other members of their household unit and so these people are seen as dependants. In relation to the poll tax returns, dependants are the people for whom the head is expected to pay, such as his wife and servants. However, fiscal units remain the poll tax assessors' main concern. If a person pays separately, he or she is listed separately, whether part of the same household or not. For example, in the York poll tax return of 1377 some servants are listed as paying separately from their masters:[17]

William Tailor, his wife and one servant	12d
One servant of his	4d
. . .	
Roger de Selby junior and his wife	8d
One maid [*ancilla*] of his	4d

---

13 Smith 'Geographical Diversity', p. 35; Goldberg, *Women, Work, and Life Cycle*, pp. 305 ff., 308, 310f.
14 Jennifer I. Leggett, ed., 'The 1377 Poll Tax Returns for the City of York', *Yorkshire Archaeological Journal* 43 (1971), pp. 128–46, p. 131; Maryanne Kowaleski, ed., 'The 1377 Dartmouth Poll Tax', *Devon and Cornwall Notes and Queries* 35 (1985), pp. 286–95, p. 289.
15 Sarah Rees Jones has suggested that this was also the case for rentals: private communication, meeting of the interdisciplinary Urban Household 1300–1550 research group, Centre for Medieval Studies, University of York, 1998. This collaborative project is producing a series of studies to be published by Brepols, of which two will be *The Urban Household and its Ethos* and *Household, Neighbourhood and Town*.
16 Olivia Harris, 'Households as Natural Units', *Of Marriage and the Market*, ed. K. Young, et al. (2nd edn; London, 1984), pp. 136–55, p. 146 (author's italics). Amy M. Froide, 'Single Women, Work, and Community in Southampton, 1550–1750' (unpublished Ph.D. dissertation, Duke University, North Carolina, 1996), p. 131, comments on the Marriage Duty assessments for Southampton of 1695–97 that, 'relatives of wives or other members of the household may not have been recorded as such since the assessors described the inhabitants by their relationship to the . . . household head'.
17 Leggett, '1377 Poll Tax Returns', p. 137 (although the extract given is my own translation).

It is very unlikely that unmarried servants would set up independent house-holds next door to those of their masters. What is shown in these examples are servants paying their own tax. This is implied in the less abbreviated Latin of the Hull poll tax return of 1377, for example:[18]

Alan de Miton for him and his wife	8d
Magota servant [famula] of Alan for herself [pro se ipsa]	4d.

Such examples would no doubt have been read by scholars such as Goldberg as denoting single households. However, once it has been accepted that a household might be divided up into fiscal units, then there is no reason why other people who are listed as paying separately in the poll tax returns could not also be read as households. This also applies to when people are listed sequentially, because relationships between people are not always stated. It seems unlikely, for example, that there is never a connection between people living close to each other bearing the same surname, especially when it is neither a common occupational byname nor a local place name. Living with kin was probably a common residential strategy for women without hus-bands.[19] This strategy might be even more common than a superficial reading of the poll tax returns suggests, given that one party might have married and changed her name. By cross referencing the poll tax returns with other sources, however, some possible examples of this can be found.

York is a good case study for two main reasons. First, the city's poll tax records of 1377 and 1381 are obviously compiled on a topographical basis. They are divided by parish, but a comparison of individuals found in the 1377 and the 1381 listings reveals that people are recorded in approximately the same place within the appropriate parish entry.[20] This suggests that officials conducted their assessment on a street by street basis, and that the assump-tion that people recorded next to each other in the returns probably lived next to, or very near to, each other is not negated by the lower level of recording in 1381. Secondly, there are a number of other sources, such as wills and deeds, for late fourteenth- and early fifteenth-century York which allow nominal linkages to be made and, from these, partial family reconstruc-tions. This methodology is vital when focusing on women, in that female kinship ties are often obscured because some women changed their name on

---

18 Public Record Office, London [hereafter PRO], Subsidy Rolls (E 179): E 179/206/45, m. 2d.

19 It seems to have been for other periods and countries still within the confines of the north-west European household system. E.g. Hufton, 'Women Without Men', p. 362; Michael Anderson, *Family Structure in Nineteenth-Century Lancashire* (Cambridge, 1971), p. 126; Wall, 'Woman Alone', pp. 310–14; Anderson, 'Social Position', p. 390; Cohen, 'Survival Strategies', pp. 305 ff., 308–10; Cashmere, 'Sisters Together', pp. 51 ff.

20 Beattie, 'Women Without Husbands', pp. 9f. Cf. the 1377 Hull return which is actually ordered by street name: PRO, E 179/206/45.

marriage.[21] For example, an extract from the York 1381 return could be read as two separate households (and no doubt has been by quantitative historians):[22]

William de Laycestre, Spicer	12d
Alice Pund, widow	[damaged]
Katherine, her servant [*serviens*]	[damaged].

A reading of Alice Pund's will of 1390, however, reveals that she had a nephew called Thomas Laycestre and that she had been married more than once.[23] It is possible that William de Laycestre was Alice's brother or brother-in-law, and that they were cohabiting.

Poll tax returns and other records such as wills and deeds only allow snapshots of households at a specific moment in time. By using them together it is possible to modify their essentially static nature. However, there is also a need to look at how other sources, with their differing concerns, envisage households, in terms of both their structures and their members. In the following section I will both use poll tax returns alongside other sources, and consider what a different kind of legal record, cause papers, adds to the debates.[24]

II. A Room of One's Own? Two Case Studies

The residential arrangements of two widows do not sit easily with the norms propounded by both medieval poll tax assessors and modern historians of the medieval household. The first case study is an example of how an extract from a poll tax return can become more meaningful when used alongside other sources such as wills and deeds. The second is from a disputed marriage case heard before York's consistory court in the early fifteenth century. Both cast doubt on the categories of household 'head' and 'dependant'.

The York widow Ellen de Burton is not only mentioned in the poll tax return of 1381 but we also have her quitclaim of interest in a property (1375) to which other documents relate, and her will of 1390. None of these records is directly concerned with her residential arrangements but, when put together, it is possible to make some suggestions about what these were. In

---

21 See critique by Di Cooper and Moira Donald, 'Households and "Hidden Kin" in Early Nineteenth-Century England: Four Case Studies in Suburban Exeter, 1821–1861', *Continuity and Change* 10 (1995), pp. 257–78, especially pp. 259–62.
22 Neville Bartlett, ed., *The Lay Poll Tax Returns for the City of York in 1381* (Hull, 1953), p. 73.
23 Borthwick Institute of Historical Research [hereafter BIHR], York, Probate Register 1, fol. 16v.
24 For a discussion of this source see R.H. Helmholz, *Marriage Litigation in Medieval England* (Cambridge, 1974), pp. 11–22.

the poll tax return Ellen is listed in the parish of St Crux, Fossgate, below the entry for John de Berden and his wife, Alice, and recorded as paying twelve pence. Immediately following Ellen in the return are six servants of John de Berden.[25] This suggests that all nine people were living within the same property. Possible reasons for this are suggested by the set of deeds relating to a property in Mickelgate.[26] John de Berden in a grant to a John of Beverlay refers to the property as lately belonging to one William de Burton, draper.[27] In Ellen's quitclaim, relinquishing all right to the same property to John de Beverlay, she is referred to as the widow of William de Burton, draper.[28] Clearly some connection existed between John de Berden and Ellen's former husband, William de Burton. William had presumably left John his property. Similarly, Ellen named both John and his wife, Alice, as executors to her will. However, any kinship ties between the various parties are unspecified.[29] It is difficult to do more than speculate what these could be, since Ellen's maiden name is unknown, as is Alice de Berden's. Possible explanations for Ellen's residential arrangements can be advanced, though. The connection between the Burtons and the Berdens might have been strong enough for the widow to go and live with the Berdens. Or the property in St Crux might also have been William's home and, when left to John de Berden, Ellen may have stayed in part of it as her 'free bench'.[30] In her will, Ellen bequeaths to John de Berden all her land, with buildings and appurtenances, that her former husband, John de Howsom, had left to her. It seems that Ellen possessed property of her own elsewhere.[31]

All of these sources reveal something of the functional aspects of Ellen's residential arrangements. One might expect to get at the emotional through a document such as her will. In this her only bequests, besides those to religious institutions, were to a named friar, a woman, and the Berdens. The friar was named John de Howsom and presumably was a relative of her deceased

---

[25] Bartlett, *Lay Poll Tax Returns*, p. 32.

[26] York Merchant Adventurers, Micklegate Deeds, 1–19, especially 13–17. These are calendered in David M. Smith, *A Guide to the Archives of the Company of Merchant Adventurers of York*, Borthwick Texts and Calendars, 16 (York, 1990), pp. 91–95. I am grateful to the Master and Company of the Merchant Adventurers for permission to cite these deeds.

[27] Micklegate Deeds 13 and 16; Smith, *Guide to the Archives*, pp. 94 ff.

[28] Micklegate Deed 17; Smith, *Guide to the Archives*, p. 95.

[29] BIHR, Prob. Reg. 1, fol. 10r–v.

[30] Caroline M. Barron, 'The "Golden Age" of Women in Medieval London', *Reading Medieval Studies* 15 (1989), pp. 35–58, p. 41. For other examples of widows being assigned part of a house see Derek Keene, 'Tanners' Widows, 1300–1350', *Medieval London Widows, 1300–1500*, ed. Caroline M. Barron and Anne F. Sutton (London, 1994), pp. 1–27, p. 17. On a widow's dower more generally see the essays by Loengard, Walker and Hanawalt in *Wife and Widow in Medieval England*, ed. Sue Sheridan Walker (Ann Arbor, 1993).

[31] The land was in Hertergate which was in the parish of St Mary Castlegate: Angelo Raine, *Mediaeval York: A Topographical Survey Based on Original Sources* (London, 1955), p. 202.

husband of the same name. The woman was Annabel de Holm, who can also be linked to John de Berden in that he was named as one of her executors in her will of 1391.[32] While these bequests do not necessarily represent Ellen's friendship circle, it may be that she moved in with the Berdens for companionship. However, this is the kind of motive that is not revealed in poll tax returns and deeds, and rarely in testamentary records. Nevertheless, a record of an ecclesiastical court case, where it is alleged that a widow moved into the household of a man who was apparently unrelated to her, might be a useful comparison here. This is a different kind of source, with its own problems, but it suggests that other, more dramatic, reasons for such a move were considered believable in the York of Ellen's day.

Charles Donahue, Jr., has argued that we should avoid 'the "interesting" case', because 'witnesses frequently told lies'.[33] However, the value of a case need not depend on whether the 'truth' can be established, but may lie in what stories people thought were believable.[34] Most of the surviving cause papers from the York consistory court are instance actions, private litigation.[35] Both plaintiff and defendant could bring witnesses to court who would respond to set questions. Such questions often survive and are known as articles, if produced by the plaintiff, or interrogatories, if produced by the defendant.[36] The responses of the witnesses are usually written up in a formulaic Latin and are known as depositions or attestations.[37] Goldberg has commented on cause papers that 'the way in which the evidence that survives . . . is constructed is determined not so much by actual events . . . but rather by the needs of canon law'.[38] The articles, interrogatories and depositions all obviously bear the imprint of canon lawyers but for the purposes of my argu-

---

[32] BIHR, Prob. Reg. 1, fol. 31r–v. For more on Annabel de Holm see Beattie, 'Women Without Husbands', pp. 20 ff.

[33] Charles Donahue, Jr., 'Female Plaintiffs in Marriage Cases in the Court of York in the Later Middle Ages: What Can We Learn from the Numbers?', in Walker, *Wife and Widow*, pp. 183–213, p. 184.

[34] See, for example, the work of Natalie Zemon Davis, *Fiction in the Archives: Pardon Tales and Their Tellers in Sixteenth-Century France* (Oxford, 1988), and Laura Gowing, *Domestic Dangers: Women, Words, and Sex in Early Modern London* (Oxford, 1996), especially ch. 7. Also, P.J.P. Goldberg, 'Fiction in the Archives: The York Cause Papers as a Source for Later Medieval Social History', *Continuity and Change* 12 (1997), pp. 425–45, especially pp. 435f. On the problems of court testimony as a historical source see Elizabeth S. Cohen, 'Court Testimony from the Past: Self and Culture in the Making of Text', *Essays on Life Writing: From Genre to Critical Practice*, ed. Marlene Kadar (Toronto and London, 1992), pp. 83–93; on cause papers see Gowing, *Domestic Dangers*, pp. 41–48; on criminal records generally as a historical source see Edward Muir and Guido Ruggiero, eds, *History from Crime* (Baltimore and London, 1994), tr. Corrado Biazzo Curry et al., especially the editors' Introduction and Afterword.

[35] Goldberg, 'Fiction in the Archives', p. 426.

[36] Helmholz, *Marriage Litigation*, pp. 17–19.

[37] Ibid., pp. 19 ff.; Goldberg, 'Fiction in the Archives', p. 426.

[38] Goldberg, 'Fiction in the Archives', p. 438.

ment I will refer to the statements as belonging to a plaintiff, defendant, or witness.

The cause paper to be considered here is about a disputed marriage between Agnes Grantham and John Dale in 1411.[39] John was trying to get the marriage enforced but Agnes countered that, about four months after Agnes's husband had died, she was abducted, forced to exchange words of consent with John, and raped.[40] Force is the critical issue here as Agnes was seeking to annul the marriage on grounds of 'force and fear'.[41] To do this she had to prove that the contract had been made under duress. Agnes's residential arrangements were important because she argued that it was fear of further attack that caused her to move out of her own home in Petergate, in the parish of St Michael le Belfrey, into the household of William Pountfret, in the parish of All Saints, Pavement. John denied all of Agnes's account and argued that she continued to live in her own home. What the court had to establish is whether the contract between John and Agnes was made with her free consent or under duress. Therefore, whether Agnes did or did not move from her house was considered a crucial part of her story of 'force and fear', and witnesses were questioned on this matter.

Even if, as John alleged, Agnes never moved out of her house, then her story seems to suggest that it would be considered believable for a widow to move into the house of a man who appears not to have been kin of hers. From the cause paper it is not clear what the relationship was between Agnes and William Pountfret. Witnesses normally have to state if they are related within certain degrees, but William made no such claim. However, an inventory of Hugh Grantham, Agnes's former husband, made in April 1410, reveals that he might have had dealings with the same William Pountfret. Under the heading 'Debts not cleared' it is recorded that a John Thornton and a William Pontefract owed four pounds.[42] In the court case, Agnes claimed that she had contracted marriage to a John Thornton. So the men that Agnes's husband did business with seem to have been close friends of the widow.

The statements by Agnes's supporting witnesses are clearly trying to establish two things. The first is that Agnes moved into William's house after the attack. They do this by referring to her presence there at significant times. For example, Agnes Kyrkeby, a waged servant of William's in 1410, deposed

---

39 BIHR, Cause Paper, York Consistory Court: CP F 36. Some of the depositions are translated in P.J.P. Goldberg, ed. and tr., *Women in England c.1275–1525* (Manchester, 1995), pp. 152–5.
40 The will of Hugh Grantham was both made and proved in March 1410: York Minster Library, York, Probate Register, D/C Reg. 1, fol. 154 (by kind permission of the Dean of York). According to the articles of the case, the alleged incident took place around July 1410: CP F 36.
41 Helmholz, *Marriage Litigation*, pp. 90–94; Goldberg, 'Fiction in the Archives', pp. 438 ff.
42 James Raine, ed., *Testamenta Eboracensia* 3 (Surtees Society, 45; 1864), p. 52.

that she served Agnes with food and drink and covered her in bed with sheets.[43] This was clearly to suggest that Agnes both had her meals and slept there, that is, that she was clearly a resident in William's house. The second point Agnes's supporters emphasise is that she did move out of her own house. The references to how Agnes kept her old household going in her absence, with frequent visits, are probably not to suggest that she is a strong, independent woman, but rather to counter allegations by John and his supporters that Agnes never left her own house. Any evidence of Agnes being in her old house could be explained and negated by their accounts. For example, Roger Marschall, who lived in the parish where Agnes's home was, deposed that Agnes often returned to check on her *familia* and her chattels, including great quantities of malt in the making, but took care to say that she did not spend the night there.[44]

The examples of Ellen de Burton and Agnes Grantham suggest that the categories of household 'head' and 'dependant' are not always useful when thinking about the residential arrangements of women without husbands.[45] Neither woman fits the description 'dependant'. Burton possessed a property of her own, but chose to reside instead with Berden and his household. She was assessed in the 1381 poll tax at twelve pence, when the minimum rate was four. Agnes, although living in William's household, still had a household of her own that she kept going. She also had a 'dependant' of her own, a servant. According to this servant, while Agnes was at William's she had to share a bed with a blood relative of his, dame Christina, who had 'a room and living within the dwelling house of the said William'.[46] This suggests that the women's quarters were separate to William's main household, the medieval equivalent of a 'granny flat' perhaps. Even if the depiction of Agnes's living arrangements, as presented by her supporters, is not 'true', it was clearly thought to have been a believable situation. We need to rethink definitions of the household that require there to be a head around which the household is organised and on whom the other members are dependent.

III. Women Without Husbands: Widows *v.* the Never Married

It has been argued, for other periods and countries within the confines of the northwest European household system, that there are real differences

---

43 Goldberg, *Women in England*, pp. 153 ff.
44 CP F 36; Goldberg, *Women in England*, pp. 152 ff.
45 Erickson, *Women and Property*, p. 202, in her case study of 'How lone women lived' in early modern England, commented that, 'Where they did live in someone else's household the relationship was not normally one of dependence, even if it was couched in those terms at the time because an expectation of female subservience easily elided into female dependence.'
46 Goldberg, *Women in England*, p. 154.

between the residential strategies of never married women and widows. The thesis is that generally widows become household heads, whereas the never married remain as dependants.[47] The medieval evidence is such that it is often not possible to distinguish between the never married and the widowed with any real certainty. To some degree it makes sense to assume that household 'heads' are widows and that 'dependants' might be never married. However, at this early stage of research into never-married women in late medieval England, it would be circular to identify them on the basis of similarities between their residential arrangements and those of never-married women in later periods.[48] Also, the same studies usually argue that older never-married women are often comparable to widows, and sometimes that young widows are like the never married.[49] So, to some extent, life-cycle not marital status was at issue. It is perhaps preferable to continue to question the usefulness of categories such as 'head' and 'dependant', rather than use them as a basis to separate the never married from widows.

In the previous two case studies the living arrangements of the two women can both be related to their status as widows. Agnes's house in Petergate was inherited from her husband and it was argued that Ellen might have got part of the Berden's property as her dower. However, this need not be the case. In this section the living arrangements of sisters cohabiting will be considered. These have been chosen deliberately in order to question both the household 'head'/'dependant' dichotomy and how that supposedly relates to marital status.[50] The first case study is again from a conjunction of poll tax returns and a will. One sister is a widow and the other is possibly never married. The second is from a cause paper and the marital status of both sisters is unknown, although both were single at the time of the court case.

The first example of two sisters cohabiting is derived from an explicit reference in the 1381 poll tax listings and is supported by the will of one sister. Cecilia de Yharom, who made her will in 1396, can be identified as the Cecilia de Malton of the 1381 returns. In her will she referred to her sons as Thomas and Roger de Malton. A Thomas de Malton and his wife are recorded in the 1377 poll tax listings, not only in the same parish as Cecilia is

---

47 Froide, 'Marital Status', pp. 237–43; Wall, 'Woman Alone', p. 307; Anderson, 'Social Position', p. 391; Palazzi, 'Female Solitude', p. 444.

48 Indeed Wall, 'Woman Alone', p. 307, cautions against this.

49 Froide, 'Marital Status', pp. 241–43; Wall, 'Woman Alone', p. 312; Anderson, 'Social Position', p. 391; Palazzi, 'Female Solitude', pp. 455 ff.

50 Households which consisted of unrelated women living together would presumably also be hard to divide up into 'heads' and 'dependents'. Research on women without husbands for other periods and countries, albeit within the confines of the north-west European household system, has suggested that, besides living with kin, setting up such households was a common strategy: Hufton, 'Women Without Men', pp. 361 ff.; Cohen, 'Survival Strategies', p. 310; Richard Wall, 'The Composition of Households in a Population of 6 Men to 10 Women: South-east Bruges in 1814', in eadem, Family Forms, 421–74, pp. 454 ff., although he classes one woman as the house-

listed in in the 1381 return, St Martin's, Coney Street, but around the same place in the parish listing too. Both the will and the 1381 poll tax listing refer to Cecilia having a sister called Margaret.[51] In the 1381 poll tax listing Cecilia is listed first and described by occupation, a brewster, rather than as a widow. Margaret is recorded directly under her sister's name, with the designation *soror eius*. Then there are four females described as Cecilia's servants. The impression is that Cecilia is the household head and Margaret is her dependant. It is likely that the house was Cecilia's given that she was living there with her husband, Thomas, in 1377. Cecilia's will reveals that, by 1396, she had not only remarried, to one Henry de Yharom, but had been widowed again. However, her parish was still St Martin's. It is not known at what stage Margaret moved in with her sister – whether it was before the death of Cecilia's first husband, or after, whether Margaret stayed or moved out when her sister remarried, and, if the latter, whether she moved back in when Cecilia's second husband died. In her will Cecilia not only left her sister twenty marcs but asked her favourite son, Roger, in his capacity as her executor, to use a third of the residue of her goods for the help and sustenance of her sister. The nature of this bequest perhaps suggests that Margaret could not sustain a household of her own in 1396, and was residing with her sister as she had in 1381.

This is the little that is known about Margaret. We do not know if she is a never-married woman or a widow. Both will and poll tax listing construct her as a dependant but this might be because both sources are more interested in her sister, Cecilia: the will for obvious reasons, and the poll tax because the assessors wanted a 'head' whom they could make responsible for paying the taxes for a group of connected people. Margaret thus looks like an archetypal never-married woman. Similarly, the cause paper that gives the second example of two sisters cohabiting, can be used as an example of how the construction of someone as a household 'head' or 'dependant' is affected by other concerns.

In 1432 Agnes Brignall was seeking to enforce an alleged contract of marriage to John Herford in the consistory court of York.[52] For this she needed two witnesses to the contract being made. Although it is alleged that the couple contracted before a John Jameson, one witness was not enough. The other occasion when a contract was said to have been made was in Agnes's home before two female witnesses, a Katherine Burton and Isabel Henryson,

---

hold head; Froide, 'Marital Status', p. 239, although she calls such households 'co-headed'. Evidence of this has also been found for late medieval England: Goldberg, *Women, Work, and Life Cycle*, p. 315; Derek Keene, *Survey of Medieval Winchester*, vol. 1 (Oxford, 1985), pp. 388 ff.

51 BIHR, Prob. Reg. 1, fol. 92v; Bartlett, *Lay Poll Tax Returns*, p. 41; Leggett, '1377 Poll Tax Returns', p. 137.

52 BIHR, CP F 104. Some of the depositions are translated in Goldberg, *Women in England*, pp. 114–17.

recorded as a blood sister of Agnes. John Herford's supporters countered by alleging that he was not in York at the time of this reported event. The court had to establish whether the contract was made as suggested by Katherine and Isabel. Therefore, the women, their presence in Agnes's house, and their relationship to her were of importance and other witnesses were questioned about these matters. Again, for the purposes of my argument, the value of the case does not depend on the 'truth' being established. Rather, what is of interest is how Isabel was represented by both sides.

Both sides affirm that Isabel was living with her blood sister. Both sisters were then unmarried but there is no certainty that this had always been the case.[53] The difference in names might suggest that one woman was a widow. Isabel is recorded as aged 'thirty years and more'. However, ages in cause papers are generally given to the nearest decade, so this could imply she was anywhere between her late twenties and late thirties. According to two witnesses Isabel had been living with her sister for twelve or sixteen years, so from a relatively young age.[54] This perhaps makes Agnes the more likely candidate to be the widow.

John Herford represents Isabel as her sister's dependant. The set of statements that he wanted witnesses to be asked to verify includes one saying that Isabel had nothing by which to live except what she got from selling her body, and that she was 'a household member [domestica] and known to be living with the said Agnes Brignall her sister'.[55] The term domestica seems to suggest more of a dependant than an equal member. It also had the meaning 'maid-servant'.[56] John's supporters, Thomas Midelham and William Fox, affirm both these statements. The intention was presumably to make Isabel's testimony look less objective. If she was dependent on her sister for a home then she might be supporting her cause out of self-interest. However, Agnes's set of statements countered such assertions. John's witnesses were to be asked whether Isabel and Agnes had both the same parents or just one, and whether they were equal in home and fixtures or whether one of them was superior. Presumably the purpose of these statements was to get John's witnesses to admit that Isabel was not a dependant. The question about parentage, though, might explain the sisters' different surnames.

---

[53] Isabel must have been unmarried at that stage given that she is accused by John Herford of both fornication and adultery. The medieval definition of adultery includes both lechery between a single person and a married person, and two married people, whereas fornication must be between two single people. See, for example, Venetia Nelson, ed., A Myrour to Lewde Men and Wymmen: A Prose Version of Speculum Vitae (Heidelberg, 1981), p. 165. This text was written c.1400 although it is derived from an earlier tradition.

[54] I am grateful to Jeremy Goldberg for the observation that these periods of time, rather than being random guesses, are both multiples of four, a multiple that would have been familiar from reckoning money.

[55] CP F 104.

[56] R.E. Latham, ed., Revised Medieval Latin Word-List (London, 1980), p. 155: c.1197, 1480.

Which side was telling the 'truth', if either, cannot be known. If John is believed, Agnes looks like the household head and possibly a widow, whereas Isabel appears to be the dependant and probably never married. However, if Agnes's story is followed, it seems that the sisters owned the house jointly, perhaps inheriting it from their parents. This might suggest that neither woman was a widow, and neither was a household 'head' nor 'dependent'. In Isabel's deposition, the house where she lived with her sister is described only as Agnes's home. However, it is not known what words Isabel actually used and what was added by the clerk to aid interpretation.[57] As the case was concerned with Agnes primarily, it is perhaps not surprising that events were said to have taken place in her home. However, the result of this concern is that she is perhaps misrepresented as a household 'head'.

The above case studies demonstrate that it is often not possible to distinguish between the never married and the widowed with any real certainty. This section has also argued against a simple correlation between household 'heads' and widows, and 'dependants' and the never married. This is partly because the exceptions can sometimes be more revealing,[58] and partly because 'heads' and 'dependants' are only constructs. The sources that we have were written from specific standpoints that required the household to be thought of in a certain way. Dependence, in the cause papers and the wills, as well as in the poll tax returns, is constructed as being about money. We do not know, for example, whether Isabel was a source of emotional support for her sister when John apparently jilted her, or whether Margaret was a help for Cecilia when first Thomas, then Henry, died. We are told about the functional rather than the emotional household. If we are to get closer to what women without husbands might have thought about their living arrangements, then we need to look beyond categories such as household 'heads' and 'dependants'.

Although this article focuses on York in the late fourteenth and early fifteenth centuries, it concentrates on a handful of case studies in order to make some general but important points about the residential arrangements of women without husbands. It argues, first, that a more critical approach to the legal sources that are used as evidence for medieval household structures, particularly poll tax returns, needs to be taken. One methodology advocated is that of using the returns alongside other sources so that nominal linkages can be made. Both this method and that of close readings of cause papers then were then used to address two important issues: the household 'head'/'dependant' and the widows/never married dichotomies. The former is a frequently used construct when the household is being discussed. It is a model imposed

---

57 For an example of a deposition where the language perhaps reflects the canon lawyer rather than the deponent, see Goldberg, 'Fiction in the Archives', p. 439.
58 Cf. Cohen, 'Survival Strategies', p. 304.

by both medieval authorities and modern scholars who were more interested in male-headed, conjugal units. However, this article argues that women without husbands do not always readily fit such a model. In contrast, the widows/never-married dichotomy is not readily apparent in the sources considered here but modern scholars have been criticised for not differentiating between the two groups. While interested in exploring differences between the two groups, this article's use of the umbrella group, 'women without husbands', stems from a belief that, at this early stage of research into the lives of medieval never-married women, such differences need to be uncovered carefully rather than being assumed.

Women, Testamentary Discourse and Life-Writing in Later Medieval England

KATHERINE J. LEWIS

THROUGHOUT the Middle Ages the last will was intended to perform certain legal and religious functions. Virginia Bainbridge argues that wills are 'snapshots' taken by those in authority. [1] Wills are thus embedded within a specific context which to a great extent directs their meaning and the ways in which they are interpreted. But, regardless of what wills were originally intended to accomplish we can relate them to the past in several different ways and at different levels. Testamentary evidence has been employed by a variety of scholars in order to illuminate our knowledge of legal and religious, as well as social, familial, demographic, and economic history. [2] In more recent years wills have increasingly been used to clarify our understanding of medieval women's beliefs and practices. [3] They are particularly valuable in this respect as women have left comparatively little other direct evidence about their lives in this period. This article seeks to investigate wills not as documents, but as texts, and to explore the extent to which women's wills can be understood as autobiographical compositions. [4] It draws on the wills of 19 women, and those of their husbands. [5]

These wills date from the fifteenth and early sixteenth centuries, and the testators were all based in, or had important ties with, the county of Somer-

---

[1] Virginia R. Bainbridge, *Gilds in the Medieval Countryside: Social and Religious Change in Cambridgeshire c. 1350–1558* (Woodbridge, 1996), p. 59.

[2] M.M. Sheehan, 'English wills and the records of the ecclesiastical and civil jurisdictions', *Journal of Medieval History* 14 (1988), pp. 3–12, pp. 3–4 for discussion of this point.

[3] For example, Caroline M. Barron, 'The "Golden Age" of Women in Medieval London', *Reading Medieval Studies* 15 (1989), pp. 35–58; articles in Caroline M. Barron and Anne F. Sutton, eds., *Medieval London Widows: 1300–1500* (London and Rio Grande, 1994), pp. 55–67; P.H. Cullum, ' "And hir name was charite": charitable giving by and for women in late-medieval Yorkshire', in *Women in Medieval English Society*, ed. P.J.P. Goldberg (Stroud, 1997), pp. 182–211.

[4] This leads on from Victoria Thompson's similar approach to the wills of Anglo-Saxon women discussed earlier in this volume.

[5] See Appendix.

set.[6] In general terms those who left wills and inventories in the later Middle Ages were those who could afford to, those who possessed at least some property or other goods, which they wanted to dispose of in precise ways after their death.[7] Those drawn from the upper levels of peasant society, or more affluent urban artisans did leave wills, but those which have been consulted for this study were all made by people of gentry or affluent mercantile status. In some instances we can be more precise about their status. Six of the male testators describe themselves as 'knight', three as 'esquire'.[8] At least two seem to have been involved in cloth making or dying, to judge by bequests of cloth and woad mentioned in their wills.[9] Presumably their wives originally came from similar kinds of backgrounds as their husbands, although in only a few instances are we given any indication of their status, beyond being the wife/widow of their husband.[10]

The majority of wills in this period were made by men. Although there are some extant wills made by married women, the majority of female will-makers were widows.[11] Richard Helmholz argues that by 1450 it was widely assumed that married women had no separate property or independent legal interest in chattels, and that there was a concomitant decline in the number of married women making wills.[12] This development is born out here: within this sample three women made wills within their husband's lifetime, the

6 The wills have been taken from F.W. Weaver, ed., *Somerset Medieval Wills*, Somerset Record Society, 16, 19, 21 (originally published 1901–05; reprinted 1983). Wills dating from 1350–1500 are in the 1901 volume, hereafter I, wills dating from 1500–1530 are in the 1903 volume, hereafter II. I am aware that there are problems in using a sample taken from an edited collection. In some cases the editor has clearly only taken an abstract of a will, especially where the will is in Latin, depending on his opinion of the interest/use of its contents, although he mostly makes a fairly full transcription of the English wills. But nevertheless to judge by a comparison with the form and content of other extant wills I believe that those chosen for this analysis provide a stable enough sample for the present purpose – which suggests an altenative way of approaching testamentary evidence. Here I quote from the wills that are in English, as they provide a closer representation of the 'authored voice' of the women within the wills in this collection, unlike those not in the vernacular.
7 For a general introduction to the will and testamentary procedure see Michael M. Sheehan, *The Will in Medieval England: From the Conversion of the Anglo-Saxons to the End of the Thirteenth Century* (Toronto, 1963).
8 The knights and their wills: Sir Humphrey Stafford (II, pp. 312–13), Sir Leonard Hakeluyt (I, pp. 61–2), Sir Richard Chocke (I, pp. 238–43), Sir John Byconyll (II, pp. 6–9), Sir John Newton (II, p. 272), and Sir John Speke (II, pp. 189–90). The esquires and their wills: William Grene (I, pp. 122–24), John Cammell (I, pp. 270–71), Roger Twnyhoo (I, p. 352).
9 Richard atte Welle (I, pp. 227–78) and John Hille (I, pp. 233–34).
10 For example, see the will of Joan Twynhoo, below.
11 Barron, 'The "Golden Age" of Women in Medieval London', passim; also her introduction to *Medieval London Widows*, pp. xiii–xxxiv; Anne J. Kettle, ' "My wife shall have it": marriage and property in the wills and testaments of later medieval England', in *Marriage and Property: Women and Marital Customs in History*, ed. Elizabeth Craik (Aberdeen, 1984), pp. 89–103.
12 Richard H. Helmholz, 'Married Women's Wills in later Medieval England', in *Wife and Widow in Medieval England*, ed. Sue Sheridan Walker (Michigan, 1993), pp. 165–82, esp. pp. 172–75.

others were all made between one and twenty-eight years after their husband's death.[13] To judge by the time that elapses between the date that a will was made and its probate, the majority of those consulted were made just before death.

For the purposes of this investigation I have chosen to analyse the wills of those women whose husbands' wills are also extant. In this way it will be possible to draw comparisons between female and male wills, in order to investigate the frequently voiced assertion that there are certain intrinsic, gendered differences between the contents and concerns recorded in women's and men's wills.[14] In addition, by comparing the wills of wives and their husbands, it may be possible to draw some conclusions about the ways in which women could use wills as a form of self-definition.

Thinking in terms of wills as a means of constructing an identity indicates that the main concern of this article is explicitly not to investigate the ways in which these women's wills reflect the 'reality' of their lives, beliefs, experiences or attitudes. Instead the aim here is to suggest that the female will can be perceived as a self-representational text, and the composition of it as an autobiographical act. The argument here leads on from Victoria Thompson's discussion, earlier in this volume, of the ways in which surviving Anglo-Saxon wills can be seen as 'among the few contexts in which we can see them structuring the narrative of their lives, "telling their stories" in effect'.[15] In legal terms, this suggests a type of female legal agency, not only in the act of being able to make a will, but especially in terms of being able to use the legal forum of the will as an arena within which to tell these stories. Late-medieval female wills do not present such a rare example of writing in a female voice as their Anglo-Saxon counterparts.[16] In the cases of Julian of Norwich and Margery Kempe we have female-authored texts which are explicitly concerned with 'telling their stories' and are frequently discussed within the context of women's autobiography.[17] The women whose wills we shall consider here were very likely to be able to read, if perhaps not to write, and had far greater access to a variety of texts than earlier medieval women.[18] We also have a far greater range of extant documentation which allows us to hear

---

13 Wills made before husband's death: Elizabeth Stafford (II, pp. 304–6), Agnes Grene (I, pp. 108–9), Joan Twynhoo (I, pp. 284–85). Only Joan mentions that she is making the will with her husband's permission.

14 For discussion of this see e.g. Cullum, ' "And hir name was charite" ', pp. 185–86.

15 Victoria Thompson, 'Women, Power and Protection in Tenth- and Eleventh-Century England', p. 1.

16 For a representative anthology see Alexandra Barratt, ed., *Women's Writing in Middle English* (London and New York, 1992). See also Carol M. Meale, ed., *Women and Literature in Britain, 1100–1500* (Cambridge, 1993).

17 See below n.57.

18 For an introductory survey of medieval women's education see Nicholas Orme, *Education and Society in Medieval and Renaissance England* (London and Ronceverte, 1989), pp. 161–75; see also

their voices, albeit through the medium of the male scribe.[19] Nonetheless, despite their greater visibility (or perhaps, rather, their audibility) in this respect, it is the contention of this article that wills offered late-medieval women a rare opportunity for deliberate, 'official' textual self-presentation. Similarly, Gail McMurray Gibson, in her study of East Anglian drama and society in the later Middle Ages, argues that:

> The social restraints on women and their actions probably made the female testator's will . . . a document recording, sometimes for the very first time, her own self-identity, her sense of priorities, her convictions, and affirmations of her significant personal, family, and institutional relationships.[20]

The present study is therefore not directly concerned with questions of how far wills constitute windows, or mirrors, which provide a clear view or reflection of the past and its people. Given the circumstances of a will's composition, its status as the last pious act of a Christian usually near death, it must be questioned whether its provisions can be taken as an accurate representation of the individual's concerns or priorities. Wills can only give us a partial idea of the lives and beliefs of individuals and communities. For example, the work of Clive Burgess' has demonstrated that a brief will does not necessarily indicate poverty or lack of religious enthusiasm on the part of the testator. Rather it may be that she/he died with their wishes and estate well in order.[21]

Another problematic area sometimes explored by those analysing wills is the question of whether a testator's final bequests and requests were actually undertaken by her/his executor.[22] However, this issue is not of direct relevance to the present survey, because it is concerned with the textually constructed 'reality' presented by women's wills, and therefore deliberately does not seek to ascertain what correspondence this may have had with any historical or documentary reality that exists. Indeed, in post-structuralist terms we could argue that there are no 'real' women to discover. The 'I' of the will does not and cannot exist for us outside of the text which constitutes a

Caroline M. Barron, 'The Education and Training of girls in Fifteenth-Century London', in *Courts, Counties and the Capital in the Later Middle Ages*, ed. Diana E.S. Dunn (Stroud, 1996), pp. 139–53.

[19] E.g. legal, devotional, hagiographical, etc. P.J.P. Goldberg, *Women in England c. 1275–1525* (Manchester, 1995), provides a very useful survey of the range of sources available.

[20] Gail McMurray Gibson, *The Theater of Devotion: East Anglian Drama and Society in the Late Middle Ages* (Chicago and London, 1989), pp. 71–72.

[21] Clive Burgess, 'Late-medieval wills and pious convention: testamentary evidence reconsidered', in *Profit, Piety and the Professions in Later Medieval England*, ed. Michael Hicks (Gloucester, 1990), pp. 14–33; and his ' "By quick and by dead": wills and pious provision in late medieval Bristol', *English Historical Review* 405 (1987), pp. 837–58.

[22] Sheehan, *The Will in Medieval England*, p. 219; idem, 'English Wills', p. 8.

woman's last testament.[23] But while bearing these interpretations in mind, it is also important to note that there are many instances in which we can trace connections between the pre-occupations highlighted by a will and the beliefs, experiences and connections of its maker which emerge from other documentary sources.[24] For example, Gibson has indicated the ways in which the wills of three members of the East Anglian gentry, John Baret, John Clopton and Anne Harling, constitute a continuation of individual and familial life-time practices and priorities.[25]

In problematising the nature of the will, we need to think further about its status as a personal, final statement. Michael Clanchy argues that originally the primary purpose of wills was to ensure the testator's state of grace at death, rather than to dispose of his/her effects.[26] Given the circumstances in which wills were usually composed it is not surprising that religious and devotional concerns are frequently paramount. On a basic level even the briefest of the wills here consulted contain some bequest intended to secure intercession and memorialisation for the testator's soul. For example, the single biggest bequest in Amice Gregory's will of 1457 is 8 marks of silver to pay a suitable priest to celebrate mass for her soul for one year.[27] She had been widowed for nearly thirty years and her will does not display the same levels of wealth as her husband John Gregory's, made in 1429.[28] Similarly, the largest bequest in the brief 1513 will of Margery Merifield is 9 marks to be expended on a priest to celebrate for the souls of herself and her husband.[29]

Some of these women were able to make much more lavish provision. For example, in 1405 Elizabeth Stafford, wife of Sir Humphrey Stafford, left detailed instructions for her funeral.[30] She requested 1000 masses for her soul and for the souls of her ancestors and benefactors from the church of St Giles, Stapleford and from the friars of Dorchester, Yevelchester and Abbotsbury, leaving each institution £4 3s 4d to accomplish this. There are also detailed instructions for pennies to be handed out to all the tenants and poor people who come to her burial and her trental. The clerks in attendance were to receive 6d, and everyone who attended her exequies was to be fed. The will of Elizabeth Byconyll (1504) leaves particularly precise instructions for inter-

---

23 In documentary terms this is sometimes literally true.
24 M.L. Zell, 'The use of religious preambles as a measure of religious belief in the sixteenth century', *Bulletin of the Institute of Historical Research* 50 (1977), pp. 246–49; Goldberg, *Women in England*, pp. 51–52.
25 Gibson, *The Theater of Devotion*, pp. 67–106.
26 Michael Clanchy, *From Memory to Written Record: England 1066–1307* (2nd edn, Oxford, 1993), p. 232.
27 I, p. 171.
28 I, pp. 131–32.
29 II, p. 166.
30 For the following see II, pp. 304–6.

cessory prayers.[31] She asks that as soon as her ghostly father and other clerks have administered extreme unction:

> . . . immediately as by man erthly it may be perceyved that my soule shuld be from my body separate, as soon as the lawe of holy church ordeyneth after the apperyng of the daylight by the advice of myn executors iiij discrete preestes shall secretly say dirige and masse for my soule begynnyng the trigentall of Saint Gregory, every preest to say xxxti masse xxxti diriges suceeding dayly or other in their stede till the xxxti day of partyng, and than from that howre of myn Auete betwixt the hour of the burying of my body the said iiij preests say for the helth of my soul neuer cessing, but oon of them to be occupyd nyght and day in sayng iiij tymes the Saulter of David as the Holy Church doth use it by the ordeynance of most holy Saynt Jerome every one of them to be rewarded as they deserve by myn executors.[32]

As has already been seen, in general these sorts of concerns were often a continuation of life-time beliefs and practices, but were coloured by a much more immediate anxiety for the fate of the soul. Through the various bequests specified in the will, a network of memorialisation and intercession is created, often spread over a variety of sites and individuals, and focused on the figure of the testator as benefactor. We can see this at work on one level, for example, in the 1485 will of Joan Atwell, the widow of Richard Atwell, who seems to be have been involved in cloth-making or dying in Glastonbury. (Both of their wills leave cloth as bequests and Joan leaves a quarter of woad each to Margaret Robyns and Joan Wyke.)[33] Several bequests are focused on the parish church of St John the Baptist in Glastonbury, where she and her husband were buried.[34] A gold ring and a veil of lawn are left to the image of the Virgin in the church, two other figures of Mary in the church each get a lawn veil too and each of the four lights in the church are left 20d. The church is also left one lead vessel for keeping oil and one pipe of lamp oil. Joan also leaves 6s 8d to the fabric of chapels at West Kennard, Strete and to the parish church of Walton. In addition, each poor person living in 'la spitell hous' is to be given one cartload of fuel. Everyone who carries one of these cartloads is to be given 4d for their labour. In this way Joan spreads her benefactions quite widely. According to Leland she and her husband arranged to have a permanent record of themselves erected in the church of St John the Baptist too:

---

[31] II, pp. 72–74.
[32] II, p. 72.
[33] I, pp. 255–56, Joan; ibid., 227–28, Richard.
[34] For this and the following see ibid., pp. 227–28.

Ther lyith on the N. side of the Quier one Richard Atwell that died circa 1472 [his will was registered for probate in 1476 in fact]. This Atwelle did much cost in this chirch and gave fair Housing that he had buildid in the Toune onto it . . . Johanna wife to Atwelle lyith buried in a lyke marbel Tumbe on the S. side of the Quier.[35]

Margaret Chocke, widow of Sir Richard Chocke 'oon of the Kynges Justice', displays similar concerns in her will of 1484.[36] Margaret had evidently become a vowess after her husband's death, and her will is largely taken up with devotional/intercessory bequests. She requests burial with her husband in the church of All Hallows in Aishton, and leaves the church a gown of blue velvet, a kirtle of blue damask, her professed ring and a tapestry work coverlet to lie before the high altar on principal feasts 'and other tymes to be occupied on a bedde in the chauntry house to kepe it from mothes.' This coverlet was likely a piece that she had worked on herself, and specifying its use thus was a way of ensuring that she would be brought to mind, and prayers at key moments in the Church year. In addition Margaret asks the executors to make:

. . . a wyndow in Aisheton Chuirch of iij dayes [lights] and glace yt as thodir wyndowes beth wt my husbondis armys and myn undir neth the ymages And saynt Sonday be the ton of the ymagis and saynt Gregory is the tother.[37]

Both Joan and Margaret use their wills in an attempt to establish and maintain their posthumous reputation as important, generous and devout women. In this way the very composition of the will as much as the instructions it contains constitutes the construction of a pious identity. The 'I' of the will may have been quite different to the empirical individual who dictated it, but the overwhelming impression left for posterity is of the generously pious woman.

These observations force consideration of the extent to which the will can be seen as a personal statement on the part of the testator. Thompson has already discussed the oral or nuncupative nature of Anglo-Saxon wills.[38] From the thirteenth century it became the norm for wills to be written down, and, as Clanchy observes, from this time the validity of the will was primarily dependent upon it being a correctly formulated document.[39] Despite this shift, 'the notion of the will as an oral act continued in England until well

---

35 Quoted by Weaver, I, p. 228.
36 For the following I, pp. 244–45.
37 I, p. 245.
38 Thompson, 'Women, Power and Protection', p. 7.
39 Clanchy, p. 254.

after the Middle Ages' as Michael Sheehan points out.[40] The fifteenth-century wills currently under consideration retain marked oral features. The wills begin with the formula 'I, X, make my will in this manner'. Throughout the will each bequest is specified 'I bequeath', or 'I will' and this is representative of the other wills in this sample.[41] They read like transcripts of dictated statements, and indeed later medieval wills seem to constitute the preservation of the spoken wishes of the testator in written form by a scribe, probably a cleric.[42]

We are usually given little indication in the wills themselves as to the precise circumstances under which this took place. Sometimes the composition of a will may have been dictated by special circumstances but in general it seems reasonable to assume that the testator was actually on her or his death-bed when the composition took place. Indeed, at least one testator, Isabel Fitz-James, gives us a direct indication of this as among the bequests mentioned in the 1527 codicil to her will is, 'I will that Sir Robert Rotherham, parishe prest, shal have a counterpoynt of imagery which nowe lyes upon me'.[43] In most wills the scribe gives no indication as to his identity, but there are sometimes clues. Several of the Somerset wills include clerics not only as recipients, but also as being executors, or among the list of witnesses to the will itself. For example, Humphrey and Elizabeth Stafford both name the clerics William Erkerdon and Edmund Elyot as executors and in 1498 Sybil Cammell lists as her witnesses Master William Spekenton, bachelor, Sir John Hardiberd, public notary and Sir John Barnhill, chaplain.[44] Sometimes the cleric in question seems to have been the spiritual adviser of the testator; in 1429 John Gregory refers to one of his executors, Master John Symondesburgh as 'my beloved in Christ', in 1483 Margaret Chocke makes Sir Hugh Walbrond 'my preste' one of her executors, and one of the witnesses to Sir William St. Maur's will in 1503 is 'my gostely fader', Nicholas Chaunterell.[45] It seems reasonable to assume that these clerical friends and acquaintances probably acted as scribes for the testators. Only one of the testators, William Balsham, whose will is dated 1444, explicitly states that he has written his own will.[46]

The scribe would have been responsible for embedding the final wishes of the individual testator within conventional, institutional language. This involved the employment of a recognised legal and religious formula for the

---

40 Sheehan, *The Will in Medieval England*, p. 187.
41 For one example see the will of Agnes Grene: I, p. 108.
42 Sheehan, *The Will in Medieval England*, pp. 193–94.
43 II, p. 252.
44 I, p. 305, p. 313, p. 373.
45 I, p. 132, p. 245; II, p. 50.
46 I, p. 156.

disposition of property and the articulation of concern for the soul.[47] This process has led some historians to argue that wills represent the interests of the clerical scribe rather than of the testator.[48] However, as Noël James Menuge has pointed out in a study of Bristol wills, the formulaic nature of a will does not automatically render it impersonal: 'despite the use of a scribe and the conventional legal language, [wills] are intensely personal documents'.[49] This is particularly true of female wills, which, as will be seen, frequently comprise the reiteration of very personal, familial, and wider domestic preoccupations and concerns. It is almost impossible to tell in the case of individual wills how far the scribe has influenced content as well as form, but nonetheless Gibson's description of wills as 'self-conscious and volitional documents' deserves serious consideration.[50]

Thus the nature of the relationship between the testator and the text of her will is somewhat problematic. This does not, however, preclude their identification as female-authored texts. Virtually all of the female-authored texts composed in the later Middle Ages were not physically written by the woman whose voice they represent. The Proem to *The Book of Margery Kempe* gives us a particularly detailed description of the way in which this process could work. Kempe has had one version of her narrative written (possibly by her son) which is virtually illegible, so she has asked a priest to read, and re-write it:

> þe preste, trustyng in hire prayers, be-gan to redyn þis booke, & it was mych mor esy, as hym þowt, þan it was be-forn-tym. & so he red it ouyr be-forn þis creatur euery word, sche sum-tym helpyng where ony difficulte was . . . And þerfor sche dede no þing wryten but þat sche knew ryght wel for very trewth.[51]

We are given the picture here of the priest reading back to Kempe her dictated words, in order that she can judge their 'trewth'. She is presented as being in overall control of the text of her life.[52] It seems reasonable to suggest a similar process of dictating and reading back in the case of our female testators and their scribes. These women would want to make sure that their final wishes were precisely and correctly recorded, perhaps particularly with

---

47 Sheehan, *The Will in Medieval England*, pp. 193–95.

48 J.D. Alsop, 'Religious preambles in Early Modern wills as formulae', *Journal of Ecclesiastical History* 40 (1989), pp. 19–27.

49 Noël James Menuge, 'The Infant Heir in the Urban Household: A Study of Bristol Wills' (unpublished Leeds International Medieval Congress paper, 1997), p. 2.

50 Gibson, *The Theater of Devotion*, p. 71.

51 Sanford Brown Meech and Hope Emily Allen, eds., *The Book of Margery Kempe*, Early English Text Society o.s. 212 (1940), p. 5.

52 Lynn Staley, *Margery Kempe's Dissenting Fictions* (Pennsylvania, 1994), presents a strong argument for seeing Margery Kempe as the author and controlling force behind *The Book*.

respect to valuable large-scale bequests, but arguably no less in the case of small personal items left to a favourite relative or friend. *The Book of Margery Kempe* is a very different kind of text to a female will, but it is my contention that both constitute forms of female life-writing. In the case of Margery Kempe, this was a very self-conscious act, a formalisation of the many times that she apparently used the confessional 'to be schreuyn of alle hir lyfe-tym as ner as sche cowde'.[53] We could make the further point that Margery herself was obviously familiar with the sorts of language and formulae used in wills, and what these were for. A passage from the eighth chapter of her book makes this apparent, when she says to Christ:

'Lord, sythen þow hast for-ȝouyn me my synne, I make þe myn executor of alle þe god werkys þat þow werkyst in me. In prayng, in thynkyng, in wepyng, in pylgrimage goyng, in fastyng, er in any good word spekyng, it is fully my wyl þat þow ȝeue Maystyr R. halfyndel to encres of hys meryte as yf he ded hem hys owyn self. And þe oþer haluendel, Lord, sprede on þi frendys & þi enmys on my frendys & myn enmys, for I wyl haue but þi-self for my mede.' [and he replies] 'Dowtyr, I xal be a trew executor to þe & fulfyllyn all þi wylle, & for þi gret charyte þat þow hast to comfortyn þin euen-cristen þu schalt haue dubbyl reward in Heuyn.'[54]

Here Margery displays not only her knowledge of the legal processes of the will, but in employing Christ as her executor sanctions her life's behaviour in short, she uses this legal forum symbolically in order to write her character as she sees it. She probably had to make a proper will of her own when she was motally ill after the birth of her first child – it is likely that her 'ghostly father', who comes to hear her final confession, might also have been there to take down her will[55] – and would thus have had the experience to employ this formula when it suited the autobiographic purposes of her later life.

Nevertheless, in ordinary cases I do not wish to suggest that the composition of a will signifies such an absolutely self-conscious act on the part of the female testator. Certainly this was far from being the 'official' function of wills, and, again, we have little way of knowing the motivating factors that would govern the range of bequests made. But just as, in some senses, the nature of the bequests can be more useful to an historian than the issue of whether they were actually carried out, so the question of motive becomes less important if we return to the idea of the will as text. For there is an iden-

---

[53] *Book of Margery Kempe*, p. 7.

[54] *Book of Margery Kempe*, pp. 20–21.

[55] Some of the women in my sample evidently used their confessors to take down their wills: see above, p. 64.

tifiable typology to female wills, allowing us to look upon them as in some senses akin to a literary genre, or discourse. As has already been indicated, in this case the most appropriate comparative genre is autobiography.

The study of autobiography has flourished over the last fifty years, but feminist scholars have recognised that the expectations and definitions of autobiography have been almost exclusively based on the reading of men's.[56] Since the 1980s several studies devoted exclusively to the subject of female autobiography have provided a variety of definitions and analyses of female life-writing.[57] This has served to deconstruct the dichotomy which holds autobiography to be a positive term when applied to men, but which holds 'negative connotations when imposed on women's texts'.[58] Historical surveys of women's autobiography invariably include discussion of *The Book of Margery Kempe* and Julian of Norwich's *A Revelation of Divine Love* as the only two medieval examples.[59] However, one of the most important points that emerges from this scholarship is the necessity of exploring not only those texts that are self-consciously autobiographical in intent, but any texts that contain female-authored life accounts.[60] Wills do not seem to have been used as a source by those studying female life-writing. We have seen that Gibson makes autobiographic claims for female wills, although in the course of her study she only applies the actual term autobiography to the will of John Clopton.[61] Wills certainly fit into Sidonie Smith's definition of autobiography as 'written or verbal communication that takes the speaking "I" as its subject rendering the "I" both subject and object'.[62] For this reason it seems valid to treat them as such, especially given the comparative lack of more self-conscious medieval female life-writing.

---

56 Domna C. Stanton, ed., *The Female Autograph: Theory and Practice of Autobiography from the Tenth to the Twentieth Century* (Chicago and London, 1984), pp. 3–20; Estelle C. Jelinek, *The Tradition of Women's Autobiography from Antiquity to the Present* (Boston, 1986), pp. 1–8; Sidonie Smith, *A Poetics of Women's Autobiography: Marginality and the Fictions of Self-Representation* (Bloomington and Indianapolis, 1987), pp. 3–19. I am grateful to Sarah Williams for her help and advice on the subject of women's autobiography.

57 See works cited in the previous note. Also Bella Brodzki and Celeste Schenck, eds., *Life-Lines: Theorizing Women's Autobiography* (Ithaca and London, 1988); Sidonie Smith and Julia Watson, eds., *De-Colonizing the Subject: The Politics of Gender in Women's Autobiography* (Minneapolis, 1992); Leigh Gilmore, *Autobiographics: A Feminist Theory of Women's Self-Representation* (Ithaca and London, 1994).

58 Stanton, *Female Autograph*, p. 4.

59 Janel M. Mueller, 'Autobiography of a new 'creatur': female spirituality, selfhood and authorship in *The Book of Margery Kempe*, in Stanton, *Female Autograph*, pp. 57–69; Jelinek, *Tradition of Women's Autobiography*, pp. 11–22; Smith, *Poetics of Women's Autobiography*, pp. 64–83. The writings of other medieval female visionaries and the writings of Christine de Pisan certainly deserve more attention in this respect.

60 Gilmore, *Autobiographics*, p. ix.

61 Gibson, *Theater of Devotion*, p. 90.

62 Smith, *Poetics of Women's Autobiography*, p. 19.

From a methodological point of view it is also appropriate to consider wills as forms of autobiography. On the one hand both can be regarded as texts whose form and meaning is grounded in the experiences of the women who authored them, and interpreted via the framework of what we know about women's lives to understand them as self-representative texts.[63] On the other, they can both be read as construing the self simply as a textual construction which may bear no resemblance to historical 'reality'.[64] In the case of both autobiography and wills we are dealing with a discourse that is based to a greater or lesser extent on the actualities of its author's life, but that can be manipulated to leave a particular impression behind.

But if at least some measure of textual self-construction is at work in these wills, do we need to ask at whom it is directed? Who is the intended audience? Many of these fifteenth-century wills were evidently written down during the testator's lifetime – six of the women explicitly state that they have affixed a personal seal to the document.[65] Furthermore, over half of the wills contain reference to witnesses as well as to executors.[66] It is not entirely clear whether they witness the actual composition of the will itself, although that must be a possibility. They are certainly witness to the contents of the will, and to the affixing of a seal, where appropriate. They would be aware of the nature and recipients of the various bequests, and, I would argue, of the representation of continuous identity that the testator seeks to create for him/herself.[67]

These female will-makers would also have been aware of a wider audience. Of the sixteen women who were alive at their husband's death all but one were made executor of his will.[68] They would thus have been responsible, either solely, or alongside others, for presenting the will to the appropriate ecclesiastical authority for probate.[69] All of these wills are extant as copies of the originals preserved in what their editor described as 'tall thick volumes' which signifies their enrolment before the bishop of Bath and Wells for probate.[70] When the time came for these women to make their own wills they would thus have a precise idea of the hands through which their dictated text

---

[63] This formulation was influenced by Gilmore, *Autobiographics*, p. 18.

[64] Ibid. See also Smith, *Poetics of Women's Autobiography* pp. 44–62. This has already been suggested in the case of wills, see above, pp. 59–60.

[65] Elizabeth Stafford, I, p. 306; Agnes Grene, I, p. 109; Alice Balsham, I, p. 173; Isabel Newton, I, p. 375; Joan Twynhoo, I, p. 285 and Isabel Fitz-James, II, p. 252.

[66] For the importance of witnesses, see Sheehan, *The Will in Medieval England*, pp. 178–79, p. 191.

[67] 'Continuous identity' is a concept borrowed from Smith, *Poetics of Women's Autobiography*, p. 47.

[68] The exception is Elizabeth Speke. Her husband Sir John Speke makes his son George his sole executor in his will of 1516, II, pp. 189–90.

[69] For women as executors see Rowena E. Archer and B.E. Ferme, 'Testamentary procedure with special reference to the executrix', *Reading Medieval Studies* 15 (1989), pp. 3–34.

[70] Weaver, *Somerset Medieval Wills*, p. xvii. These are registered in the Prerogative Court of

would pass as its contents were ratified and its instructions carried out.[71] Their contents would be known not simply by the immediate witnesses, but by probate officials, as well as by the intended recipients, some of whom probably already knew of their inclusion. The will would eventually be included in a probate register, thus leaving a permanent textual record and representation of the testator for posterity. These women would be well aware of the different audiences that would have access to their testamentary self-presentation, which in turn may have affected the nature of that construction.

Comparisons between autobiography and wills also make sense in terms of the perceived differences between the male and female forms of both. There is a perceptible binary opposition between male and female autobiography, as several scholars have observed. According to Stanton, the male autobiography is associated with public, professional achievements.[72] The male autobiographer thus presents himself as the mirror of his era.[73] Conversely the female autobiography is associated with personal, intimate and essentially private concerns.[74] Thus it is not held to be 'representative' in the same way that a man's is.[75] Estelle C. Jelinek, in one of the first systematic studies of women's autobiography, identified a 'consistent pattern of similar characteristics'; 'the subjects women write about are remarkably similar', comprising the family, close friends and domestic activities.[76] The men's wills in this sample are often generally taken up with the question of land and other considerable properties, and bequeath sums of money rather than personal items.[77] Similarly to male autobiography, this would emphasise the author's powerful public status above all. In most cases, as in our sample, men died first, leaving their wives, as executors, to ensure that their husband's final wishes were carried out, hence men did not need to specify any but the most important matters – she would take care of anything else.[78] On the other hand women's wills are far more likely to be taken up with bequests of very personal posses-

---

Canterbury, hence the exclusively aristocratic and mercantile nature of the sample. Wills were proved within the Probate Canterbury Court where the testator held property in more than one diocese (and hence could not be proved in the local bishop's court). I am grateful to P.J.P. Goldberg for information concerning this point.

71 For the probate procedure and implementation of the will see Sheehan, 'English wills', passim.

72 Stanton, *Female Autograph*, p. 11; Smith, *Poetics of Women's Autobiography*, p. 16.

73 Bdodzki and Schenk, *Politics of Gender*, pp. 1–2; Smith, ibid., p. 8.

74 Stanton, *Female Autograph*, p. 11.

75 Smith, p. 8.

76 Jelinek, *Tradition of Women's Autobiography*, pp. xii–xiii.

77 For example, the wills of William Balsham (I, pp. 155–56), John Hille (I, pp. 233–34), John Newton (I, p. 272) and John Speke (II, pp. 189–90).

78 Burgess, 'Late medieval wills', pp. 20–21.

sions such as clothes and jewelry.[79] Some representative examples will serve to illustrate this point.

The codicil to Elizabeth Stafford's will, written in 1413, is almost completely taken up with bequests of this nature.[80] Her daughter-in-law, also Elizabeth Stafford, is left a gown of scarlet furred with miniver, a hood of scarlet and a mantle furred with grey. Margaret Beer is given a red gown, Juliana Hillary a blue, as is Alice, Elizabeth's chambermaid. By contrast Humphrey Stafford's codicil bequests, also written in 1413 (apparently just after Elizabeth's death) all take the form of precisely specified sums of money to men, from £20 to the Abbot of Abbotsbury to 6s 8d each to the two boys who serve in the chapel.[81] The only exception is Alice the chambermaid, who is left 20s, and Elizabeth his daughter-in-law, who is left a charger, twelve dishes and six silver saucers, which would seem to underline the testamentary connection between women and material objects.[82]

Elizabeth Speke's will of 1518 constitutes a very detailed list of her personal belongings.[83] For example, her unnamed daughter-in-law is left 'a bee of gold with stonys', and her two sons by her first marriage, William and Walter, are left particular items of silverware. Silverware is also left to two cousins, John Rowe and John Soumaster. The latter's wife is left

> my lytull rope of perells with the bedstone of gold. Also to hir my litull
> paire of beides of gold, and my best purfle fot a bonet sett with perells
> and my best pyncasse, also a crosse of gold that hyng aboute my necke
> usually, my secound best frontlet and a demy girdell the coorse of venys
> gold.[84]

Several women are left gowns: Elizabeth Colshill 'a tawny gowne of cloth purfeled with black velvet', Elizabeth Speke's sister Alice Gere 'a gowne of violet ingrayned, furred with black bogie', Alice Gere 'a gowne of violet ingreyned and furred with whyte leetes', Margaret Trowbrigge 'a gowne of black chamlett purfelyd with cremsyn velvet and my best bonet garnysshed and my best frountlet embrouded'. Alice Gere also gets 'my second best bonet', as well as '3½ yerdis of fyne tawny clothe and a blak kirtill of wolsted'. Amy Ashe is left 'my thyrd best bonet and a chaced pece of silver' and Alice Uppeton, 'my cheff woman-servant', 'and a gowne of tawny clothe purfeled

---

79 The following does not give an exhaustive account of the contents of the representative wills in question, but highlights their disposition of personal items, which in each case forms a significant part of the whole.

80 For the following, I, pp. 305–6.

81 Ibid., pp. 312–13.

82 Ibid., p. 313. These are left jointly to her husband, but as they are household items their use presumably falls under that of the house mistress, Elizabeth.

83 II, pp. 195–96 for the following.

84 Ibid., p. 195.

with crymsyn velvet and to her an old bonet of black velvet and 40s'.[85] These women are all left a very personal reminder of Elizabeth. Perhaps some of them are left gowns that they had particularly admired during her lifetime.

Sir John Speke, who had made his will two years earlier in 1516, does mention personal items in his will, but in a very general way. For example, Peter Markenfeld and John Joyner are left between them 'all my wering gere, gownes, dobletts, hosys, jaketts and shirts'.[86] This is a practical, rather than a personal bequest though. John has not singled out particular items that he would like them to have. Other than that, the will follows the typical male pattern of arranging the inheritance of his lands, and bequeathing sums of money to named beneficiaries.[87]

A final representative example is provided by the will of Isabel Fitz-James, made in 1525. She makes very precise provision for the disposal of personal items to her daughters and their families in particular.[88] Her daughter-in-law Lady Fitz-James is left 'a gurdell of gold harnesyd with golde', her daughter Elizabeth Fitz-James the younger 'a gowne of chamlet purfilled with crymson velvet'. Her son-in-law Hugh Mallett and his son Thomas, Isabel's godson, are both left particular goblets, one decorated with a leopard, the other with a portcullis and a rose. Hugh is also left a bed, its sheets and covers, and various other furnishings such as cushions and coffers. Hugh's wife Isabel, the testator's daughter, is left 'a nutt gilt, with a cover to the same, a mary mawdelyn box gilt with a cover to the same . . . a blak gowne of chamlet furryd with martyrns, my tryangle of gold'. Isabel leaves another daughter, Joan Michell 'my gowne of chamlet furryed with shanke, another tawny chamlet gowne purfilled with blak velvet and my best beads with a broche of gold'. Joan's husband Thomas Michell is left a comprehensive list of furnishings: two beds and their covers, cushions, coffers, hangings, basins, hangings, and cupboards. In the codicil dated 1527 Isabel further mentions two priests who are to receive bedcovers (including the one now lying on her, as we have seen), as well as two female cousins, and the wife of a male cousin, who are to receive gowns, and the latter 'a harte of golde which I have used to were about my necke'. Isabel also leaves money to support two scholars.

At no point in her will does Isabel mention her son John Fitz-James, who is mentioned in the will of her husband, also John, made in 1510.[89] This will is largely taken up with the disposition of the family silver, of which there seems to have been a considerable amount.[90] It is distributed between Isabel and John junior. The latter was presumably the husband of the Lady Fitz-James

---

[85] Ibid.
[86] Ibid., p. 190.
[87] For the whole will, ibid., pp. 189–90.
[88] II, pp. 249–252 for the following.
[89] Ibid., pp. 143–45.
[90] Ibid., p. 144 for the full list of plate.

referred to in Isabel's will and actually one of its witnesses.[91] As his father's heir perhaps Isabel felt that there was no material need to leave her son anything in her will. By the time she made it his father had been dead for fifteen years. Instead she chooses to use her will to benefit, and thus stress her ties with, her female relatives.

There is one will in this sample which departs markedly from the accepted female will 'blue print'. This is the 1489 will of Joan Twynhoo.[92] She describes herself as the wife of Roger Twynhoo, and states that she is making her will with his license.[93] However, she first defines herself as Joan, daughter of Thomas Rooley, merchant, and Margaret his wife, late of Bristol.[94] The will itself is also interesting because it does not follow the expected female testamentary formula discussed above, instead the primary emphasis is on land. These two anomalous features are linked. It transpires that Joan, who was presumably an only child, holds several messuages, lands and tenements in Bristol which were left to her by the terms of her parents' wills.[95] Joan does not appear to have any children or automatic heirs to inherit these properties,[96] and it is likely that the will was composed because she was very ill and needed to make sure that her considerable possessions would pass to her husband after her death. There are none of the customary references to personal belongings, female relatives, friends or servants. As an independent property owner Joan makes a will which reflects the concomitant masculine aspects of her status.

How are we to account for the differences between female and male wills? In part women's wills are different because of legal constraints upon them; they have less to leave than their husbands. Hence an emphasis on chattels such as clothing and jewellery which were perhaps the only items that many women could definitively call their own.[97] They are also different as a result of women's differing life-cycle experiences, roles and priorities.[98] Through the will they map out the connections that have been of particular importance to them, through the medium of personal and intimate bequests.[99] Women's wills thus frequently reveal a female network of relations, friends and servants, women who helped and supported the testator during her lifetime, and

---

91 Ibid., p. 252.
92 I, pp. 284–85.
93 Ibid., p. 284. For wives needing their husband's license to make a will see Helmholz, 'Married women's wills', pp. 165–66.
94 I, p. 284.
95 Ibid., p. 285.
96 None are mentioned in her will, nor in the will of her husband, Roger, made in 1497. He leaves all of these properties to his brother, George, ibid., p. 352.
97 Helmholz, 'Married women's wills', pp. 172–75.
98 Cf. Cullum, 'And hir name was charite', p. 185.
99 For other examples see the wills of Thomasine Hille (I, pp. 246–48), Elizabeth Byconyll (II, pp. 72–74), Isabel Newton (I, pp. 374–75).

were now being relied upon to continue that support after her death, by remembering her in their prayers. These women would be prompted to memorialise their mother/sister/friend/employer thus whenever they made use or caught sight of the bequest that she had left them.

Through her will the female testator seeks to project her key affective relationships onto the afterlife in very precise terms. Indeed, the composition of the will gives her a unique opportunity to give that largely informal network textually concrete and even 'official' status. This suggestion may provide the key to the final will I wish to examine, that of Amice Gregory. As has been mentioned, she had been widowed for almost thirty years by the time she made her will in 1457.[100] Her husband, John Gregory, had been married before, and asks to be buried next to his late wife Eleanor.[101] It is likely that Amice, who was made her husband's executor and left the residue of his goods, was a good deal younger than John.[102] The two appear not to have had any children, and Amice evidently did not remarry after John's death. The length of her widowhood seems to have taken its toll on her financial status, as has already been suggested. Apart from the fact that she still bears his surname there is no direct reference to John Gregory in Amice's will, or to her status as his widow. Perhaps after so much time had passed Amice no longer perceived herself in these terms. Indeed, her will strongly indicates that another family, the Westons, had become very important to her. A certain Richard Weston is her executor, and he and his son, John Weston, who is Amice's godson, are left the residue of her goods.[103] Richard Weston was apparently John Gregory's godson, and was bequeathed the latter's armour, a gown and 10 marks.[104] John also receives several pieces of silver, including a girdle, and his sisters Agnes and Eleanor receive a silver pot and 10 marks of silver, respectively.[105] Beyond knowing of Richard Weston's spiritual relationship to John Gregory, and John Weston's to Amice, we have no way of knowing much more about the nature of her relationship with the Westons. No wife of Richard Weston is mentioned, nor mother of John, Agnes and Eleanor. Whether or not she ever actually fulfilled these roles to some degree it could be argued that Amice's will writes her into them. Perhaps this is how she wanted to be remembered by the people who took the place of a family she never had, and by the others who would read and know of the contents of her will.

Thus it can be seen that the emphasis placed by the female will on its author's intimate, domestic relationships and concerns is a central common

---

100 I, pp. 171–72.
101 I, pp. 131–32 for John Gregory's will.
102 Ibid., p. 132.
103 Ibid., p. 172.
104 Ibid., p. 131.
105 Ibid., p. 171.

feature that it shares with other forms of female autobiography. Leigh Gilmore writes: 'autobiography demonstrates that we can never recover the past, only represent it'.[106] Arguably wills, and women's wills in particular, perform a similar function. But they do demonstrate that later medieval women had opportunities for writing their life-stories, for textually recording their most valued beliefs, relationships, and, indirectly, experiences and were able to use a legally-sanctioned forum in which to do so. It has been seen that wills contain a whole web of allusions to many different aspects of women's lives and experiences which can be variously interpreted: religious, devotional, familial, domestic, economic and so on. It is important to consider that any or all of these allusions may not have been included for straightforward religious or practical reasons. As a closing point I would suggest that given later medieval women's comparative lack of access to other forms of textual self-presentation, combined with the concerns and priorities articulated in their wills, it may be more useful in many respects to see a female will not as a direct reflection of its author, but as an indication of the ways in which she wanted to be remembered and commemorated.

APPENDIX

Wills consulted

1405 Elizabeth Stafford (173 Arundel II), II, pp. 304–06
1413 Humphrey Stafford (173 Arundel II), II, pp. 312–13
1414 Margaret Hakeluyt (29 Marche f. 230), I, pp. 66–67
1413 Leonard Hakeluyt (27 Marche f. 213), I, pp. 61–62
1423 Agnes Grene (2 Luffnam f. 12), I, pp. 108–09
1427 William Grene (8 Luffnam f. 57), I, pp. 122–24
1457 Amice Gregory (9 Stokton f. 66), I, pp. 171–72
1429 John Gregory (12 Luffnam f. 93), I, pp. 131–32
1457 Alice Balsham (9 Stokton), I, p. 173
1444 William Balsham (29 Luffnam f. 231), I, pp. 155–56
1485 Joan Atwell (18 Logue f. 137), I, pp. 255–56
1475 Richard Atte Welle (21 Wattys f. 154), I, pp. 227–28
1483 Thomasine Hille (18 Logge), I, pp. 246–48
1481 John Hille (4 Logge), I, pp. 233–34
1489 Joan Twynyhoo (3 Vox f. 23), I, pp. 284–85
1497 Roger Twynyhoo (15 Horne), I, p. 352
1498 Isabel Newton (23 Horne), I, pp. 373–75
1487 John Newton (8 Milles f. 70), I, p. 272

---

[106] Gilmore, *Autobiographics*, p. 86.

1498 Sybil Cammell (34 Horne), I, pp. 372–73
1487 John Cammell (6 Milles f. 53), I, pp. 270–71

Wills of Chocke family

1483 Margaret Chocke (9 Logge), I, pp. 244–45
1483 Richard Chocke (21 Logge), I, pp. 238–43
1487 Thomas Chocke (4 Milles), I, pp. 267–70. Son of Margaret
 and Richard.
1488 John Chocke (11 Milles), I, pp. 273–75
1493 Elizabeth Chocke (28 Doggett), I, pp. 305–07. Wife of John.
1504 Elizabeth Byconyll (13 Holgrave), II, pp. 72–74. Daughter
 of Margaret and Richard.
1500 John Byconyll (5 Blamyr), II, pp. 6–9
1503 William St Maur (6 Holgrave), II, pp. 48–50. Elizabeth
 Byconyll's son by her first marriage.
1513 Margery Merifild (17 Fetiplace), II, p. 166
1511 Nicholas Meryfeld (8 Fetiplace), II, pp. 158–59
1517 Joan Gryme (4 Ayloffe), II, p. 193
1509 John Gryme (26 Bennett), II, p. 139
1518 Elizabeth Speke (17 Ayloffe), II, pp. 195–96
1516 John Speke (9 Ayloffe), II, pp. 189–90
1528 George Speke (39 Porch), II, pp. 275–77. Son of John Speke
 by a previous marriage.
1525 Isabel Fitz-James (24 Porch), II, pp. 249–52
1510 John Fitz-James (34 Bennett), II, pp. 143–45
1528 Joan Carter (33 Porch), II, p. 273
1521 John Carter (22 Porch), II, pp. 209–10
1521 Margaret Quarre (14 Mainwaring), II, p. 211
1521 Richard Quarre (14 Mainwaring), II, p. 210

References in brackets are to the MSS. Volume and page numbers are to
Weaver's edition where the transcriptions can be found: F.W. Weaver, ed.,
Somerset Medieval Wills, Somerset Record Society, 16, 19, 21 (originally published 1901–05; repr. 1983). Wills dating from 1350–1500 are in the 1901
volume (I); wills dating from 1500–1530 are in the 1903 volume (II).

A Few Home Truths: The Medieval Mother as Guardian in Romance and Law

NOËL JAMES MENUGE

A NY SCHOLAR of medieval wardship will be aware of the ambiguous role of the mother within guardianship arrangements, but may not be fully aware of alternative ways in which to read that role. Most recent studies of wardship naturally focus almost entirely upon the legal aspect of it, that is, upon legislature, the pronouncements of legal treatises, and the content of legal cases themselves.[1] Another group of wardship literature exists, however, and we find it in the discursive medium of romance.[2] Romances, as I shall show, have the potential to inform and complement legal, historical and ideological readings of wardship, and throughout this article I shall use them to illuminate the ambiguous and often misogynist stance we find in the legal sources, where they concern mothers as guardians. Primarily I consider

[1] On feudal wardship, which I discuss in this paper, see esp. Sue Sheridan Walker, 'Royal Wardship in Medieval England' (unpublished Ph.D. thesis, University of Chicago, 1966); eadem, 'Violence and the Exercise of Feudal Guardianship: The Action of *Ejectio Custodia*', *American Journal of Legal History* 16 (1972), pp. 320–33; eadem, 'Proof of Age of Feudal Heirs in Medieval England', *Medieval Studies* 35 (1973), pp. 306–23; eadem, 'The Marrying of Feudal Wards in Medieval England', *Studies in History and Culture* 4.2 (1974), pp. 209–24; eadem, 'Widow and Ward: The Feudal Law of Child Custody in Medieval England', *Women in Medieval Society*, ed. S.M. Stuard (Philadelphia, 1993), pp. 159–72; eadem, 'Free Consent and Marriage of Feudal Wards in Medieval England', *Journal of Medieval History* 8 (1982), pp. 123–34; eadem, 'The Feudal Family and the Common Law Courts: The Pleas Protecting Rights of Wardship and Marriage c.1225–1375', *Journal of Medieval History* 14 (1988), pp. 13–31; Scott L. Waugh, 'The Fiscal Uses of Royal Wardships in the Reign of Edward I', *Thirteenth Century England I: Proceedings of the Newcastle upon Tyne Conference, 1985*, ed. Peter R. Coss and S.D. Lloyd (Woodbridge, 1986); idem, *The Lordship of England: Royal Wardships and Marriages in English Society and Politics 1217–1327* (Princeton, New Jersey, 1988); S.F.C. Milsom, 'The Origin of Prerogative Wardship', *Law and Government in Medieval England and Normandy: Essays in Honour of Sir James Holt* (Cambridge, 1994), pp. 223–44.

[2] Elsewhere I have defined a group of six romances as 'wardship romances', owing to their concern with feudal wardship. They are: *King Horn*, ed. R. Allen (New York and London, 1984); *Horn Childe and Maiden Riminild*, ed. M. Mills (Heidelberg, 1988); *Havelok the Dane*, ed. D. Speed, *Medieval English Romances*, 2 vols. (Durham, 1993); *The Romance of Sir Beues of Hamtoun*, ed. E.

extracts from two legal treatises, the late twelfth- to early thirteenth-century *Très ancien coutoumier*[3] and the mid-thirteenth-century *Bracton on the Laws and Customs of England*,[4] alongside the romances of *Beues of Hamtoun* (Southampton, c. 1300) and *William of Palerne* (south-west Midland, c. 1350–61). Previous studies of wardship have considered how and when mothers gained and were denied wardship of their children, and while I reiterate some of this evidence in order to provide a framework of real mothers employing legal action as guardians, I concentrate mainly upon the hitherto neglected areas of the treatise and romance polemic. In conjunction they tell us much about the ideology underlying the apparent legal misogyny some mothers as guardians appeared to have faced. While individual legal cases show us how some mothers were able to exercise effective agency as guardians, the discursive sources obscure this from the modern-day reader. The object of this article is not to prove that this agency existed, but to explain why contemporary lawyers and romanciers sought to contain it through the powerful medium of the written word.

In our modern-day society the mother is often considered the best person to care for her infant until it reaches maturity. We make much of the bonds of emotion and nurture; understanding what such bonds may have meant in medieval feudal society is a more difficult task. Legal treatises obfuscate the importance of these bonds, and consider them threatening. They provide us with an unbalanced view, which appears, in many instances, to belie what we actually find happening in legal cases. Romances, as Fellows suggests, give us an insight into contemporary attitudes to mothering.[5] Wardship romances give us a further insight into contemporary attitudes to mothers as guardians. An understanding of the way relationships between mother and ward were

Kolbing, Early English Text Society, Extra Series, nos. 46, 48, 65 (1885, 1886, 1894); *William of Palerne*, ed. G.H.V. Bunt (Groningen, 1985); *The Tale of Gamelyn*, in *Robin Hood and Other Outlaw Tales*, ed. Stephen Knight and Thomas Ohlgren (Kalamazoo, 1997). All extracts and line numbers are from these editions. Here, however, I discuss only *Beues of Hamtoun* and *William of Palerne* as they offer the fullest examples of mothers as guardians in this genre.

[3] *Le Très ancien coutoumier*, in *Coutoumier de Normandie*, ed. E.J. Tardif, 2 vols. (Rouen, 1881, 1903). The Latin text of this treatise was written in Normandy during the late twelfth to early thirteenth century, probably by a clerk of the seneschal William fitz Ralph: G.D.G. Hall, *The Treatise on the Laws and Customs of England commonly called Glanvill* (London, 1968), p. xv; Walker, 'Royal Wardship', p. 18, Tardif, *Coutoumiers de Normandie*, vol. 1, pp. 1–57. Much of early English wardship practice was drawn from the Norman, and so it is pertinent to study this Norman text: Walker, 'Royal Wardship', p. 18; Hall, *Glanvill*, p. xv.

[4] *Bracton on the Laws and Customs of England*, ed. George E. Woodbine and tr. Samuel E. Thorne, 4 vols. (Cambridge MA, 1968), hereafter Bracton.

[5] Jennifer Fellows, 'Mothers in Middle English Romance', *Women and Literature in Britain, 1150–1500*, ed. C.M. Meale (Cambridge, 1993; repr., 1996), pp. 41–60, and pp. 42–43 for a brief overview of theoretical views of motherhood in the Middle Ages. See also Shulamith Shahar, *Childhood in the Middle Ages* (London, 1989), p. 115; Clarissa W. Atkinson, *The Oldest Vocation: Christian Motherhood in the Middle Ages* (New York, 1991), and the various essays in J.C. Parsons and Bonnie Wheeler, eds., *Medieval Mothering* (New York, 1996).

defined and presented within the legal and romance sources sheds much light upon the social and political roles expected of aristocratic parents and guardians.[6]

A mother did not automatically assume guardianship of her children after the death of their father. Depending on the value of the inheritance, and on the type of tenure her husband held land by, a mother might have to contend with several lords, or even the king, for the wardship of her child. Feudal guardianship entitled the immediate feudal lord to possession of the ward's estates and body until he or she came of age, and as tenure of lands could be multiple, this could mean that the land itself could be held by a number of different guardians. The wardship of the heir was not divisible in this manner, but could be held by a different guardian from those who held the land. The mother of the heir might hold one or both of these wardships, including the wardship of the body of the heir, but this was not guaranteed; a mother could not expect any guardianship of her heir as a given legal right.[7] Walker writes that:

> Because the child and the feudal lands returned to the overlord on the death of the tenant and father, the mother had no right to the guardianship of her child. Not sentiment as to who would most suitably nurture the infant shaped minority in medieval England, but rules which governed land tenure.[8]

This lack of an automatic legal right to guardianship did not, however, prevent a mother from seeking custody of either land or heir or both through the courts. The Pipe Rolls, the Fine Rolls, and the Patent Rolls offer several examples of mothers doing just this, and succeeding.[9] This involved the mother paying to receive the body or the lands of the ward (or both) from the overlord or other guardians;[10] a mother might also sell this guardianship at a later date.[11] The same might apply to the ward's mar-

---

6   As mentioned I concentrate here only upon aristocratic wards and guardians. This is because the wardship romances engage only with feudal wardship.

7   See Walker, 'Widow and Ward: The Feudal Law of Child Custody in Medieval England', for a thorough discussion of the legal position of mothers as guardians within feudal society.

8   Walker, 'Widow and Ward,' p. 160. Cf. London guardianship law where widowed mothers were preferred as guardians of their own children: Barbara A. Hanawalt, *Growing up in Medieval London: The Experience of Childhood in History* (New York, 1993), p. 16.

9   I shall give individual examples of these below. See also Walker's article for several unpublished examples: Walker, 'Medieval Wardship', pp. 156–57; Waugh, *The Lordship of England*, p. 195.

10   As in *Calendar of the Patent Rolls (1232–1509)*, 52 vols. (London, 1892–1954) hereafter *CPR* (date): *CPR (1258–1266)*, pp. 291, 304; *CPR (1266–1272)*, p. 13. See also Waugh, *The Lordship of England*, pp. 226–67.

11   As in CP 40/5m 96 (1274); KB 27/110 m 16d (1288), cited in Walker, 'Widow and Ward', p. 166, nn.52 and 53.

riage.[12] This does not preclude maternal feeling, but rather demonstrates the ethos governing the high financial stakes of feudal wardship. A mother could not always afford to buy custody for sentimental reasons alone.[13] Mothers could, however, remain or become the child's *de facto* guardian if this was in accordance with the guardian's wishes.[14] This period in the child's life was for the benefit of nurture and usually lasted until the child was about seven.[15] John Trevisa's translation of Bartholomaeus Anglicus opines that 'The modir hatte *mater* for he[o] profreþ and puttiþ forþ þe brest to fede þe child and is busy to norische and kepe þe childe.'[16] Walker notes that children usually remained under the care of the mother in the first instance after the father's death, although this would not always be apparent in records. If the mother continued this *de facto* care with the guardian's approval, then the guardian was obliged to pay the mother a sufficient amount for maintenance.[17] The office of *de facto* guardian gives us some insight into maternal attachment to infant heirs, and suggests that mothers who claimed *de facto* guardianship may have done so for emotional reasons. Trevisa notes that the mother usually 'loueþ' her children 'tendirliche', holding and kissing, feeding and nourishing them, which suggests emotional attachment.[18] There are many instances of mothers seizing custody from guardians, and being forced in the courts to answer the writ of *quod reddat custodia* (right of ward).[19] In many cases the mother answers only that her right is that of 'nurture'.[20] Often

---

12 As in Gouthorp c. Skete (1310), where the mother bought the guardianship and marriage of her son from one William de Couzoun, only to have her ward 'ravished' (abducted) 'with swords, bows, and arrows' by one Ralph and accomplices, before she could do anything with it: F.W. Maitland, et al., eds., *The Year Books of Edward II*, 27 vols., Selden Society 17–104 (London, 1903–1988), hereafter *Year Books* (vol.): *Year Books* 4, pp. 216–17.

13 See Walker, 'Widow and Ward', pp. 160–1; Walker, 'Medieval Wardship', pp. 133, 155; Waugh, *The Lordship of England*, pp. 195, 227.

14 Walker, 'Widow and Ward', pp. 161, 163.

15 Walker documents this practice in some detail. See Walker, 'Widow and Ward', esp. p. 161; Walker, 'Medieval Wardship', pp. 154–55; Waugh, *The Lordship of England*, p. 196. See also Shahar, *History of Childhood*, esp. pp. 115–16 for the basic function of the mother as prime nurturer until this age in the 'normative literature'. See also Nicholas Orme, *From Childhood to Chivalry: The Education of the English Kings and Aristocracy 1066–1530* (London and New York, 1984), pp. 7–8.

16 Bartholomaeus Anglicus, *On the Properties of Things. John Trevisa's translation of Bartholomaeus Anglicus 'De Proprietatibus Rerum'. A Critical Text*, ed. M.C. Seymour, et al., 2 vols. (Oxford, 1975), vol. 1, p. 302, ll. 31–33. The focus of the remainder of this passage is upon biological function, and to a small extent, upon emotional attachment to the young child.

17 Walker notes that royal records are full of examples of such payment: Walker, 'Widow and Ward', p. 161, and n.10; Walker, 'Royal Wardship', p. 54, and nn.3 and 4 for illustrative cases in the Public Record Office.

18 *De Proprietatibus Rerum*, vol. 1, p. 303, ll. 7–8.

19 Walker, pp. 163, n.28, 164 gives several examples of these. See also Waugh, *The Lordship of England*, pp. 235–36.

20 Walker, 'Widow and Ward', p. 163.

she had to yield up the ward to its guardian *de iure*; the act of the mother's abduction of her child might then suggest a deeper maternal concern than the legal records make explicit.[21] But this image of Trevisa's caring mother may be ideological. The nurturing, emotional mother may be deployed for commercial or strategic reasons in the legal context. Mothers themselves may have exploited this.

Abduction by mothers does not necessarily imply emotional attachment, nor does the office of *de facto* guardian prove maternal emotion. There are cases of mothers of wards gaining forceful entry into property, and of seizing property and wardship (body and land) by armed force. This might indicate a desire for financial gain, or a determination rightfully to seize a guardianship which has been denied.[22] There are also cases where a mother as *de facto* guardian abducted her child in order to arrange, force, or sell the marriage.[23] We may find an echo of such behaviour of the mother in John Marrays c. Alice, daughter of Gervase de Rouclif (1365).[24] As I have argued elsewhere, the underlying issue in this case is over who has the right of marriage of the allegedly under-aged Alice de Rouclif, the guardian *de iure* (probably one Sir Brian de Rouclif) or the mother (probably the guardian *de facto*).[25] Alice's mother arranged for her a marriage with one John Marrays for a dowry of 100 marks; Sir Brian (possibly Alice's legal guardian) abducted Alice on the grounds of her age and contested this marriage in the case brought by John Marrays for the restitution of his conjugal rights. Alice's mother may have arranged the best possible marriage for her child, but her motives, although perhaps emotionally sound, were legally questionable given that she apparently only had *de facto* care. Any emotional motivation here was also likely to be influenced by financial considerations. 100 marks was a lot of money.

This brief sample of cases from the text and notes shows us mothers who were in some ways legally vulnerable, but by no means legally ignorant or inept. They show us that mothers were as capable as wealthy lords and other potential guardians of dealing in the traffic of wardship, whether for financial or emotional fulfilment, or both. The mother may not have been the automatic or even the preferred guardian, but she was certainly capable of maintaining her heir's inheritance in this way. She could fulfil the role of surrogate father herself. It is illuminating to consider how legal treatises and romances view such agency, indeed even such autonomy.

---

21 Walker, 'Widow and Ward', p. 161; Waugh, *The Lordship of England*, p. 195.
22 See Walker, 'Widow and Ward', p. 164, n.39 for several examples, and also pp. 164–65.
23 Walker, 'Widow and Ward', pp. 164–65.
24 BIHR CP E 89 (1365). This case is one of several marriage cases, known as cause papers, held in the Borthwick Institute for Historical Research, York.
25 See Noël James Menuge, 'Female Wards and Marriage in Romance and Law: A Question of Consent', *Young Medieval Women*, ed. Katherine J. Lewis, Noël James Menuge and Kim M. Phillips (Stroud, 1999), pp. 153–79, esp. pp. 161–63.

*

Feudal law favoured the position of the feudal overlord as guardian, as we have already seen. The attitudes inherent within certain treatises pertaining to feudal law reveal a concern with inheritance, rather than welfare. The interests of the lord-as-guardian are promoted to the detriment of the mother, her character, and the characters of those with whom she will begin a second family. It is this second family, and the mother as its instrument, which represent the threat to a patrilineal family.[26] Consider the following passage, which I have taken from the *Très ancien coutoumier*:

> A fatherless heir must be in ward to someone. Who shall be his guardian? His mother? No. Why not? She will take another husband and have sons by him and they, greedy of the heritage, will slay their first born brother, or the step-father will slay his step-son. Who then shall be his guardian? The child's blood kinsman? No. Why not? Lest, thirsting for his heritage, they destroy him. For the prevention of such faithless cruelty, it is established that the boy be in ward to one who was bound to his father by the tie of homage. And who is such an one? The lord of the land who can never inherit that land in demesne; for heirs of a noble race always have noble heirs.[27]

This passage concerns the role of the father-lord ideal in relation to wardship. However, it also concerns the issue of family care, and more specifically in this light, the issue of motherhood. According to this contemporary of *Glanvill*, a mother is not a fit guardian for her children once her husband is dead, and the implication in fact seems to be that she is not fit to provide any kind of care for them at all. The passage states that a widow will remarry; no alternative is given. She will *take* another husband, she will act so far as it pertains to further procreation, but she will not protect her initial progeny by

---

[26] For widows re-marrying and buying the rights to the wardship of their children, see Walker, 'Royal Wardship', pp. 58–59. For medieval legal opinion concerning kin as unsuitable guardians see Waugh, *The Lordship of England*, pp. 195–96.

[27] *Orphanus heres, quoniam debet esse in custodia alicujus, quis eum custodiet? – Mater. – Non. – Quare? – Quia sponsum accipiet et inde filios habebit; filii, propter cupidatatem hereditatis habende, possent occidere fratrem primogenitum vel heredem, vel sponsus occidere fiastrum suum, ut daret hereditatem filiis propriis. – Quis igitur custodiet eum? – Consanquinei eju. – Non. – Quare? Ne forte morti ejus inhyantes et hereitatem ejus cupientes oprimerent innocentum. Ad hujusmodi infidelitatem et crudelitatem evitandam, statutum est orphanum esse in custoda ujus, qui patri oephani fide connexus fuerat per homagium et ligatus. – Quia est ille? – Dominus terre, qui hereditatem illam non potest habere in dominio: hujusmodi enim heredes de nobil genere multos habent heredes.*
Le *très ancien coutoumier*, part one, cap. xi, 'De Custodia Orphani', pp. 10–11.

remaining chaste.[28] Therefore, the treatise implies, it is in the nature of widowed mothers to remarry. They cannot help it. Moreover, it is in the nature of mothers to follow the desires of their current husbands; only if she can resist the urge to procreate will the children from her first marriage be safe from the greedy machinations of their half-siblings. The only way of providing fit care and custody is if the mother can stay respectably widowed against the odds, but the passage suggests that remarriage is inevitable. This is how the text constructs mothers as widows and as second wives. They are the starting point for the whole chain of destructive action which follows, although the entire family (except the father and heir) is also undermined. This family (the surviving first kin and subsequent second kin) are responsible for the 'faithless cruelty' which the heir will almost certainly, according to the treatise, be subjected to. This 'faithless cruelty', which consists of a complex of betrayals – by the mother through remarriage and subsequent procreation, by the step-father and step-siblings through envy and murder, and by the greedy blood relatives who prize property over blood ties – is another construct, a baggage of stereotypes which elicits pathos for the heir and outrage at his predicament. This is neatly undercut by the presence of the lord who will prevent these betrayals; the lord is represented as a legitimate source of justice and care, whereas the family is represented as a place of destruction.

The actual motive of the passage is to defend the lord's right to the financial benefits of prerogative wardship against any possible rights of the ward's remaining kin. Waugh draws attention to similar edicts in the *Leges Henrici Primi* (no kin claiming inheritance should be given custody of minors), and in an explanation of Henry II that allowing elder sisters to have the custody of their minor co-heirs was similar to 'entrusting sheep to wolves'.[29] By undermining the motives of the family, patriarchal feudal society is justified (by patriarchal feudal law). The lord's financial interest in the ward is concealed under the guise of care; indeed, this financial interest is encouraged, because the ward's *person* is in no danger from the lord's interest in his or her lands. As the passage explains so beautifully, a lord cannot inherit the land his ward holds from him, whereas a relation, encouraged by ulterior motives, might. Thus we have a rhetorical reinforcement of the power of patriarchal feudalism, at the expense of the reputation of the family.[30] More importantly, it is at the expense of the reputation of the mother. Thus the mother represents, as

---

28 Walker notes that prospective husbands often purchased the marriage of wealthy widows along with the wardship of their chidren from the lord (often the king) who held the rights. So we see that such widows could be 'bought' if they chose not to pay for their own right to marriage or to remain widowed: Walker, 'Royal Wardship', pp. 58–59.

29 L.J. Downer, *Leges Henrici Primi* (Oxford, 1972), p. 223; *Close Rolls of the Reign of Henry III (1227–1272)*, 14 vols. (London, 1902–1938), 3, pp. 375–6; Waugh, *The Lordship of England*, p. 196.

30 On medieval rhetoric, see J.J. Murphy, *Rhetoric in the Middle Ages* (Berkeley, 1974).

Fellows suggests, 'a threat to patriarchal values'.[31] She is the means by which a second family will issue to threaten the patrimony of the first. This helps to explain why the vilification of the mother is central to this passage. She is a threat to smooth patrilineal inheritance, and thereby to the feudal order. We find this sentiment echoed in *Beues of Hamtoun*. Shortly after her marriage to the elderly, but noble Sir Guy, Beues's mother gives birth to him. Finding her husband old, unattractive, and without sexual passion she decides not only to 'Take a young knight,' who 'wold loue me both ny3t and day' (ll. 83–84), but to dispose of Beues's father, and to 'sle him with som gyle!' (l. 88). The lover she chooses is Sir Mordur of Almeyn. She has endured seven years of marriage and motherhood when she reaches this decision.[32] Beues is the sole heir to his father's estate, and is in obvious need of guardianship care. As in the passage from the *Très ancien coutoumier*, his mother takes a second husband. Later in the text (l. 2745) we see she has had a son with Sir Mordour. No description is given of this relationship between mother and son. Sir Mordour is devastated when their son is killed, but his wife is given no dialogue at this point and expresses no grief, almost as if, as with Beues, no nurture took place.

No 'appropriate' maternal relationship exists with Beues either. His mother makes no attempt to gain custody of Beues. Instead she attempts to have him killed, in order to remove his bloodline. He, after all, represents the oppression from which she has escaped; her allegiance, if not affection, now lies with the second son, the blood of the step-father. Seven-year-old Beues bears little filial affection to his mother, either, addressing her in the language of an angry and thwarted misogyny: ' "I-wys, moder, thou semeste full well / To be an hore, an old Brothell!" ' (ll. 245–46). The feudal ethos seems to be speaking through him: the words put into the mouth of this babe carry the same sentiment as those in the legal text I have just discussed.

The sentiment within the romance echoes that within the legal treatise, although the *Très ancien coutoumier* is rather more subtle in its misogyny. A romance serves a different narrative purpose to a polemical legal treatise. Texts such as the *Très ancien coutoumier* justify an already existing attitude, one which is held within feudal society, and one which would be recognised in the society in which romances were intended to be circulated. It is worth noting here that although mothers would have had contact with romances as readers and listeners, they would have had minimal, if any, exposure to the genre of the legal treatise. This confines them to its textual boundaries, thus limiting their discursive, if not actual, power. The legal discourse within the

---

31 Fellows, 'Mothers in Middle English Romance', p. 52.
32 I have already mentioned that mothers usually had the care of their children as wards until the age of seven. This was considered to be the period during which they required nurture. This is actually the period after which Beues becomes a ward. This is perhaps a further comment about the mother's unsuitability to be a guardian after this age.

romance serves as a point of recognition, rather than enforcement, of the discourse within the treatise. The message is similar, but it serves a different purpose.

Here we have an example of contact between the two different types of genre. The romance makes use of the legal discourse as far as it is recognisable within the milieu of the romance. It is not the voice of Beues we are meant to hear; in a legal sense he does not yet have one. Nor is it an authorial attempt to supply us with the feelings of the unfortunate seven-year-old. It is the voice of an outraged patrilineal feudal society which we are meant to hear, the voice of a society which is threatened by the vulnerability of Beues's infancy, and a society which is threatened by the advantage his mother is willing to take of this vulnerability. The romance has used the legal perspective, copied it, parodied it, and incorporated it into the plot in such a way as to make light entertainment with a serious social message, or messages.

The romance perpetuates the myth about mothers of wards, but in such a way as to make it almost absurd. The moments of comedy come in precisely the same places as those in which the feudal message is echoed. When Beues speaks to his mother in the voice of patriarchy it is also extremely funny; do we take seriously a message which has been put into the mouth of a cheeky, angry boy? And yet how can we deny the serious and real implications of his position in terms of wardship concerns? It is the same when Beues, in his fury, beats his stepfather with a stick, and runs back proudly to his guardian, shouting ' "I wyll you tell all to geder: / Bete I haue my stepfader! / With my staff I smote hym on the hede, / That I lefte hym all ffor dede!" ' (ll. 344–47). The moment is as rich in comedy as in revenge, and we identify with the actions of Beues. We feel, at this point, the outrage of thwarted feudal patrilineage. We applaud the physical punishment of the step-father. Is the romance thus designed to serve feudal identification? Although it uses a different *modus operandi* to the legal treatise, we are nevertheless expected to identify with the feudal voice. The comedic point of contact between the two discourses brings this home. Is this one of the social functions of wardship romance – to force recognition of appropriate and inappropriate feudal behaviour?[33] Apparently so.

Beues's attempts to reinforce the patriarchal view drive his mother to pure hatred. Just as she symbolises the threat to the feudal establishment, so does he threaten her security and new found, though ill-gotten, freedom. The infant voice of patriarchal feudal society must be removed, and so she plots to have Beues killed. When this plan fails, and Beues is instead sold as a slave, his mother and step-father fulfil the warning in the *Très ancien coutoumier*, and gain control of Beues's inheritance. Thus far we find the romance in

---

33 For the function of romances as edificatory, as well as for their social function in general, see Stephen Knight, 'The Social Function of the Middle English Romances', *Medieval Literature: Criticism, Ideology and History*, ed. David Aers (Brighton, 1986).

perfect sympathy with the legal antipathy shown by the treatise towards the mother.

Nevertheless, unlike the treatise, there are certain points during the romance, where, although not explicit, we are given possible motives (with which women might be able to identify) for the actions of Beues's mother. There is a possibility here that we are given to read a different story from the patriarchal – an alternative, 'hidden' narrative. We are told early in the romance that Beues's mother is young and beautiful, in love, and married against her will to an aged and infirm knight ('Ageyn the wyll of his doughter bryght', l. 59).[34] We are made aware that her plans for a love-match with Sir Mordour, who 'Wold haue wed that lady ffayn' (l. 54), have been thwarted, that before her marriage to the aged and infirm Sir Guy, 'She had lever haue had that other knyght, / For he was yonge and also bold, / And Sir Guy was waxen old' (ll. 60–62). At this point we could read her as an innocent party, wronged by the very feudal society which she ends up trying to destroy.[35] She rails against the father of her child (old enough to be her own father; does she rail against him also?) because she has been denied personal happiness for his financial gain and political good. Not only this, she is a princess; she has been married to a knight.[36] She is young and passionate, and she does not desire her husband. It is implied that he may be impotent ('He lovith not with me to rage;' l. 82). Her situation is appalling enough, and yet not unusual. We could feel pity for Beues's mother; we have her story, we have her motives, and in a sense they are not unreasonable. In this reading she is not evil; her actions are reactions. Yet the latent pathos of her situation is not developed. It shows us the cost of maintaining patrilineal descent.

As soon as she expresses intent to murder, she becomes all things evil in womanhood, in motherhood. She is a bad woman, so she is a bad mother. Beues represents to her the constraints within which feudal society binds her, and therefore he is not a thing she can love or take delight in. Surely females within a romance audience might have identified with this position: Beues's mother represents a point of tension, of the suppression of female agency by those forces which seek to control her behaviour through her marriage. Females such as Beues's mother are dangerous and must be confined within the boundaries of 'appropriate' behaviour. Given that such women would not have read the warnings in texts such as the *Très ancien coutoumier*, such identification may indeed be possible, and may even have been deemed necessary.

---

[34] On consent in marriage and forced marriages, particularly where this pertains to female wards, see esp. Menuge, 'A Question of Consent'; Walker, 'The Marrying of Feudal Wards'; eadem, 'Free Consent and Marriage of Feudal Wards'.

[35] Cf. *Le Bone Florence of Rome*. Florence rejects marriage to an aged sultan. In romance, heroines are allowed to reject old men. Beues's mother, however, is not supposed to be a heroine.

[36] She herself could probably argue disparagement here. Sir Mordour, although himself only a knight, is also the brother of the Emperor of Almeyn, and is therefore a socially superior match to Sir Guy.

This is the untold story which we can reconstruct from the narrative itself. It is a story we could identify with, but there are key points at which we are prevented from doing so. The first of these occurs when she considers her husband too old to fulfil her desire for sex (l. 77). This type of marital relationship is of course the staple of *fabliaux*: the reader connives in the lusty young wife's deception of her husband.[37] He gets what he deserves. The romance audience might recognise this archetype, and the writer might acknowledge it, but the romance is not *fabliau*, and Beues's mother is not lauded. She is constructed, at this point, solely in terms of that much feared, voracious, female sexuality which knows no bounds or discretion. This, we know, is a particularly misogynist view; it is one which is implied in the *Très ancien coutoumier* (a woman's loyalty is controlled by her sexual appetite), although the text of the legal treatise is more neutral than this.[38] It does not say for what purposes a widowed mother will take a new husband; the implication is sexual, but not explicit. Perhaps the narrative of Beues's mother is one approach towards an explanation. Romances can offer several alternatives: there are many different legal and social perspectives present in the text, and for some reason the author, after exploring all to some degree, settles on one 'appropriate' ending. Why choose this ending?

The motive given to Beues's mother for taking Sir Mordour as a lover is not because their youthful love was thwarted, with which we might at least be allowed some sympathy, but because of lust. The first words she utters within the text are those which present her as a purely sexual being, one who would overthrow the legitimate patriarchal order for the pleasures of the body:

> The lady be-thought her on a day
> And to her selfe can she say:
> 'My lord is old and may not worche,
> All day he courit in the churche:
> What for bresyng and for age,
> He lovith not with me to rage;
> But had I take a younge knyght,
> That had not bene bryssud in fight,
> He wold me love both ny3t and day
> And make me all the myrth, he may:'   (ll. 77–86)

Operating here is, of course, the stereotype raised in the *Très ancien coutoumier*, not yet fully recognised (she has yet to remarry and procreate), but already signalled. The second key point follows shortly, when it becomes clear that the lady has murder in mind ('Certes it shall be this no while, / I

---

[37] Cf. Chaucer's *The Miller's Tale* and *The Merchant's Tale*.

[38] See also esp. Alcuin Blamires, ed., *Women Defamed and Women Defended: An Anthology of Medieval Texts* (Oxford, 1992).

shall sle hym with som gyle!' ll. 87–88). From this point she is constructed as devious, cunning, deceitful and murderous. Sir Mordour does her bidding through love for her ('Certes, nowe I may see / Thinge, that I love, nowe lovis me! / . . . All her wyll wull I do;' ll. 121–25) and although he kills Sir Guy, we are to understand that Beues's mother has engineered the plan:

> '[to a messenger] And byd hym [Sir Mordour], in the furste day,
> That comythe in the month of May,
> That he in oure foreste be,
> Well armed with his meyne;
> Bid hym, that it be not belevid,
> That he smyte of my lordus hede
> And send it me in present:'   (ll. 103–9).

(The sinister sexual echo of Salome is surely intentional.) Her dialogue, of which there is much, shows her to be devious, cunning and deceitful, just as her earlier dialogue showed her to be driven by sexual motives. This is surely an authorial ploy to give her autonomy in her actions and desires; in this sense *he* is not damning her as an enemy of patriarchy, thus removing himself from the type of stereotypical propaganda we find in the legal treatise, but causing her to damn herself. Thus must the audience, also, damn her. Nor should we forget that she is Scottish: xenophobia against the Scots was still riding high after the war against them under Edward I (1296) when the Middle English *Beues* was composed (c. 1300).[39] Contemporary treatment of Scottish noblemen's wives and widows during this time was often atrocious. So she is twice damned. How much more evil the sexually voracious, murderous mother who is also a Scot? Beues himself seems to avoid such judgement since his father was English. Not surprisingly, the father's line is seen to be the true one.

When her second son meets an untimely and accidental death at the hands of her second husband, no lines are wasted upon parental grief; it seems an appropriate kind of justice that the usurping half-brother dies by the hand of the usurping step-father at the moment when the rightful heir himself becomes known:

> Whan syr Mordour herde that worde,
> He cast his knyfe ouer the borde,
> To haue hit the messengere,

---

39 Cynthia J. Neville, 'Widows of War: Edward I and the Women of Scotland During the War of Independence', *Wife and Widow in Medieval England*, ed. S.S. Walker (Ann Arbor, 1993), pp. 109–40, esp. p. 121. See also F.J. Watson, 'Settling the Stalemate: Edward I's Peace in Scotland, 1303–1305', *Thirteenth Century England VI: Proceedings of the Durham Conference 1995*, ed. M. Prestwich, R.H. Britnell, and R. Frame (Woodbridge, 1997), pp. 127–44.

But he fayled, as ye may here,
And smote his owne son in the brest . . .   (ll. 2741–45)

Any challenge to the patriarchy must self-destruct. Of course, this is another feudal comment, as is the laughter of Beues when he hears of the event. That the usurping step-father unintentionally kills his own usurping son restores the feudal order. The usurper thus makes way for the true heir. The irony is indeed heavy.

His mother is quick to counsel battle rather than display grief; she speaks now in the terms of a warlord:

> The countesse sayde: 'Drede ye nought,
> Of good counsel I am bethought:
> Ye shal sende, in certayne
> After the power of Almayne . . .
> . . . After my fader into Skotlande,[40]
> He wyl come to you redely
> Wyth a ful great company,
> And we may haue many mo
> Out of England and Wales also:
> Wherfore shulde ye drede then,
> Whyle ye haue so many men?'   (ll. 2967–78)

Such dialogue could almost be gendered masculine; it reconstructs her as a feudal overlord type, even while she is, in a sense, its nemesis.[41] She reacts against this system by donning its masculine mantle, and thus attempts to subvert it. She has essentially taken upon herself the role of the man, as indeed she has since she first plotted murder; her second husband has hung upon her every word and rushed to do her bidding. She displays no maternal feeling for either son; in her masculinity she is an even greater threat to the patriarchy, and she steps beyond the boundaries of the female in thrall to her second husband. In adopting such masculinity she further rejects the ideals of motherhood and good guardianship. She only regains a femininity with death, when she displays grief (for the first time) at the death of Sir Mordour.

---

40 The maternal line is skewed even here; her father fights on the side of the step-dynasty, and yet Beues is the first of his grandchildren.

41 Kim Phillips notes that Susan Crane denies active feminine roles in romance by character-ising femininity as passive, pious and timorous, in opposition to masculinity as brave, severe, and led by initiative. Phillips remarks that romance actually opens up active roles within femininity: Kim Phillips, 'The Medieval Maiden: Young Womanhood in Late Medieval England' (unpub-lished D.Phil. Thesis, University of York, 1997), p. 153, n.77; Susan Crane, *Gender and Romance in Chaucer's Canterbury Tales* (Princeton, 1994), pp. 18–23. Beues's mother herself avoids such gender classification by donning the aegis of 'masculine' characteristics.

She is so distraught that she flings herself from a tower and breaks her neck.[42] Thus is she damned again, eternally, for her suicide. We are warned that we should not feel sympathy for her ('I beshrewe hym, that therfore doth recke', l. 3192), lest we suffer the author's curse. That an alternative response is offered, i.e. to sympathise, suggests that the alternative or 'hidden' narrative of the maligned or repressed female is actually recognised within the text. However, the feudal position is again declared in a moment of black humour when Beues hears the news:

> Whan syr Beuys tydynges herde
> Of his moder, howe she fared,
> As sory was he for hyr,
> As he was for his stepfader.   (ll. 3193–6)

We find ourselves laughing with Beues, and any sympathetic tension we might have felt for the tragedy of his mother's life is dispelled; we can laugh away her terrible existence and that of her second family. The rightful line has triumphed in spite of the curse of unnatural motherhood.

The main focus of wardship romances is naturally the male feudal heir, yet, as we see in the narrative I have offered of the mother of Beues, they contain other, less 'appropriate' narratives. It is easy to overlook the significance of these other stories given the prominence of the feudal protagonist, yet they also tell us much about legal perceptions. The untold anti-patriarchal stories of the mother (as in *Beues*) and of the stepmother (as we shall see in *William of Palerne*) are as legitimate as the feudal narratives with which we are supposed to identify, and may help us to understand further the negative image of the mother which we find in legal treatises and some romances.

Bracton also contains somewhat misogynist opinions concerning the nature of mothers with an heir in ward, including an interesting section entitled 'Of supposititious birth and when a woman claims to be pregnant though she is not, to the disherison of the true heir'.[43] This passage is not dissimilar to that offered by the *Très ancien coutoumier*, in its supposition that women have inherently deceitful natures, especially where an inheritance is concerned. Some guardians may also be untrustworthy:

> We have said above that one is presumed to be the heir since he is born of the wife, and that he is heir whom the marriage shows to be such. Since a child is sometimes substituted by a wife, who pretends to be pregnant when she is not, sometimes by a guardian, who substitutes a stranger after the death of the true heir, and raises him as heir to the

---

[42] This action of course brings to mind the drama of Macbeth in which Lady Macbeth attempts to thwart the feudal order. She meets her death in the same way.
[43] Bracton, 2, p. 201.

inheritance, though he is neither son nor heir, to the disherison of the true heir, we must therefore consider suppositious births and how fraud of that kind may be proved in the royal court. Suppose that a wife, in her husband's lifetime, or after his death, claims to be pregnant when she is not, to the disherison of the true heir, or though she is pregnant it seems unlikely that the offspring can be that of her deceased husband, in which case she must be questioned as to the time she conceived and the time of her husband's death or departure from her.[44]

Walker points out that if the woman comes to term and a wardship is declared necessary for the infant at the cost of the next heir (i.e. the person who would have been due to inherit), then this wardship could be 'terminated if the next heir had been successful in demonstrating before the courts that the child was not the child of the father claimed for it, and was therefore no heir'.[45] In offering an example of the pregnant mother, Bracton substantiates the notion that some mothers will employ such deceit to retain an inheritance within their family, or within their own hands. Similarly, it is possible that *Beues of Hamtoun* hints that part of Beues's mother's murderous guile is, through sickness and craving, to feign pregnancy in order to lure her husband into the hunt that will result in his death:

> In the ffurste weke of May
> The lady ffeyned her seke and laye;
> She made her lord to her callyn
> And said, an evill was on her ffallyn
> . . . [he] axid, yf she wold ought.
> 'Sir,' she said, 'yf I myght gete,
> Of a borys hede I wolde ete!'. (ll. 142–52)

The text seems to be playing with discourses of pregnancy. If it is, then

---

44   *Dictum est supra quod præsumiter quod quis sit heres eo quod nascitur de uxore, et quod heres est quem nuptiæ demonstrant. Et quoniam aliquando supponitur partus ab uxore quæ se facit prægnantum cum non sit, et aliquando a custode qui mortuo vero herede supponit extraneum, et nutrit ut heredem ad hereditatem et ad exheredationem veri heredis cum non sit filius nec heres, ideo de partu suppositio videndum, et qualiter huiusmodi malitia in curia regia convincatur. Esto igitur quod uxor alicuius in vita viri se prægnantem fecerit cum non sit, vel post mortem viri prægnantem se fecerit cum non sit, ad exheredationem veri heredis, vel forte cum prægnans sit, non sit verisimile quod partus possit esse viri defuncti.* Ibid.
Paul Brand notes that the presumption that the wife's children were the father's was very strong. Apparently this could only be 'rebutted' if the husband was proven impotent, the husband was not in the country at the time of conception, or if the husband and wife were not living together: 'Family, inheritance, women and children', *An Illustrated History of Late Medieval England*, ed. Chris Given-Wilson (Manchester, 1996), pp. 58–81, p. 73.
45   Walker, 'Royal Wardship', p. 108, n. 2. See also pp. 106–7. She notes also that occasionally the marriage of unborn children was bought: ibid., p. 60.

Beues's mother invites her husband to his death under the misapprehension that she is carrying his child; if we read this discourse, we understand the awful irony that Sir Guy is, in effect, killed by the progeny of his usurper. How much better then the irony, that Sir Mordour avenges the death of his rival by the accidental killing of his own son.[46]

Bracton posits that some mothers will claim to be carrying the children of their husbands when in fact they are someone else's – making the mother also a fornicator and an adulteress – in order to retain the patrilineal inheritance. Will she then marry the real father of the child? Bracton does not say, but *Beues of Hamtoun* does. He stresses, though, like the *Très ancien coutoumier*, that the inheritance of the true heir is in danger, especially after the death of the father, and especially through the medium of the wife. The Crown here is held up as the force of justice (patriarchal feudal law) and the woman is to be subjected to an examination 'by responsible matrons, by feeling her breasts and abdomen, in order to discover the truth'.[47] At the slightest suspicion of fraud the mother is kept in custody: every threat to the true heir must be removed. This passage claims to be an exposition of actual circumstance, rather than a diatribe against the mother, and as such provides a legal plan for the appropriate action and writ. Yet like the *Très ancien coutoumier* it still constructs the mother-as-guardian as villain. It supposes the behaviour of mothers in general terms which explain her motives in anti-feudal terms. Wardship romances such as *Beues of Hamtoun* take these motives one step further than such supposition, and play them out with dialogue.

Beaufitz c. Faukener (1310) presents us with a mother (Gillian) who has married twice, and produced a son by each husband (as in *Beues*). The inheritance in this case, however, had been gifted to Gillian 'and the heirs of her body issuing' in fee simple by one Henry, someone other than her husband.[48] After her death, Robert, her first son, entered into his inheritance. He subsequently alienated it to one William Beaufitz. William Faukener, son to Gillian and her second husband, Hugh le Faukener, claimed to be heir to Gillian and her son Robert, William Faukener's step-brother. After the deaths of Robert and Gillian he brought a writ against William Beaufitz to reclaim what he saw as his inheritance. Although step-brother to the heir, he forced his (false) claim as next heir, but this backfired. The lawyers spent most of the case arguing whether or not William (Faukener) could claim to be heir to Robert, as he was 'not of the whole blood'. They decided he could only be heir to Gillian, because two different fathers were involved. They decided that the writ was worded incorrectly; the judge intervened and

---

[46] For irony see Dennis Howard Green, *Irony in the Medieval Romances* (Cambridge, 1979).
[47] . . . *et faciet eam videri a discretis mulieribus, et tractari per ubera et per ventrem, as inquirendam veritatem* . . . Bracton, 2, p. 201.
[48] *Year Books* 4, pp. 58–61.

demanded that the writ be understood as it was intended, i.e. for intention, rather than wording. Robert was then declared the rightful heir, and so William Beaufitz kept the land.

While this case has little in common with *Beues of Hamtoun* apart from the relationship of the brothers, it explains for us the complexities at law which were brought about by half-blood and whole-blood families, especially where inheritance was at stake. It helps us to understand the sentiment within treatises such as the *Très ancien coutoumier*. What it does not and cannot do though, is provide us with the narrative behind the case. Romances such as *Beues* do, by exploring these issues within the controlled environment of a rounded-out, complete, narrative. They work out legal complexities in a way which the lay person would find more accessible. By exploring these complexities within the portrayal of a family environment such as that with which the legal cases engage, they are also resolving problematic legal issues. *Beues of Hamtoun* gives us the mother who will take a second husband to the detriment of the first husband's heir, as indeed does the *Très ancien coutoumier*. Gillian le Faukener is a woman whose actions in taking a second husband and having issue by him, damage only the prospects of that second issue (as eventually happens in *Beues*). Even though she is the means through which the inheritance passes, it is adjudged that only the issue of her first husband can be heir. This judgement, in essence, is the same as that which we find in *Beues of Hamtoun*. Unfortunately, we know only this narrative of Gillian's life. We do not know why Robert chose to alienate his inheritance. We do not know how he viewed his step-father and brother. We do, however, know how Beues felt, and the motives of his mother.

In Thackstede c. Freebarn (1310), Emma and her husband brought a case against the guardian of her father's step-brother Ralph.[49] Emma was the granddaughter of Sir Ralph by his first wife, Isabel. After the death of Isabel, Sir Ralph married Maud, and had two sons, Thomas and Ralph. Emma's unnamed father (Sir Ralph's first son by Isabel) died some time after her birth, and while she was still an infant Thomas (Sir Ralph's first son by Maud) entered into the patrimony following the death of Sir Ralph. After the death of Thomas, Ralph (second son of Sir Ralph and Maud) entered into the inheritance under the auspices of his guardian. By this time Emma was of age, and able to bring an action against the infant Ralph. As the daughter of the first-blood son, she believed that she should be next heir. The defendant,

---

[49] *Year Books* 4, pp. 24–25. We might briefly compare Emma and her husband to Goldborough and Havelok in *Havelok the Dane*. Havelok regains his wife's heritage for her, but through marriage it becomes his, as Emma's will probably become her husband's. So even though the heiress regains her land, she is dispossessed by her husband. The romance simplifies what is happening in cases such as Thackstead c. Freebarn, but also shows that it is serving the interests of the man.

however, argued that she was 'not of the whole blood', and that she was 'a stranger to them' and 'cannot say anything to estrange them'. In effect, she is accused of being the step-sibling, when in fact she is 'of the whole blood'. It is interesting that it is the second family who claim rightful descent; Emma's father died before he could inherit, so Thomas entered into the land, and Emma, as a female minor, was conveniently overlooked, and presumably unable to bring an action due to her minority.

The judge requires explanation of the genealogy, and orders that the mothers be named. Emma declares her willingness to prove that she is next heir, and it is judged that she is. It is not in this case the mother who has remarried and caused dynastic confusion, but the father, who has apparently favoured the male descendants of his second union. Here we see a set of males threatening the correct feudal succession of the inheriting female, a case of step-families inheriting as if this was the feudal norm. Sons may indeed be preferable heirs to daughters, but in the court, which acts for the deceased father, this is not the case if they are step-brothers. The court may indeed be speaking for Sir Ralph and his first son, but it is also speaking for Emma. The threat of the step-sibling, even that engendered by the father, is all too real. This is a situation that is also explored in *William of Palerne*.

William of Palerne tells the story of two protagonists; the eponymous William, and his werewolf foster-parent, Alphouns. Each protagonist is a first son, a rightful, yet disinherited, heir. As such, each has a mother. These roles bear close and significant comparison. William's mother is a virtuous, aristocratic ideal, an icon of motherhood for the romance audience. The step-mother of Alphouns, on the other hand, is the calculating, disinheriting archetype, the mother who promotes the interests of her progeny (her first-born, but the patrilineal second-born) over the interests of the heir.

The importance of the role of Alphouns has, in the past, been dismissed as merely supernatural.[50] By default, the role of his mother has often been over-looked as part of this supernatural element. She is, however, more than the obligatory wicked witch who bewitches her step-son. As an example of moth-erhood she is as important as, or more than, William's mother, in that she provides us with a complex set of emotions and motives to read. These pro-vide us with a dual narrative of motherhood, that of the good mother and bad step-mother. She threatens the smooth succession of the rightful dynasty, but, like Beues's mother, attempts to create her own. The supernatural element of her behaviour only adds a further dimension to her character. It is not her

---

[50] See the complaints of Tibbals and Hibbard, and the comments by Bunt: Kate Watkins Tibbals, 'Elements of Magic in the Romance of *William of Palerne*', *Modern Philology* 1 (1903–4), pp. 355–71, pp. 355–56; Laura Hibbard, *Medieval Romance in England: A Study of the Sources and Analogues of the Non-Cyclic Metrical Romances* (New York, 1960), p. 217; Bunt, *William of Palerne*, p. 105.

whole character, nor does it undermine the importance of her role. Rather, it may tell us about the helplessness of mothers and step-mothers as second wives in feudal society.[51]

A step-mother may provide care for children from her husband's first marriage along with her own, should he meet an untimely death.[52] Siblings who were not the next heir were often cared for by the mother.[53] A step-mother should be no different. There is no reason to expect that step-mothers did not care for their step-children. In a sense the step-mother even fulfils the role of *de facto* guardianship (perhaps in the sense of 'nurture') in that she is providing *de facto* care for someone else's child. As *William of Palerne* shows, this situation causes problems of its own, similar in many ways to the concerns voiced by the *Très ancien coutoumier* about step-fathers and step-families and the weaknesses of mothers as the guardians of their own children. *William of Palerne* is an example of romance reaching areas which the law does not reach. The step-mother does occur in legal cases in disputes over property, but she does not seem to appear often in cases to do with guardianship or care, which is not surprising if the father is still alive.[54] She does, however, appear in this role in the romances. This suggests that the relationship of step-mother to child may have been deeply problematic, but not in a way with which the law was concerned. We must therefore rely upon our readings of the wardship romance to enlighten us.

We are introduced to the story proper of Alphouns and his step-mother well into the plot, quite some time after we have already become acquainted with the stories of William, his mother, and his sister, Florence. Alphouns's father remarries after the death of his first wife (Alphouns's mother). His step-mother gives birth to a son, Braundinis, and thus feels threatened, in herself and for Braundinis, by Alphouns's position as heir. Her solution is to bewitch Alphouns and change him into a werewolf. She then tells her husband (the father of Alphouns and Braundinis) that Alphouns is drowned. He is devastated, yet consoled by the knowledge that he still has an heir, in the surviving second son. Meanwhile, Alphouns is cast into the wilderness to fend for himself. In so doing he takes it upon himself to rescue another endangered heir, William. Sometime after meeting William, he tells him (and us as readers) of these trials.

What do these actions tell us about Alphouns's step-mother, the mother of Braundinis? What can they tell us about the perception of the step-mother where the livelihood of the rightful heir is at stake? Alphouns is not a ward.

---

51 I shall return briefly to this idea below.
52 This is implied in Walker, 'Widow and Ward', pp. 159–60.
53 Walker, 'Widow and Ward', p, 160.
54 For a tangential example of a step-mother appearing in such a case, see *Year Books* 2 (1309–10), p. 163 (1310), where Agnes the widow of John le Rus brings a writ of dower against the Earl of Gloucester, guardian of the land of her husband's heir from his first marriage.

His chief relationship with the wardship topos is in his rescue of, and relationship with, William. Yet his situation may be paralleled with wardship. Let us consider the passage from the *Très ancien coutoumier* once more, and reverse the male and female roles. Alphouns's father is still alive, yet powerless to act against, or even detect, the apparently inherent evil which exists within the step-family. The passage from the *Très ancien coutoumier* implies that *all* step-family situations carry their danger, and that all rightful heirs placed within a step-family will be threatened by such danger. It would appear that the notion of the step-family was a threat to correct feudal succession. We find that this is the case in Thackstead c. Freebarn, as seen.[55] Although Emma is overlooked in favour of her uncles, and is accused of being 'not of the whole blood', it actually transpires that her uncles are the step-family, and she is adjudged to be the rightful heir. This case alerts us to the notion that 'step-family', or 'half-blood', depends upon which family one happens to belong to. Any family environment that involves the production of different heirs from two different bloodlines, male or female, must create an atmosphere of danger, of jealousy and of destruction. This atmosphere is part of what the step-mother represents. If the true heir can be in danger from the actions of his own mother on remarriage, then how much more potent is the danger if the new female head of household is not his own.[56]

This step-mother is a danger to the first-born of another woman, but inverts the warning in the *Très ancien coutoumier* that a woman is weak when it comes to the protection of her offspring. Alphouns's step-mother shows that she is as well able as a man to protect and further the interests of her own offspring. Nevertheless, this image of strength could be misleading. Although the example of Alphouns's step-mother suggests that certain women will stop at nothing to protect their children, witchcraft and lycanthropy were not, one suspects, available options to most protective mothers in the Middle Ages. Rather, the familiar topos of the resort to witchcraft underlies and underlines the fact that mothers were less able to protect the best interests of their children when faced with a strongly patriarchal legal system. The woman who does so is therefore demonised (as is Braundinis's mother).[57] The fact that it is the 'wicked step-mother' who (typically) commits the crime against the rightful heir on behalf of her own child or children also tells us

---

[55] *Year Books* 4, pp. 24–25.

[56] David Blamires notes that the story of the evil step-mother was a popular motif in folk and fairy tales during the Middle Ages, as well as in romance. Indeed, a fifteenth-century manuscript contains a fairytale entitled *The cheylde and his step-dame*: David Blamires, 'Folktales and Fairytales in the Middle Ages', *Bulletin of the John Rylands University Library of Manchester* 74 (1992), pp. 97–107, pp. 104–5.

[57] For considerations of how such 'unsuitable' mothers are demonised in the Breton Lay, Margaret Robson, 'Feeling Women: An Exploration of Women's Viewpoints in the Middle English Breton Lay' (unpublished D.Phil. Thesis, University of York, 1994), ch. 5, 'The Demon Mother: A Reading of Sir Gowther', pp. 158–84, esp. pp. 163–65.

that the creation of female scapegoats is more important to the patriarchal ethos than is any concern with nurture, or with a will to nurture. Crimes against the male heir, the prime focus of sympathy, are typically blamed on the female. This is true both in the legal treatise, and in *William of Palerne*. Romances frequently take the part of the rightful heir, and consequently any attack on the rightful heir is represented as (a) issuing out of perverse or unnatural feeling, or (b) motivated by the illegal ambitions of 'unrightful' claimants, or both. The wicked step-mother is thus the creation of the perspective of the plot: she is both (a) and (b) together.

The step-mother, as a type, presents us with an interesting duality to consider. As step-mother, we are shown a woman who symbolically and actually maltreats her charge. As a mother, we are shown a woman with boundless love and ambition for her offspring, coupled with a protective urge to destroy any threat to the survival of her child, even if that means the destruction of the child of another. She contains both evil and good; yet her good is judged relatively and alongside feudal requirements. When the truth comes to light in *William of Palerne*, the step-mother is punished and publicly humiliated. Alphouns's father, on the other hand, is not blamed for his gullibility, weakness and lack of vigilance. Such is the power of a woman's deceit.

Alphouns's step-mother has only three main episodes of dialogue, which occur during the recognition of Alphouns. Until this point her motives, actions, and character are constructed by Alphouns, and by the author. She first speaks to the court at large when she fears attack by Alphouns, who has entered, accompanied by William. Thus when she is allowed dialogue, in the first instance it is, literally, to cry wolf:

> 'A! leve lordes, mi lif lengþes ȝut a while!
> Socoures me nouþe, or ful sone I deiȝe:
> for þis ilk breme best bale wol me wirche,
> ac I wite him no wrong, witeþ wel alle.
> I have served þe deþ; ȝif ȝou dere þinkes,
> lengþeþ now my lif, for love of hevene King!
> And meke me in þour mercy, I mai do nouȝt elles.' (ll. 4348–54)

It is probably safe to assume that she knows who he is; so her first dialogue is one of deceit, and denial. William speaks next, and explains the situation to the court, whereupon Alphouns's step-mother, realising that she is only in moral danger, admits all, and begs for repentance:

> 'Swete Alphouns,' sche seide, 'mi semli lorde,
> I have brouȝt here þi bote to bring þe of sorwe.
> Sone schal þe puple se þi semli face
> in manhede and in minde as it out to bene.
> I have þe gretli agelt, to God ich am aknowe,
> For redili þe reve þi riȝt eritage:

þat þis man, min owne sone, miȝt it have hadde
feiþli after þi fader, ich forscop þe þanne
in þise wise to a werwolf and wend þe to spille;
but God wold nouȝt þat þou were lorne.'   (ll. 4387–96)

Are we to read this as genuine repentance, or as repentance and admission of guilt because there is no other way out? Is she merely practising more deceit? Either way, through this dialogue we are given to understand that patriarchal feudal society will force its will in the end, because from its own perspective its will is righteous and just. We may read deceit in her words, but we also read an acceptance that the legitimate order of things will not be overturned; in the humiliation of her admission is her punishment. She takes the discourse of the legal treatise for her own. She is made to admit its polemic as her own truth, and her untold story is that of the warning within the discourse of the legal warning.

Alphouns's step-mother should be compared with William's mother. William's mother is shown as the altruistic, fiercely protective, completely selfless and ultimately desirable mother-figure. She has all the instincts of Alphouns's step-mother when it comes to the care of her own children, but none of the thwarted biological intensity. Although she does not know of William's survival until the end of the plot, she nevertheless protects his interests through her protection of her daughter and the family inheritance. She is constructed in terms of his interests, and is represented as the perfect mother. After the loss of William and the subsequent death of her husband she does not consider the option of remarriage. This short-circuits the dangers for herself and her daughter of the second family scenario, and thus rejects the legal model as found in the *Très ancien coutoumier*. Instead she devotes herself to raising her daughter and protecting her kingdom. Of course the actions of William's mother as his sister's guardian are part of the wider plot; William's mother needs to remain widowed and in control of her estates so that William can re-claim his heritage when he finally returns home. It is not, therefore, surprising that his mother is held up to the audience as a paragon of motherhood and female guardianship. She is constructed entirely in feudal terms, and although the care she gives to her daughter when protecting her from an undesired marriage is in itself exemplary, it is only a necessary part of the wider scheme. It does, however, have its own tale to tell.

William's mother is a queen. She is ruler of her land, and as such, answers to no higher feudal power.[58] She can therefore maintain the guardianship of her daughter, who, given William's supposed death, is now the next heir. In

---

58 For some secondary sources concerning the privileges of medieval Queenship, see John Carni Parsons, 'The Intercessionary Patronage of Queens Margaret and Isabella of France', *Thirteenth Century England VI*, pp. 145–56; idem, 'Ritual and Symbol in the English Queenship to 1500', *Women and Sovereignty*, ed. L.O. Fradenburg (Edinburgh, 1992), pp. 60–78; idem, 'The Queen's

contemporary English feudal society, a female royal might well have had such power over wardship.[59] In 1364 Isabel, the daughter of Edward III, leased the wardship of the inheritance and body of Edmund, heir to Roger Mortimer, the Earl of March, over whom Isabel apparently had initial custody, to his mother Phillipa, wife of the deceased Roger Mortimer. A complex financial arrangement was agreed, in which Isabel would pay Philippa 100 marks a year for the upkeep of the heir; Philippa might have had to repay the same for every year in which Isabel had custody. Philippa, as the new guardian, was not to be held responsible for any waste previously carried out by Isabel.[60] Therefore Isabel leased to Philippa the right to have custody over her own son. As a queen, William's mother is not answerable to royal caprice, favour, or design, as an aristocratic widow such as Phillippa might be. She is able to care for Florence's body and property without arranging complex financial agreements, and without fear that Florence, as next heir, will be taken from her.

During the reign of Henry III, Mabel Torpell, a noblewoman, was not so fortunate. After the death of her husband, the king gave full guardianship and marriage rights to the bishop of Chichester. While the heir William was alive, and thus in guardianship custody, Mabel retained *de facto* guardianship of her remaining child. Unfortunately, William died, and the king sent a message to Mabel,

> as she loves herself and her goods, not to eloign Acelota, sister and next heir of the said William, whom the chancellor [also the bishop] committed to her ward to nurse, but to deliver her to the messenger of the said bishop bearing these letters with letters of the bishop testifying that he is his messenger.[61]

Mabel resisted this order, perhaps because of her attachment to her daughter. We know she had no power over the lands or the marriage of Acelota, so her resistance seems to have been in order not to lose the custody of a daughter who was still in infancy. She was denied the right to retain *de facto* guardianship, and was forced by the sheriff of Northampton to surrender the girl to the bishop.[62] This legal case, as do many, denies us the emotional context, and conceals the reason for disobedience, but we can guess at it. It is not unreasonable to suggest a mother's distress at the loss of her remaining child after

---

Intercession in Thirteenth-Century England', *Power of the Weak: Studies on Medieval Women*, ed. J. Carpenter and S.B. Maclean (Illinois, 1995), pp. 147–77; idem, 'The Pregnant Queen as Counsellor and the Medieval Construction of Mothering', *Medieval Mothering*; idem, ed. *Medieval Queenship* (Stroud, 1994).
[59] See, for example, Queen Eleanor, who received at least sixteen wardships before she died in 1290: S.L. Waugh, 'The Fiscal Uses of Royal Wardship in the Reigns of Edward I', p. 57.
[60] CPR (1364–67), pp. 37–38.
[61] CPR (1232–1247), p. 301.
[62] Ibid.

the death of her husband and her son. She had been allowed to 'nurse' the child. In the sense of 'nurture' this may mean no more than *de facto* guardianship. *De facto* guardianship as we have seen, however, was a means by which mothers may have emotionally nurtured their children. We feel a sense of this fear of loss in William of Palerne's mother when Florence is threatened with abduction and undesired marriage. Part of the story of Florence's mother may be to show us how vulnerable mothers as guardians, and as *de facto* guardians, really were.

The relationship between Florence and her mother shows us at the very least the existence of an emotional tie between mothers and their *de facto* wards. Even as a patriarchal construct, William's mother can be read as a symbol of the threat to the maternal role which some women might have faced from feudal law and society. In a sense we have two versions of William's mother, and two narratives which come out of these portrayals. First and foremost we have William's mother, the feudal and patriarchal construct who keeps the feudal inheritance safe for the return of the rightful heir. Secondly, we have *Florence's* mother, who within the bounds of a feudally constituted society, must protect and nurture the maternal relationship she has with a female heir; a female heir who is especially threatened by the feudal and patriarchal society within which she has her identity. Her inheritance is threatened by would-be suitors and ravishers, as is her virginity and her relationship with her mother. Equally important and more subversive is that all of these are actually threatened by the safe return of her brother, the rightful feudal heir, who will remove her from her relationship with her mother, remove her from her own position as heir, choose a husband for her, and despatch her out of her own family environment. In the patrilineal narrative, Florence herself is the cuckoo; in the narrative which results from William's absence, William is the threat. Once untangled, we see that each narrative can be valid within its own set of circumstances. The narrative we are supposed to choose, however, is that of *William's* mother. This is the narrative borne by treatise and case and convention. We perhaps catch a glimpse of the narrative of Florence in the case of Thackstede c. Freebarn (1310), even as we catch a glimmer of her mother's emotion in the case of Mabel Torpell.[63] Nevertheless, the narratives of Florence and her mother, as with those of Beues's mother and Alphouns's step-mother, are to remain embedded within the layers of the romance, for they are subversive. This does not prevent certain members of the audience from reading them, nor from identifying with them, however silently. This hidden narrative could be another reason why the mother must be vilified in the genre of the legal treatise. Carol Meale argues that the readership includes women, so if women are understanding and identifying with subversive narratives, then it is even more important

---

63 *Year Books* 4, pp. 24–25; CPR (1232–1247), p. 301.

that they receive the message that these narratives, while co-existing with patriarchal narratives, are unacceptable.[64]

Owing to the unfortunate absence of the first three folios of the Middle English *William of Palerne*, we do not have the reactions of William's mother to his abduction by the werewolf; nor do we know if there was any dialogue expressing their anguish at his loss. William's mother is, however, given emotional dialogue towards the middle and the end of the romance. She expresses grief at the loss of her son to William himself, before she knows who he is. This demonstrates appropriate maternal feeling for her first-born male child. Her sorrow is brought on by William's likeness to his father:

> 'Forsoþe, sire,' sede þe quen, 'Þe seyn al þe treuþe;
> þe make me mater inow mirye to bene.
> I wot, for I so wept, I wrouȝt nouȝt þe best,
> but I miȝt nouȝt þerwith, iwisse, sire, and, treþe,
> so þroli a sori þouȝt þirled min hert!'   (ll. 3692–96)

Her grief is described by the author, for this is legitimate grief, a grief which stresses feudal lineage, unlike the feelings of Beues's mother and step-father. William, for the moment covering his identity, does his best to comfort her. His dialogue is also highly emotional. When William's identity is later revealed to her by Alphouns, 'þer nys man upon mold miȝt telle þe joye / þat was made bitwene in þe mene while, / betwene þe dame and þe douȝter and hire dere sone, / wiþ kesseng and oþer kind dede.' ll. 4662–65). This relationship is in sharp contrast to that shared by Beues and his mother, or to that shared by Alphouns and his step-mother.

This kind of maternal-filial emotion is allowed because the devotion strengthens the feudal claim, rather than threatening it. True-feudal family love is allowed; anti-feudal family love is not. In further contrast to Beues's mother and Alphouns's step-mother, William's mother has little dialogue. As she clearly supports the feudal ideal there is no need for her to speak. Nor is it seemly for this feudal icon to express her own opinions; she is constructed as the feudal ideal. Whereas undesirable mothers and step-mothers need a discourse to demonstrate their dissonance with the feudal ethos, and thus to vilify themselves with their 'own' words, a perfect feudal model does not require one. It is, according to contemporary feudal and religious models, seemly for her to remain silent. She only speaks out when the system she represents is in danger, for example, when her daughter's honour and inheritance are at stake or when the system becomes unbalanced (ll. 2663–76). At these times her voice is calm, reassuring, and instinctively on the side of patriarchal

---

64 C.M. Meale, ' "gode men / Wiues Maydenes and alle men": Romance and its Audiences', *Readings in Medieval Romances*, ed. C.M. Meale (Cambridge, 1994), p. 209.

right. Nor is her position as a strong widow at odds with the patriarchal ethos. By refusing remarriage for the sake of her estate and children's inheritance she preserves the feudal ideal. Unlike the mother in the *Très ancien coutoumier*, she ensures that the line will continue. Contrary to the legal stereotype, she proves that she is a very fit guardian indeed.

The construction of William's mother as feudal entity implies that feudal motherhood is defined in terms of the protection of the heir, especially the male heir. The mother must subsume her own desires in the interests of her son. Indeed, she does not have independent desires. William's mother is the aristocratic and patriarchal ideal, the type of female guardian widowed mothers should aspire to be, for she protects the rights of the rightful heir. On the other hand, Alphouns's step-mother is represented as a sinner who is split with a more human duality. She is a sinner who eventually repents and submits to the greater good – in this case the right of the *husband's* first born to succeed, not her own. Because of this duality she presents a more effective feudal warning: it is easier to follow by example, or by warning through identification. A contemporary female audience might have identified with at least some aspects of each of these two stereotypes. Women may even have been expected to receive some such moral instruction from the truths to be found within these tales. Thus there is no room for (safe) identification with the mother of Beues. The only ending for her within the dictates of this constructed feudalism is death: a severe warning for any woman contemplating defiance of the patriarchal line.

We seem to have two conflicting issues at stake here, the interests of a patrilineal, primogenitive feudal society, and the question of the suitability of the family to provide adequate care for inheriting wards. The *Très ancien coutoumier* deploys stereotypes which we recognise in romances to strengthen its point about the right of the lord against the claims of kin. It uses that type of legal rhetoric which will not admit argument: all women will remarry, all step-sons will seek to supplant their first-born brothers and all stepfathers will try to kill their stepsons. The child's blood relations are no better: they too will try to kill him. Only the lord is exempt from this cycle of destruction because he stands outside the family. The family – the obvious source of care – is thus represented as hostile, destructive, and loveless. But this representation is strategic: it is designed to serve the interests of the feudal ethos and to reiterate the obligations of homage. Romances serve different interests. They are not disinterested either; they have their own perspectives on the family. Although they promote patriarchal feudalism they do explore the family as a source of affective relations in a way that the law cannot. We are shown a system in which the rights of the first born are paramount, but also a system in which there is a submerged second plot, that of the second son. This provides us with reasons for the behaviour of step-mothers and step-parents and step-families. They protect the interests of their *own* heirs, so in a sense these romance step-parents are good parents, even though for the sake of the society in which they operate (and perhaps for deeper moral considerations) they are held up as predominantly bad examples. Romances thus depict the family as a place in which care, as well as destructiveness, can operate. They concern the family as both a source of affective relations, and as a place of danger.

Romances and legal treatises tap into deeply rooted areas of mistrust and patriarchal anxiety: intimacy breeds fear. To a patriarchal society the mother is frightening. The function of these texts is to ascribe to her certain explicable characteristics, and to contain her within them. The legal treatises gag her because she can speak and the dead father cannot, so they give her motives for speech and damn her while she has no access to the texts in which she is damned. Romances, while containing potentially subversive narratives, also contain the legal discourse of the treatise, but gag the subversive mother by the very act of *allowing* her to speak.

The mother's survival beyond the father ensures, or at least represents, a closure to the relationship between ward and father, and an opening to a whole series of longer relationships and experiences which will not be governed by the father unless a legally-sanctioned guardian is able to take his place. The voice in the treatise serves the purpose of this legally-sanctioned guardian (or lord). The father can no longer speak for himself, and so the legal discourse speaks for him, and it speaks against the mother, apparently on his, and the heir's, behalf.[65] The case examples I have used throughout this paper, however, show that mothers could be acceptable as guardians, and that legal courts were capable of accepting her as such. In actuality the courts may have been more liberal and more reasonable in their outlook upon medieval mothers and guardians, while wardship discourse reveals romances and treatises to be deeply reactionary and oppressively conservative. Legal treatises and romances attempt to impose a stability upon the behaviour of real women who could be as powerful as patriarchs. The mother may have remarried, but the courts *allowed* her to. They allowed her wardship of her husband's heirs, if she could pay for it. They allowed her to nurture her infants. Their legal strictures may have contained her, sometimes harshly, but in allowing her agency, they liberate her from the tyranny of the text.

---

65 These texts pit the father against the mother, but this cannot always have been the case. For some instances in which it was, see Peter Coss, *The Lady in Medieval England 1100–1500* (Stroud, 1998), ch. 5, 'Lady versus Lord: Antagonistic Relations', pp. 115–49, esp. 129–30; but, see also, in contrast, ch. 4, 'Visual Representation and Affective Relations', pp. 73–114.

A Matter of Consent: Middle English Romance and the Law of *Raptus*

CORINNE SAUNDERS

T HE RELATION of fiction and reality in Middle English romance is notoriously difficult to assess. While one school of critics has identified the genre as non-mimetic, another has engaged precisely with the mimetic process of romance: romances can yield insights into the history and politics of their age as well as into the deep structures of the psyche.[1] The duality of romance allows for both modes of interpretation: romance straddles the actual and the fantastic, and offers the possibility for both social commentary and escapism. Indeed, the creativity of the genre may be seen as situated precisely in the slippage between the two modes of realism and fantasy. This duality is echoed in microcosm in the ways Middle English romances treat the issue of *raptus* of women and the associated question of female consent.[2] On the one hand, romance narratives present the topic of *raptus* with notable realism and precision. Just as the medieval law of *raptus* addresses both rape and abduction, so romance engages with these two interrelated crimes, with the complex issues of property, pollution and consent that arise from them, and with the possibility of legal contravention of violence against women.

---

[1] For non-mimetic readings of romance, see, for example, Northrop Frye, *The Secular Scripture: A Study of the Structure of Romance*, The Charles Eliot Norton Lectures, 1974–75 (Cambridge, MA, 1976) and Derek Brewer, 'Escape from the Mimetic Fallacy', *Studies in Medieval English Romances: Some New Approaches*, ed. Brewer (Cambridge, 1988), pp. 1–10. Influential mimetic readings include Erich Auerbach, *Mimesis: The Representation of Reality in Western Literature*, tr. Willard R. Trask (Princeton, 1953; first published Berne, 1946), ch. VI, 'The Knight Sets Forth', pp. 123–42, and, more recently, Susan Crane, *Insular Romance: Politics, Faith, and Culture in Anglo-Norman and Middle English Literature* (Berkeley, 1986) and Lee C. Ramsay, *Chivalric Romances: Popular Literature in Medieval England* (Bloomington, Indiana, 1983).

[2] For a study of rape in medieval French romance, see Kathryn Gravdal, *Ravishing Maidens: Writing Rape in Medieval French Literature and Law*, New Cultural Studies Series (Philadelphia, 1991), in particular Ch. II, 'The Poetics of Rape Law: Chrétien de Troyes's Arthurian Romance', pp. 42–71. Gravdal's approach is primarily a feminist revisionist one: although she refers to several cases, she in fact considers legal history only in very general terms.

The twofold emphasis of the medieval law of *raptus* is consistently reflected within the romance genre: concern to defend the virgin from corruption against her will is interwoven with interest in protecting or gaining the woman as property, irrespective of her consent. On the other hand, the mode of fantasy also allows for more creative, plastic narrative approaches to the topic of *raptus*. The precise construction of the law of *raptus* in romance does not necessarily coincide with that of medieval England: romance narratives can create an idealised, wish-fulfilment world where women may be protected in ways impossible beyond the realms of the imagination. In particular, whereas female consent is not the definitive factor in the laws of the period, in the romance genre it is decisive in shaping narrative perspective and characterisation. The withholding of consent is a critical factor in the portrayal of force and sexual violation, and the ideal of consenting marriage is placed in opposition to actions of *raptus*, with the effect of mitigating the pervasive romance notion of the woman as object to be won in battle.

In late medieval English law, rape and abduction were inextricably linked: the term *raptus*, originally meaning 'seizure', could refer either to rape or abduction, and the central issue involved was that of theft, the theft of the woman as property either of her husband or her father. This is neatly exemplified in John Gower's *Confessio Amantis*, which classifies rape not as an example of the sin of Lechery, but of Robbery: the rape of a shepherdess by a knight is depicted as theft of another man's property, 'For other mennes good is swete.'[3] Crucially, the theft of a woman could also occur with her consent, if she were abducted not against her own will but against the wishes of parents or husband.

This definition of *raptus* was, however, complicated in England as a result of the Anglo-Saxon legal heritage. Anglo-Saxon written laws are particularly clear in condemning rape, and their construction supports the argument, propounded, for instance, by Christine Fell, that the individual rights of women in England were greater in this period than after the Conquest. The laws of Alfred distinguish between rape, indicated, for example, by the term *niedhæmed* (literally meaning 'forcible coition'), and abduction, signified by phrases such as *ut álædan* ('to lead out'); rape is treated in Alfred's law code alongside lesser sexual crimes like illicitly touching the woman, whereas abduction is addressed in a different part of the code.[4] To determine how these written law codes related to actual practice is of course impossible, but

---

[3] John Gower, *Confessio Amantis*, in *The English Works of John Gower*, ed. G.C. Macaulay, 2 vols, Early English Text Society, e.s. 81 and 82 (Oxford, 1900 and 1901, reprinted 1957, 1969), vol. 2, Book V, l. 6118. I offer a discussion of the legal history of *raptus* comparable to the following in 'Woman Displaced: Rape and Romance in Chaucer's *Wife of Bath's Tale*', *Arthurian Literature* XIII, ed. James P. Carley and Felicity Riddy (Cambridge, 1995), pp. 118–24.
[4] See F. Liebermann, ed., *Die Gesetze der Angelsachsen*, 3 vols (1903–16; Halle, 1960), vol. 1, Alfred: [8] pp. 54–55; [18] p. 58; [11] p. 56; [25–26] pp. 62–66.

it is clear that two different types of offence were recognised by the Anglo-Saxon codifiers, one a sexual offence, the other a crime of property.

Early Roman law, by contrast, had focused on the devaluation caused by abduction, and used the term *raptus* to signify the seizure or theft of a woman. It was not until the sixth-century law code of Justinian that the definition of *raptus* was broadened to include rape, and then only of virgins, nuns and widows.[5] The emphasis of Roman law on abduction was very directly reflected in later Continental law, while canon law, which drew heavily on Roman law, was even more restrictive. In canon law, the term *raptus* was used exclusively to refer to cases of abduction of unmarried women until the twelfth century, when Gratian in his *Decretum* drew on the code of Justinian to extend the definition. Although Gratian recognised unlawful sex as an aspect of the crime, 'raptus est illicitus coitus', he specified that a charge of *raptus* could only be brought if the victim were also unmarried and had been abducted from her father's house, 'id est a domo patris ducta'.[6] The issue of consent was obscured by the fact that the crime could be against either the woman's will or that of her parents. Theological writings classify 'simple' rape – rape without abduction – under one of two other branches of the sin of Lechery: *stuprum*, defloration of virgins, and *fornication*, illicit sex with married women or prostitutes. Yet at the same time, the topics of will, intention and consent were of particular concern to theologians in defining the nature of sin, while discussions of virginity dealt at length with the question of sexual violation of the woman against her will. Consent was therefore a marked issue despite its secondary role in theological writing on *raptus*.

Although English law was to move closer to Roman and canon law, in the period immediately following the Norman Conquest English legal theorists appear to have attempted to maintain the distinction between rape and abduction made in the Anglo-Saxon law codes. The *Leis Willelme*, an Anglo-Norman collection of laws that claims, probably falsely, the authority of William the Conqueror, echoes Alfred's distinctions between rape and attempted rape; similarly, the laws of Henry I appear to refer to two separate crimes, *raptus* and *violentus concubitus*.[7] In the earliest English legal treatise,

---

5   Justinian writes, 'castitas corrupta restitui non possit' ('chastity defiled cannot be restored'). See Justinian, *Codex Iustinianus*, in *Corpus Iuris Civilis*, ed. Theodore Mommsen, Paul Krueger and Rudolf Schoell, 3 vols (Berlin, 1877–95), vol. 2, Book IX, titulus xiii.i, 'De Raptu Virginum', p. 378. The fourth-century Theodosian code, which was known to the Anglo-Saxons, treats *raptus* in very similar terms, but does not mention chastity specifically. See Clyde Pharr, tr., *The Theodosian Code and Novels and the Sirmondian Constitutions*, Corpus of Roman Law I (Princeton, 1952), Book IX, tituli 24 and 25 (354 AD).

6   Gratian, *Decretum magistri Gratiani*, in *Corpus iuris canonici*, ed. Æmilius Friedberg, 2 vols (Leipzig, 1879 and 1885), vol. I, part II, XXXVI.i. 2, 1288. For discussion of punishment, see part II, XXVII.ii.48, 1077.

7   Liebermann, ed., *Leis Willelme*: [12] p. 500; [18] pp. 504–505 (MS Pseudo-Ingulf); *Leges Henrici*: [10.10.1], p. 556; [13] p. 558.

the late twelfth-century work known as Glanvill, the crime of *raptus* seems to be equated solely with rape:

> Raptus crimen est quod aliqua mulier imponit uiro quo proponit se a uiro ui oppressam in pace domini regis.

> In the crime of rape a woman charges a man with violating her by force in the peace of the lord king.[8]

This definition, which seems far narrower than in Continental law, is further elaborated in the early thirteenth-century treatise attributed to Henri de Bracton.[9] Bracton equates the appeal of *raptus* specifically to the rape of virgins, and the discussion of the penalty plays rhetorically on the sexual nature of the crime:

> si convincatur, sequitur pœna, scilicet amissio membrorum, ut sit membrum pro membro, quia virgo cum corrumpitur membrum amittit. Et ideo corruptor puniatur in eo in quo deliquit. Oculos igitur amittat propter aspectum decoris quo virginem concupivit. Amittat etiam testiculos qui calorem stupri induxerunt.

> If he is convicted . . . , [this] punishment follows: the loss of members, that there be member for member, for when a virgin is defiled she loses her member and therefore let her defiler be punished in the parts in which he offended. Let him lose his eyes which gave him sight of the maiden's beauty for which he coveted her. And let him lose as well the testicles which excited his hot lust.[10]

While Bracton states that the punishment for the rape of virgins is the loss of member, the treatise cites only one instance, in 1222, of enactment of this extreme punishment.[11] Most cases, it seems, were dismissed or the parties reached agreement, sometimes through financial settlements, sometimes through marriage. It is possible, as J.B. Post has argued, that some women made accusations of *raptus* for the purpose of bringing about marriages against family wishes.[12]

---

8 *Tractatus de Legibus et Consuetudinibus Regni Anglie qui Glanvilla Vocatur: The Treatise on the Laws and Customs of the Realm of England Commonly Called Glanvill*, ed. and tr. G.D.G. Hall, Medieval Texts Series (London, 1965), XIV, vi, 'Placitum de crimine raptus', p. 175.

9 The treatise is based on Glanvill and apparently upon the practical experience of two justices, Martin of Pateshull (1220–30) and William of Raleigh (1230–40).

10 *Bracton de legibus et consuetudinibus Angliae*: Bracton *on the Laws and Customs of England*, ed. George E. Woodbine, tr. Samuel E. Thorne, 4 vols (Cambridge, Ma, 1968–77), vol. 2, 'De placitis coronae', pp. 414–15.

11 Bracton, 2, pp. 402–403.

12 J.B. Post, 'Ravishment of Women and the Statutes of Westminster', *Legal Records and the Historian: Papers Presented to the Cambridge Legal History Conference, 7–10 July 1975, and in Lincoln's*

Despite the weight placed by early legal writers such as Glanvill and Bracton on rape *per se*, the legal discourse in England seems gradually to have come to follow the emphasis of Continental and canon law on social issues related to abduction. This phenomenon is evident in the statute of Westminster I (1275) on *raptus*. Here rape becomes blurred with abduction, and the woman may be a willing participant:

[c. 13]   E le roy defend qe nul ravyse ne prengne damysele *de* deinze age, par soun gre ne sanz soun gre, ne dame ne damisele de age, ne autre femme maugre soun. Et si nul le face, a la sute celuy ke suera *de* denz les .xl. jours le roy luy fra commune dreyture; et si nul *ne* comence la sute *de* deinz .xl. jours le roy suyra, e ceus qe il *en* trovera copables si averount la prisoun de .ij. aunz, e puis soynt reinz a la volunte le roy; e si il ne ad dount rendre ou de estra reinz a la volunte le roy si soynt puniz par plus grevous e plus long prisoun, solom ceo qe le trespas demaunde.[13]

[c. 13]   And the king forbids anyone to rape, or take by force a damsel under age, either with her consent or without it, or a married woman or a damsel of age or any other woman against her will; and if anyone does so the king will, at the suit of him who will sue within forty days, do common justice therein; and if no one begins his suit within forty days the king will sue in the matter; and those whom he finds guilty shall have two years' imprisonment and then shall make fine at the will of the king, and if they have not the means from which to be fined at the king's pleasure, they are to be punished by longer imprisonment, according to what the offence demands.[14]

The definition of *raptus* is widened to include abduction of married women, probably as a result of concern over highly political cases of abduction of noble wives, and, in addition, the king is given the right to sue if no other party does.[15] The penalty, however, is noticeably less severe: Westminster I treats *raptus* not as a felony, as the earlier treatises do, but as a trespass, a charge brought by writ and ordinarily resolved by fine. *Raptus* has become a lesser crime punished not by dismemberment or loss of life, but by two years of imprisonment (presumably this penalty was enforced only if the offender was unable to pay the requisite fine). The earlier emphasis on punishment

---

Inn Old Hall on 3 July 1974, ed. J.H. Baker, Royal Historical Society Studies in History (London, 1978), pp. 150–64: 152 and 152 n.7.

13 Texts for the statutes of Westminster I and II are taken from Post, 'Ravishment of Women', Appendix, pp. 162–64: 162–63. As Post remarks, there is no satisfactory text for the statutes; his is based on Corporation of London Records Office, *Liber Horn*.

14 Henry Rothwell, *English Historical Documents*, III: *1189–1327* (London, 1975), p. 400.

15 See, for example, Post's discussion of a celebrated abduction feud in Sussex recorded for 1274–75: 'Ravishment of Women', p. 154.

fitting to the defloration of virgins is completely lost, replaced by concern for rights of king and family rather than of the woman.

This statute appears to have been perceived as inadequate even at the time; most cases were dropped on technicalities, and the law was rewritten ten years later as Westminster II (1285):

> [c.34]   Purveu est ensement qe si homme ravise femme espose, damou-sele, ou autre femme deshormes par la ou ele ne se est assentue ne avaunt ne apres eit jugement de vie e de membre; ensement par la ou homme ravise femme, damoysele, dame espose, ou autre femme a force, tut seyt ele assentue apres, eit tel jugement come avaunt est dist, sil seit atteint a la swte le roy, e la eit le roy sa sywte.

> [c.34]   It is provided that henceforth if a man ravishes a married woman, a maiden, or other woman, without her consent before or after-wards, he shall have judgement of life and limb; and likewise where a man ravishes a woman – married woman, maiden, or other woman – by force even though she consents afterwards, he shall have the judgement before stated if he is convicted at the king's suit, and there the king shall have his suit.[16]

With Westminster II, cases of forcible coition become indistinguishable from those of abduction: the statute refers simply to 'ravishment', and the empha-sis is placed even more clearly on the problem of consenting abductions where the king may sue.[17] Although the crime of *raptus* is reinstated as a felony, thus once again punishable by loss of life or limb, in actuality the legal history of rape in the fourteenth century is 'even less distinguished than before'.[18] In the single known instance, in 1305, of a conviction for life and limb, the offender was allowed to pay a fine.[19] It became common for *raptus* to be pursued as a trespass, following the precedent of cases of ravishment of ward; cases of *raptus* of the woman would be brought by the woman's father or husband, just as cases of *raptus* of a child would be brought by a guardian. Instances where the woman consented to abduction and marriage, however, continued to pose legal problems throughout the fourteenth century. These culminated in a petition made to John of Gaunt in 1382 by Sir Thomas West, whose daughter had been abducted and subsequently married. Although the charges specify forcible coition as well as abduction, West's concern is very evidently over the non-contractual nature of the marriage to which his

---

16   Post, 'Ravishment of Women', p. 164; Rothwell, p. 447.

17   Post, 'Ravishment of Women', pp. 157–58.

18   Post, 'Ravishment of Women', p. 157.

19   Post, 'Ravishment of Women', p. 157. Post argues that the clause making ravishment of women a felony is 'an ad hoc addition', since it is written sloppily in French rather than in the Latin of the rest of the statute.

daughter has consented; the charge of sexual violation seems to be used rhetorically, for shock value and to mask a much more political agenda. West's petition led to a further statute, which legally extended the object of the wrong done in *raptus* from the woman, 'afterwards consenting', to her family, whose right to reprisal was equal to that of the woman under the old laws.[20] Consent was thus further decentred in a law that primarily emphasised property, even while social awareness of abduction and non-contractual marriage increased, and the law of *raptus* became increasingly complex and nuanced.

Given the legal and social impact of *raptus*, perhaps it is unsurprising that both aspects of the crime, rape and abduction, should figure largely in Middle English romance writing. Issues of gender more generally are central to the romance genre, and while the structures of chivalry depend on male prowess, women play indispensable and often startlingly powerful roles in the romances. The interplay of force and consent in romance narratives can illuminate vividly the dynamics of gender and the predicament of women in a male-centred world. Middle English romances mirror the contemporary legal concern regarding property in their repeated engagement with the motif of abduction, and with the chivalric custom of winning a lady in battle. The threats of rape and abduction tend to blur into each other as in medieval law, and, indeed, the term *raptus*, rather than the more specific 'rape' or 'abduction', often seems most appropriate to describe the crimes against women portrayed in romance. Romances do, however, demonstrate concern regarding the specific crime of sexual violation, and regarding the nature of force and the desirability of consent. The code of protection of the lady's person becomes an important romance ideal, while laws against rape mark a good king. The nobility or villainy of a knight is demonstrated by whether he adheres to such laws, and although romance is predicated on a male, military ethic, the lady's consent even when she is won in battle becomes imperative. Thus Middle English romance both reflects and responds to, sometimes radically, the law of *raptus*.

Although it is difficult to generalise about the differences between early and late Middle English romances, because of the continuing circulation and redaction of early works in the later period and the frequent existence of Anglo-Norman or French sources for later works, earlier romances seem to demonstrate a keener, more detailed engagement with the legal issues associated with *raptus* and particularly with sexual violation. This emphasis may perhaps be linked to the closeness of the earlier works to a period when very clear legal provision was made against rape *per se*. The early romance of *Havelok* (c.1290), for example, depicts laws protecting women from violence

---

[20] See J.B. Post, 'Sir Thomas West and the Statute of Rapes, 1382', *Bulletin of the Institute of Historical Research, University of London* 53 (1980), pp. 24–30, for discussion of this later development.

as a manifestation of admirable social order in the land, and, strikingly, the poet indicates some familiarity with early English law. The work refers with considerable legal realism to the enforcement of strict laws regarding rape in the time of King Athelwold:

> And who dide widwen wrong,
> Were he nevre knight so strong,
> That he ne made him sone kesten
> In fetteres and full faste festen;
> And who-so dide maidne shame
> Of hire body or brought in blame,
> Bute it were by hire wille,
> He made him sone of limes spille.[21]

These specific laws against rape and 'wrong' assert Athelwold's excellence as king.[22] The details recall the explicit condemnation against rape in the Anglo-Saxon laws, and perhaps indicate the poet's familiarity with Alfred's law code, or with early post-Conquest legal writing.

The *Havelok*-poet's evocation of Athelwold's laws is not unlike the historical perspective of Bracton, which refers to the laws of Æthelstan:

> Raptus mulieris ne fiat defendit tam lex humana quam divina. Et sic fuit antiquitus observatum, quod si quis obiaverit mulieri vel alicubi invenerit, si sola vel socios habuerit cum pace dimittat eam, quam si per inhonestatem tetigerit, frangit edictum regis, et emendabit secundum iudicium comitatus. Si autem contra voluntatem eius iactet eam ad terram, forisfaciat gratiam suam: quod si impudice discooperuerit eam et se super eam posuerit, omnium possessionum suarum incurrit damnum: quod si concubuerit cum ea, de vita et membris suis incurrit damnum. Adelstane.

> Man-made as well as divine laws forbid the rape of women. In ancient times the practice was as follows: if a man meets a woman or comes across her somewhere, whether she is alone or has companions, he is to let her go in peace; if he touches her indecorously he breaks the king's ordinance and shall give compensation in accordance with the judge-

21 *Havelok*, in Donald B. Sands, ed., *Middle English Verse Romances*, Exeter Medieval English Texts and Studies (Exeter, 1986) pp. 55–129: ll. 79–86. All subsequent references to *Havelok* will be from this edition and will be cited by line number.
22 The *Peterborough Chronicle* specifically remarks the punishment of rape as a manifestation of William I's excellence: 'Gif hwilc carlman hæmde wið wimman hire unðances, sona he forleas þa limu þe he mid pleagode'; see Cecily Clark, ed., *The Peterborough Chronicle, 1070–1154*, 2nd edn (Oxford, 1970), pp. 108 [7], 12, ll. 93–94. Similarly, William of Malmesbury approves the laws of Henry I against rape; see *Gesta Regum Anglorum: The History of the English Kings*, ed. and tr. R.A.B. Mynors, R.M. Thomson and M. Winterbottom, vol. 1 (Oxford, 1998), III, 245.4, pp. 458–59.

ment of the county court; if he throws her upon the ground against her will, he forfeits the king's grace; if he shamelessly disrobes her and places himself upon her, he incurs the loss of all his possessions; and if he lies with her, he incurs the loss of his life and members.
    Æthelstan.[23]

Although there is no known law of Æthelstan that fits this reference, the details of sexual violation in Bracton, like those in *Havelok*, do echo the phrasing of Alfred's laws. Both passages suggest that the Anglo-Saxon period was envisaged by those looking back after the Conquest as one when rape was rigorously controlled. In neither *Havelok* nor Bracton, however, is rape punished by fine, as it would have been under Anglo-Saxon law, but rather by death or mutilation, the penalty for felony in early post-Conquest law. As in Bracton, the reference to loss of limb in *Havelok* may specifically imply castration, the punishment appropriate to the rapist. The passage makes clear that this penalty applies exclusively to those who violate virgins, whereas the attackers of widows are only fettered; in addition, the 'wrong' done to widows is left unspecified, and may include a range of offences, such as theft of property. The narrative emphasis falls firmly on the crime of rape of 'maiden', a term that may imply women of noble status as well as virgins. Thus while rape continues to be treated as a distinctive crime, as in Anglo-Saxon laws, the perspective in *Havelok* does also reflect the gradual legal shift after the Conquest from the Anglo-Saxon distinctions to the Roman notion of *raptus*. The poet employs elements of a legal discourse rooted in the past to portray the ideal nature of Athelwold's reign. The symbolic import is clear: laws against rape signify good kingship. The fairly contemporaneous moral romance *Amis and Amiloun* similarly refers to the 'londes lawe' and the penalty of death for rape, with the implication again that a law against rape is a necessary part of the ideal chivalric world.[24] *Havelok*, however, is particularly unusual in its legal specificity, and implies some knowledge of a characteristic early English law against rape on the part of its writer.

    The linked motifs of rape and abduction also function more generally as moral indicators in romance, to distinguish the good from the bad. As increasingly in the English law, the crimes of rape and abduction tend to be conflated in depictions of unelaborated actions of *raptus* or seizure of a lady's person. While great knights win the love of their ladies by performing great deeds, less heroic figures resort to force in order to gain their desired objects: instances of *raptus* and the associated threat of enforced marriage recur throughout the genre. Adventure is repeatedly occasioned by the duty of knights to rescue ladies threatened with possession against their will, most

---

[23] Bracton, 2, p. 418.
[24] *Amis and Amiloun*, in Jennifer Fellows, ed., *Of Love and Chivalry: An Anthology of Middle English Romance*, Everyman's Library (London; Rutland, Vermont, 1993), pp. 73–145: l. 635.

often when their castles are besieged and their hands sought in marriage; the threat of rape is rarely voiced, but consistently implied in such scenes of attempted forcible possession. While the rescue of a lady tests and proves the knight-protector, it also illustrates the underlying romance assumption that military victory is decisive; once the lady's castle and lands or those of her father have been won, she has no choice but to submit to the victor. Such instances are very evidently not subject to the laws of *raptus* even if, as in *Havelok*, the existence of these has been remarked, and the predicament of the woman forced to marry against her will is explored with particular immediacy and drama by romance writers. *King Horn*, one of the earliest romances extant in Middle English (c.1225), and like *Havelok* based on an Anglo-Norman text, conveys the unpleasantness of forced marriage vividly, making clear the lack of legal redress. Horn is told by a palmer of Rimenhild's distress at her prospective wedding to King Modi of Reynes:

> Ne mighte heo adrighe
> That heo ne weop with ighe.
> Heo sede that heo nolde
> Ben y-spused with golde.[25]

Rimenhild's response to the undesired match is dramatic and assertive: she conceals a knife in order to kill both her new husband and herself. The narrative creates suspense by playing on the threat to the woman's will, and the absence of legal redress is acutely evident. Death is portrayed as the only way to escape undesirable marriage: the knight who wins the lady's lands or the consent of her parents has the right to her person. Lack of consent on her part would not render marriage illegal but only unpalatable, and the intervention of a protector is required, who in this instance conveniently turns out to be Horn himself, Rimenhild's true 'husbonde' (1047).

Romance narratives thus underline the lady's need for a defender and lord, if only to save her from other would-be defenders and the threat of *raptus*. Rather ironically, a knight's successful defence of a lady's castle from its attackers is frequently followed by the swift conferral of her hand and lands on him. This phenomenon is particularly evident in the early fourteenth-century English rewriting of Chrétien de Troyes' *Yvain*, *Ywain and Gawain*. After Ywain has killed Alundyne's protector, Lunete warns of her lady's vulnerability:

> 'If twa knyghtes be in the felde
> On twa stedes, with spere and shelde,
> And the tane the tother may sla:

---

[25] *King Horn*, in Sands, ed., *Middle English Verse Romances*, pp. 15–54: ll. 1043–46. All subsequent references to *King Horn* will be from this edition and will be cited by line number.

Whether es the better of tha?'
Sho said, 'He that has the bataile.'

. . . The lady thoght than, al the nyght,
How that sho had na knyght,
Forto seke hir land thorghout,
To kepe Arthur and hys rowt.[26]

The narrative intimates the impossibility of independent female existence: within the chivalrous society depicted here, women cannot defend themselves, and there is no recourse against the man who wins the woman in battle. Thus Alundyne swiftly accepts the expedient of marriage with the very knight who has killed her husband, while later the lady whom Ywain rescues from her besieger, Sir Alers, prays him to marry her:

'Sir, if it be yowre will,
I pray yow forto dwel here still;
And I wil yelde into yowre handes
Myn awyn body and al my landes.' (1959–62)

These lines make explicit the link between lady and lands, and the virtuous hero is equated with the able defender. In the numerous examples of ladies threatened with marriage against their will, the issue of rape lurks beneath the surface of the text as it tends to do in charges of *raptus*: it is the lady's person, as well as her lands, that is at stake and that her defender is to preserve – ironically enough, most often for himself. The fictional world is conspicuously not that of fourteenth-century law, for despite references to an independent law of the land in romance, the chivalric ethic depends on the individual strength of the knight in battle and the alignment of might with right. The lady requires military protection against rape, but also protection against the notion that her body belongs to the victor in battle irrespective of her own desires.

This situation is acutely realised in the early fourteenth-century romance of *Sir Percyvell of Gales*, which depicts the siege of the lady Lufamour's castle by a heathen sultan. Perceval himself identifies a familiar romance pattern, that of the hostile pagan outsider's desire to possess the woman:

'That scho may have no pese,
The lady, for hir fayrenes
And for hir mekill reches,

---

26 *Ywain and Gawain*, in Maldwyn Mills, ed., *Ywain and Gawain, Sir Percyvell of Gales, The Anturs of Arther*, Everyman's Library (London; Rutland, Vermont, 1992), pp. 1–102: ll. 999–1003; 1021–24. All subsequent references to *Ywain and Gawain* will be from this edition and will be cited by line number.

He wirkes hir full woo!
He dose his sorow all hir sythe
And all he slaes doun ry[f]e;
He wolde have hir to wyfe,
And scho will noghte soo.'[27]

Although Perceval responds according to the precepts of chivalry, the ensuing battle in fact becomes a battle for Lufamour's hand. She herself views her person as the right of her defender, and, rather startlingly, employs the same terminology as the Sultan, 'Scho thoght hym worthi to welde, / And he myghte wyn hir in felde / With maystry and myghte' (1310–12). The military action of winning the lady in battle is made acceptable by the romance alignment of victory and love. This pattern is echoed in numerous romances: in the late fourteenth-century Sir Degrevant, the lady Melidor's hand is the prize to be won by Degrevaunt in the lists against the Duke of Gerle, and again, the woman's consent aligns with the victor's desire for her in a highly idealistic equation of might with right, 'Welcome, Syre Aunterous'.[28] The lady may be gained through force, but not force enacted against her person, for her consent is necessary in order to rewrite as love what could otherwise be construed as enforced marriage. In this way, episodes of raptus and threats of enforced marriage in romance stand in opposition to those where the lady is won through the honour and prowess of the knight, and military achievements for the lady are contrasted with attacks on her.

The crime of raptus also figures more overtly in romance, in the numerous episodes where women are abducted by hostile opponents, often as much because of their value as property as because they provoke desire. Such actions of raptus are frequently associated with the heathen and hostile world beyond the court, a world where no legal and chivalric structures exist to defend women from the action of raptus. The early romance of Floris and Blancheflour (c.1250) is constructed around the abduction of its heroine and the resulting threat of enforced marriage, with its silent suggestion of rape. The pagan king of Spain, angered by his son Floris' love for his childhood companion, the Christian maiden Blancheflour, sells her to merchants in a nearby harbour, 'Ther have they for that maide yolde / Twenty mark of reed golde, / And a coupe good and riche . . .'.[29] For the merchants, the Christian virgin is a valuable commodity to be sold to the highest bidder, and Blancheflour is eventually bought by the Emir of Babylon. Her virginity both

---

[27] Sir Percyvell of Gales, in Mills, ed., Ywain and Gawain, pp. 103–60: 4177–90. All subsequent references to Sir Percyvell of Gales will be from this edition and will be cited by line number.
[28] The Romance of Sir Degrevant, ed. L.F. Casson, Early English Text Society o.s. 221 (London, 1949 for 1944) l. 1385.
[29] Floris and Blancheflour, in Sands, ed., Middle English Verse Romances, pp. 279–309: ll. 161–63. All subsequent references to Floris and Blancheflour will be from this edition and will be cited by line number.

increases her value and marks her as the ideal candidate when the Emir comes to make his yearly choice of a wife from among his harem. The story, with its Eastern setting, its magical garden where Blancheflour's virginity is tested, and its charming depiction of Floris' appearance concealed in a basket of flowers, forms an exotic variant on the enforced marriage motif.

In the later *Sir Isumbras*, written in the early fourteenth century, women are similarly viewed as a commodity by the pagans: the heathen king offers to buy Isumbras' wife from him, 'Wylt thou thy wyfe sell me? / I wyll yefe for here golde and fe, / And ryche robes sevenne . . .'.[30] On Isumbras' refusal, the heathens attack him and abduct his wife, 'His wyfe they toke hym fro. / On the londe they dede hym caste / And beten hym and hys rybbes braste, / And made his flessh full blo' (291–94). As in *Floris*, the implication is that noble Christian women, rendered eminently desirable by their looks, fetch a high price: the king attempts to make Isumbras' wife his queen on account of her celestial fairness, 'Hym thowghte an angell that she were, / Komen out of hevenne that day' (275–76). By representing a hostile world outside the chivalric order, these romances silently assert the need for a law of *raptus* in order to limit commodification of women, while they suggest too the importance of the woman's consent.

Malory's *Morte Darthur*, written some two centuries after most of these works, in many ways offers a retrospective on the romance genre, and treats with particular acuteness and practicality the need for a law defending women from *raptus*, and the possibility that consent rather than force should form the foundation for gender relations. Malory was himself accused of *raptus* of a certain Joan Smith on two occasions in 1450, in conjunction with a number of other crimes.[31] The records specify the act of rape, 'felonice rapuit & cum ea carnaliter concubuit' ('he feloniously seized and carnally lay by her'), and Malory is also charged with breaking into the house of Joan's husband Hugh Smith and with theft of his 'goods and chattels'.[32] Although charges were twice brought against Malory (at Nuneaton in 1451 and then in London in the King's Bench in 1452), he was never tried; his case was repeatedly deferred and he spent eight years in London prisons before being freed when the Yorkist forces defeated the Lancastrians in 1460.[33] The truth of the charges is difficult to gauge. There was no trial, nor, in keeping with the procedure of bringing a charge of *raptus* by writ rather than appeal, did the

---

30 *Sir Isumbras*, in Mills, ed., *Six Middle English Romances*, pp. 125–47: ll. 277–79. All subsequent references to *Sir Isumbras* will be from this edition and will be cited by line number.

31 P.J.C. Field, *The Life and Times of Sir Thomas Malory*, Arthurian Studies XXIX (Cambridge, 1993), p. 97.

32 Records taken from Edward Hicks, *Sir Thomas Malory: His Turbulent Career* (Cambridge, Ma., 1928), p. 96; my translation. See also A.C. Baugh, 'Documenting Sir Thomas Malory', *Speculum* 8 (1933), pp. 3–29, and Field, *Sir Thomas Malory*, p. 97.

33 See Field's discussion of this period: *Sir Thomas Malory*, pp. 105–25.

woman herself offer any evidence. The coincidence of rape and theft, however, suggests that the charges may mask a crime of property.[34] They must also be placed in the context of the troubled political period during which Malory wrote: the quarrel may have been caused by a political disagreement, or the accusations may have been linked to a series of political attacks intended to damage the status and power of public figures.[35] We can only finally be certain that, at the very least, the legal nuances of the crime of raptus were familiar to Malory. Indeed, it is very striking that over the course of the Morte Darthur, Malory carefully establishes and elaborates a law of raptus as part of his chivalric vision, and repeatedly employs the motif of raptus to explore both the contrast between villainy and nobility, and the importance of female consent in marriage.

The responsibility of the knight to defend women is made explicit in the Morte following the first quest, in the institution of the chivalric oath sworn by all the knights at Pentecost each year. This oath is one of Malory's most striking additions to his sources and encapsulates the several aspects of the chivalric ideal: service to God, king, lady and fellow-knight. We are made aware of the need for law, order and the promotion of mercy even within the Arthurian kingdom. The possibility of rape is specifically stated and forbidden as the knights swear 'allwayes to do ladyes, damesels, and jantilwomen and wydowes [socour:] strengthe hem in hir ryghtes, and never to enforce them, uppon payne of dethe'.[36] The specificity of the reference suggests the symbolic import given the crime in the Morte: it figures as the most extreme form of dishonour to a woman and as a betrayal of chivalric duty. As in earlier Middle English romances like Havelok, a stern law of rape becomes a quality indicative of an ordered land and a good king.[37] The oath also has a material foundation in the courtly culture of Malory's period; the inclusion of chivalric oaths in contemporaneous treatises on knighthood attests to the conventional nature and popular appeal of such codes of behaviour, although their emphasis tends ordinarily to fall on loyalty and obedience rather than the

---

34 Christine Carpenter has suggested that the husband's appeal was his way of seeking redress in an adulterous affair, Bulletin of the Institute of Historical Research 53 (1980), pp. 31–43: 37–38 n.55. Field makes a similar point: Sir Thomas Malory, p. 106.

35 See Field's discussion: Sir Thomas Malory, pp. 96–104.

36 Sir Thomas Malory, The Works of Sir Thomas Malory, ed. Eugène Vinaver and P. J. C. Field, 3rd edn, 3 vols (Oxford, 1990), I, p. 120, ll.20–23. All subsequent references to Malory will be from this edition and will be cited by volume, page and line number. This detail is removed in Caxton's edition: Vinaver suggests that he either saw it as incongruous or unnecessary: III, p. 1335, n.120.

37 See by contrast the romances of Chrétien, which specify the protection of women from rape, but do not indicate a legal punishment for rape; they state the custom that the knight may honourably take a lady from another knight in battle: Chrétien de Troyes, Le Contes du Graal (Perceval), ed. Félix Lecoy, 2 vols, Les Romans de Chrétien de Troyes V and VI, Les Classiques français du Moyen Age (Paris, 1975; 1984), vol. 2, ll. 6872–85; Le Chevalier de la Charrete, ed. Mario Roques, Les Romans de Chrétien de Troyes III, Les Classiques français du Moyen Age (Paris, 1972), ll. 1302–16; see also Gravdal's discussion of rape in Chrétien's romances, pp. 42–71.

protection of women. The closest parallel to Malory's oath, noted by Richard Barber, appears to be a clause in Boulton's *Knights of the Crown*, 'ye schall sustene wydowes in ther right at every tyme they wol requere yow and maydenys in ther virginite and helpe hem and socoure hem with yowre good that for lak of good they be not mysgovernyd'.[38]

Malory's version, however, does not simply suggest desirable chivalric behaviour, but actually writes the obligation of knights to defend women into the law of the land. Beverly Kennedy notes that to what was 'a commonplace of the treatises on chivalry . . . Malory gives . . . a distinctly judicial colouring when he adds that Round Table knights must undertake to champion the rightful causes of women in trial by battle'; this law redresses the vulnerability of women in a world where 'legal quarrels could be settled only by means of battle'.[39] Although it has been suggested that Malory tends to follow French law in his detail, here the phrase 'never to enforce them, upon payne of deth' seems rather to engage with the English legal tradition of Malory's own period, according to which the potential punishment for rape was death – although this was a potential, as he would have been only too aware, that was not often realised.[40] The oath also echoes the legal preference given to upper-class women in cases of *raptus* by specifying 'ladyes, damesels and jantyll-women'; crimes against lower-class women thus fall outside its jurisdiction.

Despite the formal proscription of *raptus* of ladies, however, the crime does exist within Malory's Arthurian kingdom; rape and abduction, as so often in romance, function as emblems of villainy, placing a knight outside the strictures of chivalry, and providing a focus for the defence of the chivalric ideal. Thus in the Book of Sir Launcelot (Caxton's Book VI), Launcelot encounters Sir Perys de Forest Savage, a knight specifically condemned as a rapist: 'here by this way hauntys a knyght that dystressis all ladyes and jantylwomen, and at the leste he robbyth them other lyeth by hem' (I, p. 269, ll. 19–21). Although Perys' crimes are sexual, the link between rape and theft, and the notion of violation of property so central to the medieval understanding of *raptus*, are acutely evident. In the French *Prose Vulgate*, the 'wicked knight' is 'merely a robber and a horse-thief';[41] the semantic field of *raptus*, however, allows Malory to include rape among Perys' crimes of theft, and thus to exploit the symbolic import of this offence against women in his characterisa-

38 See Richard Barber, 'Malory's *Le Morte Darthur* and Court Culture Under Edward IV', *Arthurian Literature* XII, ed. James P. Carley and Felicity Riddy (Cambridge, 1993), pp. 133–55: 149.
39 Beverly Kennedy, *Knighthood in the Morte Darthur*, 2nd edn, Arthurian Studies XI (Cambridge, 1992), p. 39.
40 See Ernest C. York's discussion of Malory's use of French law, 'Legal Punishment in Malory's *Le Morte Darthur*', *English Language Notes* 11 (1973–74), pp. 14–21, p. 21; Kennedy, by contrast, compares the terms of the oath to the punishment of rape by loss of 'life and member', and instances a fifteenth-century manuscript of 'seremons et ordonnances' which forbids rape: p. 39, n.16.
41 See Vinaver, *The Works of Sir Thomas Malory*, III, p. 1420, n.269, ll. 21–24; pp. 34–36.

tion. Launcelot suggests that Perys has betrayed his own noble blood, 'who dud lerne the to distresse ladyes, damesels and jantyllwomen!' (I, p. 269, ll. 35–36). By contravening the law regarding protection of ladies, Perys becomes a 'traytoure unto knyghthode', who merits only death, and Launcelot shows no mercy to him, 'Now haste thou thy paymente that longe thou haste deserved!' (I, p. 269, l. 35; p. 270, ll. 7–8). The knight's duty to defend the honour of women is upheld over the possibility of mercy, and Launcelot thus enacts the legal punishment for rape that in Malory's own period is never put into practice.

The act of *raptus* functions similarly to mark Malory's Sir Breunys Sanze Pité as 'a grete foo unto many good knyghtes of kyng Arthures courte (I, p. 406, ll. 6–7). Sir Dinadan encounters a lady 'makyng grete dole' as a result of her violation and abduction by Breunys:

> Sir knyght . . . I am the wofullyst lady of the worlde, for within thys fyve dayes here com a knyght called sir Breuse Saunz Pité, and he slewe myne owne brothir, and ever syns he hath kepte me at hys owne wylle, and of all men in the worlde I hate hym moste.   (II, p. 553, ll. 8–12).

The episode is a clear instance of *raptus*: Breunys has seized the lady from her protector in order to keep her as his paramour. She appears to be one of the very few victims of actual rape as well as abduction in the *Morte* and indeed in the romance genre as a whole, and it is notable that even here the sexual element of the crime is masked by the convention of winning the woman through combat. The erotic potential of the scene is ignored, and the focus is Breunys' theft and possession of the lady's person, rather than her sexual violation; the phrase 'at hys owne wylle' implies his use of force and the lady's lack of consent. That her rescuer Sir Dinadan defines his battle as for the 'honoure of all women' reiterates the public and illegal nature of the offence of *raptus*.

The indiscriminate seizure of women becomes a dramatic assertion of the villainy of Breunys and Perys, and their rejection of the chivalric code. But the motif of *raptus* also functions more subtly in the *Morte* in the numerous episodes of ladies threatened with enforced marriage, and it is here that Malory engages most directly with the issue of consent, so often marginalised in the legal discourse of *raptus*. The familiar pattern of the woman whose lands are besieged by an unwanted suitor and who bestows love on her protector receives its most sustained treatment in Malory's tale of Sir Gareth of Orkney (Caxton's Book VII). The central action of the tale is Gareth's rescue of Dame Lyonesse from the Red Knight of the Red Launds: 'she is beseged with a tirraunte, that she may nat oute of hir castell' (I, p. 296, ll. 21–22). The Red Knight's villainy is proven by the way that he conducts his siege, and in particular his practice of putting defeated knights 'to this shamefull deth withoute mercy and pyté' (I, p. 320, l. 9), by hanging them on trees

with their shields and swords. Gareth specifies the Red Knight's contravention of the code for honourable conduct of battle: 'he may be well a good
knyght, but he usyth shamefull customys . . .' (I, p. 320, ll. 20–21); the most
shameful of these customs is his siege of Lyonesse.

The focus of the tale, indeed, becomes the possibility of marriage based on
active consent rather than force. The Red Knight enlists the power of military victory to claim Lyonesse, 'she is my lady, and for hir I have done many
stronge batayles' (I, p. 321, ll. 36–37). For Gareth, however, precisely these
battles indicate that she is not the Red Knight's lady, 'For and I undirstoode
that she were nat ryght glad of my commynge I wolde be avysed or I dud
batayle for hir; but I undirstonde by the segynge of this castell she may forbere
thy felyship' (I, p. 322, ll. 4–7). Whereas the earlier Middle English
romances, like other sections of the *Morte*, tend to be constructed around the
customary law that the knight who wins the woman owns her, the tale of
Gareth rewrites this archaic pattern of marriage rooted in force with the
possibility of courtship based on consent. Lyonesse herself states the need for
active consent and love in her description of the Red Knight, 'he attendyth
unto nothyng but to murther, and that is the cause I can nat prayse hym
nother love hym' (I, p. 318, ll. 25–26). In this tale, as for example in *Sir Percyvell of Gales*, the knight who successfully defends the lady from enforced marriage in fact does gain her hand, but although Lyonesse is dependent on
physical protection, she does not unquestioningly associate military victory
and love. Despite Gareth's claims that he has won her love lawfully, 'well I am
sure I have bought your love with parte of the beste blooode within my body'
(I, p. 327, ll. 15–17), Lyonesse sends him away, ostensibly for a year, so that
she may assure herself of his identity and general worthiness. The tale thus
revises in proto-feminist terms the familiar pattern of the lady's offer of her
hand to the knight who saves her from enforced marriage. The narrative
seems to engage with the actuality of marriage, the emotional importance of
the woman's consent, and the undesirable nature of force.

In the Tristram section of the *Morte*, the episode of the abduction of Sir
Epinogrus' lady demonstrates acutely the dangers of a chivalric custom based
on force and possession. We learn that Epinogrus himself has originally won
his lady through battle, at the cost of her father's life (II, p. 771, ll. 2–10); her
will is irrelevant, rather as it might be in a contemporary legal case of *raptus*.
The problems inherent in this chivalric custom quickly become evident,
however, for Epinogrus reveals that on the very day after his victory, the lady
was in turn won from him by a stronger knight, Sir Helior, 'at the laste sir
Helyor wounded me so that he lefft me for dede, and so he toke my lady with
hym' (II, p. 771, ll. 16–17). To free the lady, Palomides must confront not
Helior but a third knight, Sir Saphir, to whom the defeated Helior has had to
offer the lady: he 'prayed hym to save his lyff and bade hym take his lady' (II,
p. 772, ll. 12–13). Upon Palomides' attempt to return the lady to Epinogrus,
Saphir claims a right to her for himself, 'Thou wenyst, sir knyght, to have that

lady away fro me so lyghtly? . . . thou shalt wyn her more derar than ever ded I' (II, p. 772, ll. 31–32; p. 773, l. 2). By defeating Saphir, Palomides in fact becomes the lady's fifth possessor, but, by returning her to the first knight, Epinogrus, he subsequently overturns the military ethic. This action is justi-fied by the fact that, although Epinogrus has formerly won the lady in battle, their relationship has been transformed into one of mutual love, and is char-acterised as something other than non-consenting *raptus*. The lady herself laments the loss of Epinogrus in rather tragic terms, notwithstanding the fact that he has killed her own father: 'Alas . . . that evir I knew hym other he me! For I have for his sake loste my worshyp and also hys lyff; that greveth me moste of all' (II, p. 772, ll. 20–22). She places on Epinogrus' life a value even higher than her own honour, and Epinogrus seems to move from subscribing to one mode of possession according to which the woman is a chattel to be won, to a more progressive mode rooted in love, consent and the notion of monogamy. In accordance with this new mode, Epinogrus' lady is returned to him despite his military defeat; their relationship has become one equivalent to marriage. Although military prowess remains the definitive quality of the knight, then, Malory sets up a new ethic of the Round Table, an ethic that protects women from *raptus* and promotes consent in marriage.

The negative consequences of *raptus* are acutely explored by Malory near the end of the book, in his depiction of the most extreme instance of the crime imaginable, the abduction of the queen herself by Sir Meliagaunt (Caxton's Book XIX). Meliagaunt's ambush of Guinevere and her company during a peaceable Maying expedition is memorable for its vivid realisation:

> So as [the quene] was oute on-mayynge wyth all her knyghtes whych were bedaysshed wyth erbis, mossis and floures in the freysshyste maner, ryght so there cam oute of a wood sir Mellyagaunte with an eyght score men, all harneyst as they shulde fyght in a batayle of areste, and bade the quene and her knyghtis abyde, for magré their hedis they shulde abyde.   (III, p. 1122, ll. 1–7)

Like the Knight of the Red Launds and Sir Breunys, Meliagaunt perpetrates his violence against a defenceless opponent. Not only does his action deny the importance of female consent and contravene the chivalric duty to protect ladies, but also, in abducting the queen, he commits an act that in Malory's time would have been considered one of high treason. According to the Statute of Treasons of 1352 a treasonable action occurred, 'si homme violast la compaigne le Roi, ou leisnesce filt le Roi nient marie, ou la com-paigne leisne fitz & heir du Roi . . .' ('if a man violates the king's wife or the king's eldest unmarried daughter, or the wife of the king's eldest son . . .').[42]

---

[42] *The Statutes*, 2nd revised edition, vol. 1 (London, 1888), p. 110; translated in A.R. Myers, ed., *English Historical Documents IV 1327–1485* (London, 1969), p. 403.

The term 'violast' here is ambiguous in something of the way the term *raptus* is: violation might include abduction and intended rape. Malory in fact is careful to show that Guinevere suffers the public violation of abduction and the threat of sexual violation, but is not actually raped: sexual violation of the queen would be irremediable.

Although Meliagaunt is eventually defeated and order is restored, ensuing events are constructed around further abductions of the queen, and we are made increasingly aware of the social threat such actions represent. Indeed, even when she consents, the seizure of her person stands as an act of high treason. Thus Launcelot's rescue of Guinevere from death by fire after their adultery has been discovered, and his flight with her to Joyous Gard, are portrayed compassionately, but the problematic nature of what is in effect *raptus* becomes acutely evident. Launcelot himself states the danger of taking the part of the queen, 'I must do much harme or I rescow her, and peradventure I shall there destroy som of my beste fryndis, <and> [that shold moche repente me. . . .] And if so be that I may wynne the quene away, where shall I kepe her?' (III, p. 1172, ll. 27–33). Yet he has no choice but to uphold his responsibility to defend his lady. His action proves even more destructive than he feared, in that it leads to the death of Gawain's two brothers, Gareth and Gaheris, and hence to Gawain's promotion of the war between Arthur and Launcelot. Notably, Launcelot himself is willing to yield Guinevere to Arthur: the social unnaturalness of keeping the queen even with her consent is clear, and she is eventually returned to the king at the request of the Pope, with a great show of ceremony. In this final section of the *Morte*, the ramifications of abduction, even when consensual, become progressively more ominous, and the motifs of betrayal and treachery dominate. As Peggy McCracken suggests with regard to French romance, the queen's adultery threatens the body politic. The public opposition to the king's order represented by the *raptus* of Guinevere dramatically increases this threat, and although the queen consents to her own abduction, the action remains one of high treason.[43]

The socially threatening quality of *raptus* becomes still more evident for Launcelot's *raptus* of the queen culminates in the fall of the kingdom. Mordred takes advantage of the absence of Arthur and Gawain to seize the English crown, and abduct the queen:

And aftirwarde he drew hym unto Wynchester, and there he toke quene Gwenyver, and seyde playnly that he wolde wedde her (which was hys unclys wyff and hys fadirs wyff). And so he made redy for the feste, and a day prefyxte that they shulde be wedded; wherefore quene

---

[43] See Peggy McCracken, 'The Body Politic and the Queen's Adulterous Body in French Romance', *Feminist Approaches to the Body in Medieval Literature*, New Cultural Studies, ed. Linda Lomperis and Sarah Stanbury (Philadelphia, 1993), pp. 38–64.

Gwenyver was passyng hevy. But she durst nat discover her harte, but spake fayre, and aggreed to sir Mordredys wylle. (III, p. 1227, ll. 8–14)

Mordred's villainy is intensified by his explicitly sexual designs and disregard for Guinevere's will, his betrayal of his father's trust, and most of all the incestuous nature of his desire. As in the Meliagaunt episode, however, corruption of the queen's body is avoided and Guinevere shuts herself away in the tower of London. In a recapitulation of all the earlier attempts at enforced marriage, Mordred lays siege to the castle in order to gain both the hand and lands of the lady through military strength, 'Than sir Mordred soughte uppon quene Gwenyver by lettirs and sondis, and by fayre meanys and foule meanys, to have her to com oute of the Towre of London. . .' (III, p. 1228, ll. 24–29). The queen's person is preserved, but this time Launcelot arrives too late to fight for her; through tragic misfortune the final battle against Mordred takes place despite Arthur's warning dream. Launcelot's departure from England as a result of his own inevitable but ill-fated action of *raptus* has set in train the disastrous sequence of events, and the social disruption caused by abduction of a queen is shown to have consequences far beyond the immediate issues of honour and consent.

Romance, then, engages with the law of *raptus* in various ways and through a number of interlinked motifs. We are made aware of the legal complexities of the crime, in particular, the blurring between rape and abduction; romance texts seem to engage both with the distinctive English heritage of a separate law against rape and with the social impact of abduction. Laws against rape become the mark of a good king, and, more generally, the protection of women from *raptus* proves the chivalrous knight. But romance also moves beyond contemporary actuality to address the issue repeatedly marginalised in legal discourse, that of consent. Romance narratives treat again and again the problematic situation of enforced marriage and, although the chivalric code relies on the custom of gaining a woman through military victory, in fact the action of besieging a lady's castle in order to gain her lands is unequivocally condemned. Marriage in romance is predicated on mutual consent and love, however unlikely. Acts of abduction, by contrast, indicate villainy, rejection of the chivalric code and often hostility to the Christian, courtly world. Indeed, the social rupture caused by abduction, even when this occurs with the woman's consent, is illuminated. Romance thus reflects social and legal concern over *raptus*, the emphasis of medieval law on property and the links between rape, abduction and theft inherent in the term *raptus*. Yet at the same time, the issue of the woman's consent, so often not the focus of the legal discourse surrounding *raptus*, is placed as critical, and is upheld and explored with an acuteness, poignancy and power that speaks for the radical possibility of romance.

Written on the Body: Reading Rape from the Twelfth to Fifteenth Centuries

KIM M. PHILLIPS

B ECAUSE rape is central to many contemporary western discourses on gender relations, scholars with an interest in the relations of medieval men and women have often turned their attention to rape in that society.[1] They have encountered problems with understanding rape there, however, because medieval concepts of the crime were in many ways different from our own, because such concepts were not single in definition, and because they were subject to very significant changes over time. In this article I shall contend that there is an important difference between modern western meanings of rape and medieval English common-legal meanings, in that where the *unconsenting will* is the dominant theme of modern western definitions, the *assaulted body* is dominant in medieval English ones. While consent was almost always a consideration in definitions, whether it was implied or explicit, rape in the language of English common law from the twelfth to fifteenth centuries was above all a crime written on the body.

---

1   On the English common law on rape see J.B. Post, 'Ravishment of Women and the Statutes of Westminster', *Legal Records and the Historian*, ed. J.H. Baker (London, 1978), pp. 150–64, and 'Sir Thomas West and the Statute of Rapes, 1382', *Bulletin of the Institute for Historical Research* 53 (1980), pp. 24–30; E.W. Ives, ' "Agaynst taking awaye of Women": the Inception and Operation of the Abduction Act of 1487', *Wealth and Power in Tudor England: Essays Presented to S.T. Bindoff*, ed. E.W. Ives, R.J. Knecht and J.J. Scarisbrick (London, 1978); Ruth Kittel, 'Rape in Thirteenth-Century England: A Study of the Common-Law Courts', *Women and the Law: A Social Historical Perspective*, vol. 2, *Property, Family and the Legal Profession*, ed. D. Kelly Weisburg (Cambridge, MA, 1982); John Marshall Carter, *Rape in Medieval England: An Historical and Sociological Study* (Lanham, 1985); Roger D. Groot, 'The Crime of Rape *temp.* Richard I and John', *The Journal of Legal History* 9 (1988), pp. 324–34; Christopher Cannon, '*Raptus* in the Chaumpaigne Release and a Newly-Discovered Document Concerning the Life of Geoffrey Chaucer', *Speculum* 68 (1993), pp. 74–94.

There are very many studies of literary or hagiographic representations of rape. Most recently, see Evelyn Birge Vitz, 'Rereading Rape in Medieval Literature: Literary, Historical and Theoretical Reflections', *Romanic Review* 88 (1997), pp. 1–29; Anna Roberts, ed., *Violence Against Women in Medieval Texts* (Gainesville, 1998).

My title attempts to draw attention to the centrality of the body to meanings of rape in the period under consideration, but also to the role of legal texts, or narratives, in producing the body of the raped woman. The kind of body defined or 'written' as a raped body changed over time, and this can be shown to be due to the motives of those who controlled the production of legal discourses. This approach to the subject of medieval rape necessitates an interdisciplinary approach. A small number of scholars have begun to consider ways of producing a genuinely interdisciplinary understanding of medieval texts which describe or define rape.[2] Here I aim to take these methods further, and attempt a reading of English common law texts on rape – treatises, cases and statutes – which knits together three different disciplinary or ideological approaches.

First, literary methods of close reading will be employed with analysis of the texts as 'narratives' which plot a changing normative model of the raped woman. This section argues that close reading enables us to see that the body, more than the will, is at the centre of common-legal discourses on rape, and that this body is subject to sharp changes over time. In the article's second section these narratives will be historicised, by being read within a political and legal framework. This process will enable a more contextualised understanding of the changes in rape narratives than has previously been achieved. Finally, the article will conclude by adding an explicitly feminist dimension to the topic, in considering the implications of the article's findings for medieval feminist history in general. It is hoped that through application of these three approaches – literary, historical and feminist – a view of common law on rape will be achieved which is at once broader and more clearly focused than is possible within a narrow disciplinary framework.

As already mentioned some scholars, notably Kathryn Gravdal and Barbara Hanawalt, have begun the process of considering medieval rape from interdisciplinary perspectives. Gravdal, strongly influenced by the inspiring work of Natalie Zemon Davis on sixteenth-century French pardon narratives, argues that 'scholars must examine the "fictive elements" in medieval documents'.[3] Her own readings of the Cerisy and St Martin court registers from the fourteenth century link the lingering detail in descriptions of rapes, particularly in the St Martin register, to thirteenth-century pastourelle rape nar-

---

[2] Kathryn Gravdal, *Ravishing Maidens: Writing Rape in Medieval French Literature and Law* (Philadelphia, 1991), esp. ch. 5; Barbara A. Hanawalt, 'Whose Story Was This? Rape Narratives in Medieval English Courts', *'Of Good and Ill Repute': Gender and Social Control in Medieval England*, ed. Barbara A. Hanawalt (New York, 1998). In this essay I take 'interdisciplinary' to mean an approach to a topic which consciously employs methods of analysis across traditional disciplinary boundaries. Both Gravdal and Hanawalt use reading techniques taken from literary studies to analyse 'historical' sources.

[3] Gravdal, *Ravishing Maidens*, p. 19. See Natalie Zemon Davis, *Fiction in the Archives: Pardon Tales and their Tellers in Sixteenth-Century France* (Stanford, 1987), esp. pp. 1–6.

ratives in their voyeurism and self-conscious literariness.[4] The fictive appeal of these legal tales had, she suggests, two functions: one, 'to make images of violence against women tolerable . . . by troping them poetically'; and two, to provide pleasure for the scribe.[5] Hanawalt picks up these ideas in her close study of the three different accounts of the rape of Joan, eleven-year-old daughter of Eustace le Seler, by Reymund of Limoges, in London in 1320. While Joan's and Reymund's accounts emphasise details which would have the pragmatic benefits of aiding their respective cases, the third version, possibly by the coroner, adds new details that could be seen as salacious. It was this third version which found its way into the *Nova Narrationes*, and thus became a model rape case for aspiring lawyers. Hanawalt follows Gravdal's lead in suggesting that this most graphic of rape narratives might have held a titillating function for its readers – 'a bit of fourteenth-century soft pornography for lawyers'.[6]

Who can say whether this is a fair reading? It is impossible to do more than speculate. But it should be remarked that rape narratives containing the detail found in Joan's case are unusual in English records – most cases are recorded quite tersely – and thus that most accounts of rape probably had a function other than pornographic. Also, it is salutary to note the findings of Guido Ruggiero for late medieval Venice, where rape trials were recorded in language that was 'curiously distant and antiseptic', in strong contrast with sodomy trials, for example, which were described in explicit detail. The exceptions to this rule for rape cases were those involving violence against children or the elderly, and the detail here may have been included for moralistic reasons. Specifically, rape in Venice (as in England) was usually punished lightly if at all, and the more graphic descriptions in cases involving particularly vulnerable parties might have been linked to a greater attempt to ensure heavy penalties.[7] It is notable, in light of this, that the case of Joan discussed by Hanawalt, and most of the cases Gravdal suggests to be pornographic, involve girls aged eleven to thirteen. To read such accounts as having a moralising and shocking function requires no more, and perhaps less, of a leap of imagination than to see them as providing titillation.

The present study, then, distances itself from the 'rape narrative as pornography' model, without rejecting it completely, and aims for a more historically contextual analysis. It is limited to discussion of representations of rape in common law texts; I make no attempt to present hypotheses on the actual occurrence of rape in medieval England.[8] Certain aspects of the medieval law

---

4 Gravdal, *Ravishing Maidens*, pp. 134–40.
5 Gravdal, *Ravishing Maidens*, p. 140.
6 Hanawalt, 'Rape Narratives', p. 137.
7 Guido Ruggiero, *The Boundaries of Eros: Sex Crime and Sexuality in Renaissance Venice* (New York, 1985), p. 90.
8 For rape law in practice see Barbara A. Hanawalt, *Crime and Conflict in English Communities*

and sociology of rape are well-known and may be quickly rehearsed.[9] Rape, from the late twelfth century, was counted among the felonies, and therefore in theory punishable by life or limb. It was one of only two criminal appeals which could be brought by a woman – the other being the death of her husband 'in her arms'. English common law distinguished quite clearly between rape (forced coition) and abduction by prescribing a different proce-dure in each case (an appeal of rape in the first instance, and a writ of ravish-ment in the second), though that distinction began to be blurred by the late fourteenth century. Few appeals of rape were made to the king's courts. Of those that were made, the majority were withdrawn before the cases could be heard, and of the cases that were heard, very few indeed resulted in a guilty verdict. Of those ending in a guilty verdict, the prescribed punishment by life or limb was rarely, if ever, carried out. In terms of its actual impact on the lives of medieval English men and women, the common law on rape was full of sound and fury, signifying almost nothing.

Writing the body of the raped woman

Consent is at the heart of modern western legal definitions of rape. A pre-sumption of the right of the individual, whether male or female, to control over his or her choice of sexual partner, and the activities performed with that partner, governs the perception that rape occurs when such rights are contravened.[10] While law codes allow for variation between acts defined as rape, the matter of consent remains at the heart of the law. In turning to medieval English common law on rape, we find that lack of consent is present within definitions, but is not so central, or is defined slightly differently. Rape in medieval English common law went through a series of changes in defini-tion, but what each phase has in common is the centrality of the *body*. Texts from treatise, statute and case material intertwine and influence one another

(Cambridge MA, 1979), esp. pp. 104–110; Kittel, 'Rape in Thirteenth-Century England'; Carter, *Rape in Medieval England*; Groot, 'Crime of Rape'.
9   For general information on English common law on rape see, in addition to the works cited in note 8, F. Pollock and F.W. Maitland, *The History of English Law, Before the Time of Edward I*, 2 vols, 2nd edn (Cambridge, 1968), vol. 2, pp. 490–91; Ruth Kittel, 'Women Under the Law in Medieval England 1066–1485', *The Women of England, From Anglo-Saxon Times to the Present: Interpretative Bibliographical Essays*, ed. Barbara Kanner (London, 1980), pp. 124–137, esp. p. 130; Sue Sheridan Walker, 'Punishing Convicted Ravishers: Statutory Strictures and Actual Practice in Thirteenth and Fourteenth-Century England', *Journal of Medieval History* 13 (1987), pp. 237–50, esp. pp. 237–38.
10 Susan Estrich, *Real Rape* (Cambridge MA, 1987), p. 29; Linda Brookover Bourque, *Defining Rape* (Durham and London, 1989), pp. 97–99; Keith Burgess Jackson, *Rape: A Philosophical Inves-tigation* (Aldershot, 1996), pp. 89–93. As these studies make clear, definitions of rape are multiple within contemporary western culture, but consent is central to common-legal definitions.

128

in their production of the raped woman's body. Three clearly discernible phases are present from the twelfth to fifteenth centuries: first, the bleeding body, second, the deflowered body, and third, the abducted body.

Glanvill's[11] explanation of the felony of rape, c.1187–89, is as notable, to a modern reader, for what it leaves out as for what it includes:

> Rape [*raptus*] is a crime in which a woman charges a man with overpowering her by force [*ui oppressam*] in the peace of the lord king. A woman who suffers in this way must go, soon after the deed is done, to the nearest vill, and there show to trustworthy men the injury done to her, and any effusion of blood there may be and torn clothing.[12]

Rape according to *Glanvill* is thus characterised by violent seizure or overwhelming by force, visible injuries as a result of this, bleeding wounds and torn clothing. Note that neither absence of consent, loss of virginity, nor even a sexual act are explicitly mentioned. Lack of consent is certainly implied by the phrase '*ui oppressam*', but it seems to be the physically violent element rather than the overcoming of the victim's will which is stressed. This emphasis on the violence of the assault is also apparent in the requirement that the victim show any effusions of blood to the men of the next vill. This requirement could, and sometimes has, been read as referring to bleeding caused by the tearing of the hymen in defloration.[13] If so, *Glanvill* could be said to be making loss of virginity an element to its definition of rape. But as we shall see in a moment reference could be made to bleeding even where the victim were a married woman, implying that the bleeding, like the torn clothing, is a result of the overall violence of the assault, rather than of defloration.

Above all, in *Glanvill's* account, rape is an act of physical violence done to a woman's body. This emphasis on violent assault and/or the bleeding body is also prominent in appeals of rape made before the royal courts in the early years of the thirteenth century. While it is possible that the treatise had some influence on the phrasing of these appeals, such a direct relationship is not assumed. Rather, both belong to a common-legal discourse in which certain narrative elements were seen as relevant:

> Malot Crawe appeals Robert son of Godfrey of rape . . . It was attested

---

11 Given the disputes over authorship of the legal treatises under discussion here, terms such as *Glanvill* and *Bracton* will serve to designate the titles of the treatises rather than the names of their authors.

12 *The Treatise on the Laws and Customs of the Realm of England Commonly Called Glanvill*, ed. G.D.G. Hall, 2nd edn with additional material by M.T. Clanchy (Oxford, 1993), XIV.6, p. 175. With this and other Latin or Anglo-Norman texts I provide translations based upon, but not always identical to, the translations offered in the editions cited.

13 E.g. Hanawalt, 'Rape Narratives', p. 126.

that he so raped her and she was seen bleeding [*sanguinolenta*] (Cornwall, 1201).[14]

Marina daughter of Everwin appeals Roger de Barid of rape, that he threw her down and took from her her virginity . . . It is attested that she was seen bleeding [*sanguinolenta*] (Cornwall, 1201).[15]

Lucy sister of William Ballard appeals Stephen Hoket that when she was going to the vine on her return he took her and led her into his booth and lay with her by force . . . The serjeant of the hundred bore witness that she was seen bleeding [*sanguinolenta*] (Cornwall, 1201).[16]

Sibba daughter of William appeals William son of Hugh of Bolton that in the king's peace he took her outside the village of Wheldrake and lay with her by force and beat her and made her bloody [*sanguinolentam*] (Yorkshire, 1208).[17]

Mabel of Harley appealed Thomas Burnel in the shire court of rape of her virginity. Thomas does not come . . . The jurors say that Thomas is not guilty of that rape, so he is quit. But they say that Roger Tangwar and Thomas Tangwar beat and tied up Mabel and drew blood from her, and forced her to appeal Thomas (Shropshire, 1256).[18]

The legal linguistic culture of the early-thirteenth-century courts created a body for the raped woman in which the marks of violence, especially bleeding wounds, were as, or more, important than a damaged hymen. The last case quoted above, though it falls outside the time-frame and thus indicates that a rigid chronology would be inappropriate here, demonstrates that individuals wishing to counterfeit a raped body might do so by producing bleeding wounds through beating. The language of loss of virginity is occasionally heard, as in the second and last examples quoted above, but less than the language of violence.

But during the thirteenth century the discourses of law would gradually shift their focus from the production of the raped woman's body as a bleeding body to a deflowered body. This shift would not be smooth or absolute, but a definite trend can be marked, and is demonstrated in the table of cases below.[19] The gap between the total number of descriptions of rape in each roll

---

[14] Doris Mary Stenton, ed., *Pleas before the King or his Justices 1198–1202*, vol. 2, Selden Society 68 (London, 1949), no. 337, p. 74.

[15] Stenton, ed., *Pleas . . . 1198–1201*, 2, no. 342, p. 76.

[16] Stenton, ed., *Pleas . . . 1198–1201*, 2, no. 395, p. 92.

[17] Stenton, ed., *Pleas before the King or his Justices 1198–1202*, vol. 4, Selden Society 84 (London, 1967), no. 3491, p. 114.

[18] Alan Harding, ed., *The Roll of the Shropshire Eyre of 1256*, Selden Society 96 (London, 1980), no. 672, p. 242.

[19] Cordelia Beattie, in an unpublished study of rape in England in the thirteenth century, independently came to similar conclusions regarding the rise in importance of defloration in rape cases around the time of *Bracton*, and I am grateful to her for showing me her findings.

Table: The Language of Rape Cases before Westminster I

Date/place	total cases	bleeding	violence/ force	defloration	abduction	consent
1198–1202/various	6	3	2	1	–	–
1199–1212/various	11	1	3	1	–	–
1206/Essex	1	–	–	1	–	–
1218–19/Yorks.	74	–	2	1	–	1
1218–19/ Lincs. and 1221/Worcs.	5	–	1	–	1	–
1221–1222/Glos., Warks., Staff.	9	–	–	–	–	1
1238/Devon*	15	–	1	3	–	1
1248/Berks.	9	–	1	3	–	–
1249/Wilts.*	20	–	8	–	–	–
1256/Shrops.	4	1	1	4	1	–

* These rolls are available in printed form only in translation.

Sources: Doris Mary Stenton, ed., *Pleas before the King or his Justices 1198–1202*, vol. 2, Selden Society 68 (London, 1949); Stenton, ed., *Pleas before the King or his Justices, 1198–1212*, vols 3 and 4, Selden Society 83 and 84 (London, 1966–7); F.W. Maitland, ed., *Select Pleas of the Crown* vol. 1, A.D. 1200–1225, Selden Society 1 (London, 1887); Stenton, ed., *Rolls of the Justices in Eyre being the Rolls of Pleas and Assizes in Yorkshire in 3 Henry III (1218–19)*, Selden Society 56 (London, 1937); Stenton, ed., *Rolls of the Justices in Eyre being the Rolls of Pleas and Assizes for Lincolnshire 1218–19 and Worcestershire 1221*, Selden Society 53 (London, 1934); Stenton, ed., *Rolls of the Justices in Eyre being the Rolls of Pleas and Assizes for Gloucestershire, Warwickshire and Staffordshire, 1221, 1222*, Selden Society 59 (London, 1940); Henry Summerson, ed., *Crown Pleas of the Devon Eyre of 1238*, Devon and Cornwall Record Society n.s. 28 (Torquay, 1985); M.T. Clanchy, ed., *The Roll and Writ File of the Berkshire Eyre of 1248*, Selden Society 90 (London, 1972–3); C.A.F. Meekings, ed., *Crown Pleas of the Wiltshire Eyre, 1249*, Wiltshire Archaeology and Natural History Society Records Branch (Devizes, 1961); Alan Harding, ed., *The Roll of the Shropshire Eyre of 1256*, Selden Society 96 (London, 1980).

and the numbers employing the language of bleeding, general violence, defloration, abduction or consent is illustrative of the generally terse nature of such narratives.

The shift is clear in the *Bracton* treatise (c. 1218–1229), which greatly expanded upon the concise and sometimes opaque *Glanvill*. *Bracton's* statements on the duties of the coroner in an appeal of rape follow *Glanvill* fairly closely, including the duty to inspect the alleged victim for torn or blood-stained clothes,[20] but in other contexts brings attention to rape as an act by

[20] *Bracton on the Laws and Customs of England*, ed. George E. Woodbine and trans. Samuel E. Thorne, 4 vols (Cambridge MA, 1968), vol. 2, f. 122, pp. 344–45.

which a woman loses her virginity, even when the crime is mentioned almost in passing ['. . .as where a woman overcome by force has lost her virginity'].[21] The focus on defloration is brought into the spotlight within *Bracton's* discussion of the forms of criminal pleading:

> Among other appeals there is an appeal called the rape of virgins [*de raptu virginum*]. The rape of virgins is a crime imputed by a woman to the man by whom she says she has been violently overpowered [*violenter oppressam*] against the king's peace. If he is convicted of this crime [this] punishment follows: the loss of members, that there be member for member, for when a virgin is defiled she loses her member and therefore let her defiler be punished in the parts in which he offended.[22]

The punishment for a convicted rapist in this instance is loss of eyes and testicles, but only where the raped woman was a virgin. Rape of married women or widows, nuns or matrons, concubines or prostitutes were all counted as rape, but according to this text were lesser versions of the felony and to be punished with less severity. The text interpolates *Glanvill's* requirement of the display of blood and torn and bloodstained garments, but the inclusion seems perfunctory, as the focus has shifted emphatically from violence to defloration, as seen in the form of the appeal in which a woman had, according to *Bracton*, to make her case.[23] In short, 'to defile a virgin and to lie with one defiled [are different deeds]'.[24]

Again, as with *Glanvill*, consent is of only peripheral interest. Lack of consent is implied in the notion of violent oppression, inserted from *Glanvill*, and in a later *addicione* which mentions consent explicitly, but is of little interest to the author of *Bracton*.[25] Rape in *Bracton* is again a crime against the body, but where violence and bleeding play a part in the definition of the act, defloration is indubitably of the greatest importance. This change represents a dramatic shift from *Glanvill's* focus, while keeping the spotlight on the body.

The shift to defloration was not absolute or sudden however. *Britton* and *Fleta* provide later-thirteenth-century accounts which retain *Glanvill's* emphasis on physical violence, despite the predominant influence of *Bracton* on the works:

> If the coroner be to take an inquest of rape, let him carefully inquire into all the circumstances of the force and of the felony, and make

21 *Bracton* 2, f. 143, p. 403.
22 *Bracton* 2, f. 147, pp. 414–15.
23 *Bracton* 2, ff. 146–8, p. 416.
24 *Bracton* 2, f. 148b, p. 417.
25 *Bracton* 2, f. 147b, p. 418.

enrolment of the presumptive signs, such as stains of blood [*de saunc espaundu*], and tearing of clothes.[26]

Rape is a felony committed by a man by violence on the body of a woman [*de violence fete au cors de femme*], whether she be a virgin or not.[27]

A woman may bring an appeal . . . for rape and violence done to her body [*de raptu et violencia corpori*] . . . A. appeals F., for that, as she was etc., the said F. came with his force (or alone) and wickedly and feloniously and against the king's peace lay with her against her will [*concubuit cum ea contra suam voluntatem*].[28]

Britton suggests that signs of rape such as bloodstains should not necessarily be linked with lost virginity, given its emphasis that a woman need not be a virgin to be raped. This account, even more strongly than *Glanvill*'s, makes rape above all a physical assault. *Fleta* retains this emphasis, and makes no mention of defloration, but adds a new element; here absence of consent is for the first time in the treatises central to the definition.

These texts warn us that the move from one definition to another was not smooth or straightforward, but still the trend is clear. Despite *Britton's* insistence on the insignificance of loss of virginity as a marker of the raped body, and *Fleta's* lack of interest in the subject, texts of rape trials from the middle of the thirteenth century show a move towards a focus on defloration. In these, the raped woman's body as a bleeding body disappears from sight, while the violated virgin moves more clearly into view:

Margery daughter of Emma de la Hulle appeals Nicholas son of Geoffrey of Whatcomb that he came to her between Bagnor and Boxford in a certain place which is known as Bagnor wood in the vigil [21 July 1244] of St. Mary Magdalen at the hour of vespers in the 28th year and raped her virginity [*rapuit ei virginitatem suam*] against the [king's] peace (Berkshire, 1248).[29]

Christian daughter of John of Woodstock appeals brother Simon, lay brother of Stanley, that he came to her in a certain park which is known as Dedemore in Wicklesham on the Friday [25 May 1246] before

---

26 *Britton*, ed. Francis Morgan Nichols, 2 vols (Holmes Beach, rpt. 1983), vol. 1, I.ii.17, p. 17.
27 *Britton* 1, I.xv, p. 55.
28 *Fleta*, ed. H.G. Richardson and S.O. Sayles, Selden Society 72 (London, 1953), I.xxxiii, pp. 88–89.
29 M.T. Clanchy, ed., *The Roll and Writ File of the Berkshire Eyre of 1248*, Selden Society, 90 (London, 1972–3), no. 787, p. 317.

Whitsun before the hour of vespers in the 30th year and there raped her virginity [*rapuit ei virginitatem suam*] (Berkshire, 1248).[30]

Agnes daughter of Adam Mason of Wrockwardine appealed Adam Turner in the shire court, [alleging] that when she was in the peace of the lord king in Newport . . . Adam came there and seized her and dragged her outside that township to a place called the Weald Moors, and there he threw her down and maltreated her and raped her of her virginity by force [*et vi ei rapuit virginitatem suam*] (Shropshire, 1256).[31]

The heightened emphasis on loss of virginity is not the only new element here. Rape narratives from this period add details concerning the location of rapes which would also bear analysis. It is notable that the locations described are usually at some remove from a domestic setting – a wood, a park, a moor – and that with the third example we begin to see abduction by force to a remote place entering the narrative.

Leaving aside the matter of abduction for a moment, let us consider a narrative which could be said to describe an 'exemplary' rape from this period, as it is included in the *Placita Corone* (third quarter of the thirteenth century), a collection of cases seen as appropriate for providing precedents for procedure in royal courts. Such cases were perhaps chosen for the comprehensiveness of detail, but also because the kinds of detail included were seen as definitive. The following narrative, in a sense, represents a perfect crime of rape, as seen in the era between *Bracton* and Westminster I:

Alice de C, who is here, appeals H de P, who is there, that whereas she was in the peace of God and in the peace of our lord the king, the day after the Annunciation of Our Lady in March, at the hour of *prime*, in such a year from the coronation, in such a wood, or elsewhere: namely in such a place called N, where she went seeking her mare to carry her grain to be ground at the mill of A de C: there came this same H, who is there, feloniously as a felon and in premeditated attack, and called her vile names in that he called her, namely, whore [*puteyne*], thief, and anything but her proper name, and said; 'I have wanted you for a long time – and here you are!' and then he seized her, feloniously as a felon, and laid her down beneath an oak tree, tied her hands together with the cord of his yew bow; with his left hand he held her so feloniously by the throat that she could in no wise escape from him nor shout nor make a noise, and with his right hand he forced open her legs and thighs, and, by violence and against her free will, he raped her [virginity] in such a

[30] Clanchy, ed., *Berkshire Eyre*, no. 888, pp. 350–51.
[31] Harding, ed., *Shropshire Eyre*, no. 739, p. 258.

way as to make a thorough job of it [*a force, encontre son gre et sa bone volunte, la ravy son pucelage et en tele manire ly focyt totoutre*].[32]

This 'perfect' rape of the middle of the thirteenth century brings together almost all the elements discussed up to this point, and is indicative of points of change. The narrative emphasises the violence of the act. It brings the reader's attention to the assault on the alleged victim's body, but has moved away from making blood and wounds the sign of the raped body. The emphasis is shifting rather to the compelling effects of the force exerted – 'she could in no wise escape from him' – and this point is made clearer by the explicit reference to the woman's non-consent. Deprivation of virginity is a key element also. The remote location (in a wood, or on the way to mill) matches mid-thirteenth-century emphasis on a lonely non-domestic setting.

Note also, though, there are aspects to this exemplary crime which are missing in most recorded English rape narratives. It has been made into a more tellable tale through the inclusion of 'fictive' elements. The inclusion of a line of dialogue adds dramatic dimensions to the tale (long aquaintance between the parties, the man's frustrated lust, and the dramatic emphasis provided by the exclamation 'and here you are!'), the close detail which allows one to picture the scene (the oak tree, the cord of the yew bow, the woman's throat, legs and thighs), and the crude language ('puteyne', 'ly focyt totoutre' – the second elided by the translator).[33] What could be the point of making this tale more tellable? It bears comparison with the 'titillating' accounts quoted by Gravdal and Hanawalt, and the inclusion of crude language seems particularly to push one towards an interpretation of pornography. Other interpretations are possible, however. The literary qualities of the piece might have aided in making the case more memorable, for example, and thus easier to bring to mind while pleading before justices. I should not like to be categorical about making an interpretation one way or the other. Perhaps it is equally important to note that shorter later versions of the *Placita Corone* repeated the example but with a simplified narrative, which retains the emphasis on physical assault, loss of virginity, remoteness of location and the details of the oak tree and bow string, but omits the dialogue, attention to the victim's body and coarse language, and could only by stretching the imagination be said to have a pornographic effect even to a modern reader.[34]

The shift to a third phase in writing the body of the raped woman becomes apparent in the last quarter of the thirteenth century, and grows stronger up

---

[32] *Placita Corone, or La Corone Pledee devant Justices*, ed. J.M. Kaye, Selden Society s.s. 4 (London, 1966), pp. 7–8.
[33] For a discussion of the power of such details as strong language and the use of dialogue see Davis, *Fiction in the Archives*, pp. 2–3.
[34] *Placita Corone*, p. 29.

to the end of the fifteenth century, where this study ends. The statutes on rape and ravishment from 1275, 1285, 1382 and 1487 outline this phase:[35]

And the king prohibits that no one ravish, nor take away by force [nul ne ravie ne prenge a force], any maiden within age, neither by her own consent nor without; nor any wife or maiden of full age, nor any other woman, against her will; and if any do, at his suit that will sue within forty days, the king shall do common right; and if none commence his suit within forty days the king shall sue (Westminster I, c.13, 1275).[36]

It is provided, that if a man from henceforth ravishes [ravist] a woman, married, maid, or other, where she did not consent either before nor after, he shall have judgement of life and member. And likewise where a man ravishes [ravist] a woman, married, lady, damsel, or other, with force, although she consent after, he shall have such judgement as before is said, if he be attainted at the king's suit, and there the king shall have the suit (Westminster II, c.34, 1285).[37]

Wheresoever and whensoever . . . ladies, daughters, and other women aforesaid be ravished [rapiantur], and after such rape [raptum] do consent to such ravishers, that as well the ravishers, as they that be ravished, and every of them from henceforth be disabled, and by the same deed be unable to have to challenge all inheritance, dower, or joint feoffment after the death of their husbands and ancestors . . . and that the husbands of such women . . . [or fathers, or next of kin] have from henceforth the suit to pursue, and may sue against the same offenders and ravishers in this behalf, and to have them convicted of life and member, although the said women after such rape do consent to the said ravishers (1382).[38]

Where women, maidens as well as widows and wives of substance . . . for the gain of such wealth be often taken [prisez] by wrongdoers contrary to their will, and afterwards married to such wrongdoers or to other by their assent, or deflowered [deflorez]: Let it therefore be ordained, established and enacted . . . [that this act] be felony (1487).[39]

Post has charted the means by which the first three statutes progressively

---

[35] The statues have been comprehensively studied by J.B. Post and E.W. Ives (see n.1), and Corinne Saunders provides a summary of Post's points in the present volume.
[36] A. Luders, T.E. Tomlins, Raithby J., et al., eds., The Statutes of the Realm, [hereafter SR] 12 vols (London, rpt. 1963), vol. 1, 29, c. 13. See also Post's text in 'Ravishment of Women', pp. 162–63.
[37] SR 1, 87, c.34 and Post, 'Ravishment of Women', p. 164.
[38] SR 2, 27, c.6.
[39] SR 3, 512, c.2/3 (the chapters are numbered differently in the English and French texts).

took control over the appeal of rape from the female victim, from allowing the king to initiate the appeal with Westminster II and pursue it in the face of the alleged victim's consent after the act, to allowing the disinheritance of such late-consenting victims in 1382 and making it possible for the husbands or other relatives of such women to bring the appeal of felony.[40] The crimes of abduction and rape, previously distinct as trespass and felony respectively, become conflated within each statute – a process apparently completed in 1487 where abduction, with or without defloration, becomes felonious.[41]

The extent to which these statutes represent a profoundly different perspective on rape from the treatises should be apparent. The notion that rape is primarily a crime of violence against a woman's body, signified by bleeding wounds, has quite gone. The question of loss of virginity is almost overlooked. In their place consent takes greater importance. But still one could say that the statutes write rape as a crime against the body through their gradual conflation with the felony of abduction. The raped woman's body, in these late formulations, ceases to be primarily the assaulted or deflowered body, and becomes the absent body.

A handful of cases from the period after 1275 suffices to illustrate the changing emphasis. I have not attempted to produce a second table to chart the changes after Westminster I as the gradual conflation or rape and abduction makes the choice of cases for the purposes of comparison very difficult:

> Rose, daughter of Nicholas le Savage, appeals John le Clifford of rape [*de raptu*] . . . [while she was in a croft near her father's house] there came the aforesaid John together with other unknown men wickedly and in felony aforethought and took the aforesaid Rose in his two arms forcibly and against [her] . . . will . . . and put her on a dappled (?) palfrey and took her away from the aforesaid croft and brought her . . . to a certain vill . . . [and thence to a hall] . . . And when she was disrobed he took her in his two arms and made her sleep with him [*fecit eam concubire*] in the same bed and there held her all naked . . . and moreover he held Rose's hands with his left hand and raped her virginity so that the aforesaid Rose departed all bloody [*sanguinolenta*] from the aforesaid John (King's Bench, 1282).[42]

> Roger of Quenby was attached to answer John de Trays on the plea why with force and arms he ravished (*rapuit*) Alice, John's wife, at London and took her away (*abduxit*), along with goods and chattels belonging to John, and still keeps them from him, and inflicted other outrages upon him, to John's serious loss and in breach of the peace etc. and in breach

40 Post, 'Ravishment of Women' and 'Sir Thomas West'.
41 Ives, 'Abduction Act'.
42 G.O. Sayles, ed., *Select Cases in the Court of King's Bench under Edward I*, vol. 1, Selden Society 55 (London, 1936), no. 75 p. 101.

of the terms of the statute provided in this case [Statute of Westminster II, c. 34]. [John complains that along with his wife Roger took away] robes, linen and wool cloths, gold and silver, to the value of a hundred shillings (King's Bench, 1314).[43]

William [Athern] of [Lincoln] sued an appeal of rape [*vne appelle de Rape*] of his wife Jane against John [Bigg], recorder of Lincoln, and Richard his servant. And the writ was, *to answer the plaintiff according to the form of the statute* etc. made in the sixth year of King Richard, c. 6, *wherefore he raped his wife, wherof he appeals him* etc. (ed.'s italics. Lincoln 1422).[44]

The earlier thirteenth-century emphases on loss of virginity and the bleeding body (which in this case seems to refer to the bleeding of defloration, in contrast with earlier cases) are still integral to the first narrative presented here, but Westminster I's conflation of the crimes of forced coition and abduction is apparent in the detail with which the abduction of the maiden is recounted. That conflation is all the more apparent in the example from 1314, which would look like a conventional tale of abduction with the ravished woman's husband in the role of appellor were it not for the reference to Westminster II. This case is interesting, as it seems to place the appeal of rape in the hands of the husband long before the statute of 1382 would formalise that procedure. Acceptance of the husband's role as appellor is apparent in the final example, which refers explicitly to the 1382 statute. In these and other fourteenth and fifteenth century examples the raped woman as a victim of violent assault or defloration becomes of minor importance compared with the suffering experienced by the new victim, her husband, father or guardian, who complains of his wife or daughter's absent body as he complains of his absent robes, linen, wool cloths, gold and silver. Rape by the later Middle Ages in England is still a crime written on the body, but the true victim is no longer the violated woman but the deprived man.

Historicising the functions of rape narratives

The later part of this story is the better known, and comes as little surprise. More surprising are the earlier modes of rape narration in English common law. Definition of rape as a crime of violence in which the raped woman was

[43] Sayles, ed., *Select Cases in the Court of King's Bench under Edward II*, vol. 4, Selden Society 74 (London, 1955), no. 20, p. 59. For a very similar case from 1369 see Sayles, ed., *Select Cases in the Court of King's Bench under Edward III*, vol. 6, Selden Society 83 (London, 1965), no. 108, pp. 159–60.
[44] C.H. Williams, ed., *Year Books of Henry VI. I Henry VI. A.D. 1422*, Selden Society 50 (London, 1933), no. 1, p. 1.

clearly the suffering party is harder to explain within modern perceptions of medieval patriarchy than the later phases. But all three stages mapping a changing body for the raped woman can be explained by examining more closely the forces shaping legal narrative across these three centuries. Gravdal and Hanawalt have read rape narratives within an imagined individual context such as that described by Davis for pardon tales; that is, in which individual speakers, scribes and readers play an important role in shaping the tales. While this may be a valid approach for exceptional narratives such as Joan vs. Eustace Seler, or for the text from the *Placita Corone*, the general pattern of formulaic narratives and their changing elements over time which has been revealed here is better read within a context of wider systems of power and the shaping of legal discourse.

The twelfth- and early thirteenth-century texts are particularly intriguing because they do *not* show great interest in defloration or abduction. This seems odd, especially given Roman civil- and canon-legal traditions on rape, which always emphasised the question of consent and in which abduction was one of the key elements.[45] But consideration of wider political impulses governing the production of legal discourse in this era make the production of the raped body as the bleeding body less mysterious. *Glanvill*, of course, was produced during the reign of Henry II. The idea that the king had much direct influence on the production of the text is now generally discounted,[46] but still the impulses guiding its production and content must be linked to the general climate of Henry's political aims and legal reforms.

Like his grandfather, Henry is often viewed as a king anxious to suppress the disorder of the previous reign through greater legal centralisation. Henry I's reign had begun the process of taking criminal law out of the jurisdiction of local courts, and Henry II's reign cemented this, especially through his assizes and the development of the eyre and writ systems, and establishment of a central court at Westminster.[47] Political and legal historians debate the role of the individual king in all this, and the extent of his 'genius',[48] but these are not my concerns. What is clear is that Henry II's reign, if not necessarily the

---

45 James A. Brundage, 'Rape and Seduction in the Medieval Canon Law', *Sexual Practices and the Medieval Church*, ed. Vern L. Bullough and James Brundage (Buffalo, 1982), pp. 141–48.

46 Paul Brand, ' "Multis Vigiliis Excogitatam et Inventam": Henry II and the Creation of English Common Law', *The Making of the Common Law*, ed. Paul Brand (London, 1992), pp. 77–102, esp. p. 78. The debate is well summarised by M.T. Clanchy in *Glanvill*, Introduction, pp. lxxi–xxviii.

47 For background see H.G. Richardson and G.O. Sayles, *Law and Legislation from Aethelbehrt to Magna Carta* (Edinburgh, 1966), pp. 30–70, 88–119; M.T. Clanchy, *England and its Rulers 1066–1272: Foreign Lordship and National Identity* (London, 1983), pp. 68–82, 143–53; W.L. Warren, *The Governance of Norman and Angevin England 1086–1272* (London, 1987), pp. 65–86, 95–122; Brand, 'Multis Vigiliis'.

48 John Gillingham, 'Conquering Kings: Some Twelfth-Century Reflections on Henry II and Richard I', *Warriors and Churchmen in the High Middle Ages: Essays presented to Karl Leyser*, ed. Timothy Reuter (London, 1992), pp. 163–78.

king as individual, was concerned to enforce and centralise order, and that control of criminal law through the eyre, the writ system and the central courts was key to this.

How did this broader political and legal climate connect with twelfth- and early thirteenth-century definitions of rape as primarily a crime of violent assault against women and the raped woman's body as a bleeding body? Primarily through the crown's desire to enforce order through the realm, thereby extending centralised control and establishing a source of income. Order, or the king's peace, was strongly linked to the suppression of physically violent acts throughout the realm. *Glanvill* listed as felonies of the crown crimes which directly affected the king, including regicide, treason, falsifying, and concealment of treasure trove, and crimes of violence which were perceived to be indirectly injurious to the king through bringing disorder to the realm: homicide, arson, robbery, and rape. Simple theft was not there regarded as a felony of the crown.[49] The nature of the law on felony at the time of *Glanvill* thus accounts for that text's and subsequent cases' conceptions of rape as a violent act resulting in general personal injury. In such a context whether or not a woman was deflowered was irrelevant. Abduction was also left out, as it was largely a matter of civil dispute rather than a breach of the peace. The most important of the 'latent' functions of twelfth- and early thirteenth-century narratives of rape, therefore, was to enforce centralised royal control through suppression of physical violence.

The shift to the deflowered body with *Bracton* and mid-thirteenth-century cases can also be explained through examination of a wider legal and political climate. It is generally thought that *Bracton* was compiled between 1218 and 1229, a period closely corresponding to the minority of Henry III from 1216 to 1227. As Clanchy sees it, 'the king's absence or incapacity seemed to bring the best out of the legal system', in producing *Bracton*.[50] I would not see the changes to rape law as representing 'the best' of anything, but find the correspondence in chronology notable. Again, while not wishing to caricature the political *zeitgeist*, the middle decades of the thirteenth century (c. 1220s –1270s) show tendencies which help to explain the changing nature of rape laws and narratives at this time. Henry III's minority was one factor in a larger picture of royal weakness and baronial dissent which one could argue stretched back to Richard I and was quelled with the accession of Edward I and his early statutes.[51] In contrast with the strength of kingly government under Henry II, during Henry III's reign power from the centre was not so strong as to dominate, and this allowed the concerns of the nobility greater space for hearing. This situation was paralleled by the increasingly profes-

[49] *Glanvill*, XVI.1–8, pp. 171–77.
[50] Clanchy, *England and its Rulers*, p. 208.
[51] Warren, pp. 171–80; Alan Harding, *England in the Thirteenth Century* (Cambridge, 1993), pp. 267–309.

sional legal system which already in Richard's reign had shown itself capable of functioning without the direct influence of the king.[52] By the time of Henry III the judiciary was fairly evenly split between lay and clerical justices,[53] and was largely run by men of low to middling knightly rank.[54] Thus the middle decades of the thirteenth century see a legal system operating with some degree of autonomy from the crown, and controlled in large part by lay gentlemen.

This is the climate in which *Bracton* reintroduces defloration as a key element of the definition of rape. It is a climate in which the interests of the crown have been slightly subdued, and strong involvement by lay gentlemen in the production and practice of common law is beginning to influence meanings within law. Into this context, with no apparent prompting from common-legal precedent, loss of virginity leaps into focus as the heart of rape narratives. Such a shift in emphasis can be explained by the interests and agendas of those lay gentlemen who now hold a powerful position in the making of law. For these men, whose daughters' virginity was a treasure, a financial asset in the unsavoury world of medieval marriage-brokering, the most deplorable kind of rape was that which deprived them of such treasure. Rape was not thenceforth defined solely in terms of defloration but a greater emphasis thereon can be clearly marked, and the raped body became more emphatically the deflowered body.

The resurgence of elite lay male familial interests in defining rape in law (resurgent because of their long-dominant place in Roman and canon law) became stronger still in the period of the statutes from the late thirteenth to late fifteenth centuries. Again, this change can be thrown into relief by the wider changes in English government – in particular the rise of parliament, which placed lay gentlemen and nobles in a still more influential legal position.[55] Post's researches into the background to the 1382 statute are illustrative of the way lay elite interests vis-à-vis their daughters could directly impact upon the theory and practice of law. The statute arose from a petition made by Sir Thomas West to John of Gaunt, asking for help in avenging the abduction of his daughter Eleanor.[56] Post argues that Eleanor's ravisher, Nicholas Clifton, was viewed by West as an ineligible son-in-law due to his limited wealth and relatively low social status, and that he therefore sought help at the highest level. We may read the resulting statute as a product of a lay elite patriarchal culture and as representative of that group's attitudes towards the sexual fortunes of their daughters. It is notable that where the

---

52 Helen Cam, *England before Elizabeth*, 3rd edn (London, 1967), p. 88.
53 Ralph V. Turner, *The English Judiciary in the Age of Glanvill and Bracton, c. 1176–1239* (Cambridge, 1985), pp. 88–89 argues this had been the picture since at least the time of Richard I.
54 Turner, *English Judiciary*, pp. 205–6.
55 Ronald Butt, *A History of Parliament. The Middle Ages* (London, 1989), esp. ch. 5.
56 Post, 'Sir Thomas West'.

young victims of rape had been referred to as *damoiseles* in earlier statutes, here they become merely *filiae*, and also that the wording specifies ladies and daughters of noblemen and includes other women only as an afterthought. This document in particular, but also the other statutes to a large extent, are the product of an elite social and familial culture in which the sexuality of daughters and wives was viewed as a possession. For the statutes to have any practical force in law these attitudes would need also to be held by legal practitioners – regional justices of the peace or justices at Westminster. That justices did indeed share such values is indicated in a ravishment case from 1315, in which Justice Beresford indicated his empathy with a noble father: 'if a man come with force and arms into my close and carries away my daughter and marries her against my will he does me a wrong'.[57] The assumption that the father, not the daughter, is the wronged party, represents received legal wisdom concerning rape in the fourteenth and fifteenth centuries. For the lawmakers and practitioners of this era, their daughters' and wives' chastity was their property, and the raped body was the body absent from male familial control.

If the picture that has emerged appears too neat, that is because I have emphasised the passages and examples which illustrate my theme. As we saw in the first section, some cases, and some treatise literature such as *Britton* and *Fleta*, do not exactly fit the picture. It is of course important to acknowledge that the process of change was by no means absolutely smooth or straightforward, but despite this the evidence does consistently produce very clear overall trends. These trends in the language of rape cases, I have argued, can be explained by consideration of the changing agendas of the law-makers. It remains to consider this material from a more openly political perspective.

Feminism and medieval rape

Though I have taken issue with some of Gravdal's interpretations, her insights into rape texts do offer us something of broad value. That is, she encourages us to read medieval court records as rather more than simply bland accounts of court room events. She reminds us to be alert to the power structures deep within the language of court reporting, and to be aware that the details described, those left out as much as those left in, can reveal a great deal about the interests and agendas guiding the workings of the law. A feminist reading of English common law texts dealing with rape easily reveals the patriarchal power structures, in this case the male elite authors and enforcers of common law, guiding and producing the language of the law. Rape is a

---

57 G.J. Turner and William Craddock Bolland, eds., *Year Books of Edward II*, vol. 19, *9 Edward II*, A.D. 1315–1316, Selden Society 45 (London, 1928), no. 12, p. 29.

crime which always involves the oppression of the female victim at the level of the relationship between rapist and victim, and sometimes at the secondary level of relationship between law and victim. That secondary level has been the focus of study here, and it is clear that protection of the interests of the individual woman are generally of only minor interest in the medieval English common law on rape. As noted early in this article, at the level of actual hearing and prosecution women's interests were more absolutely subsumed.

But this study has argued for the recognition of changes over time within the theory and language of the law on rape. Is it possible to map changing degrees of patriarchy across the texts studied? Two factors militate against such an approach. First, as it has been shown that women's interests or rights in law over their bodies are of limited importance in framing the texts discussed, how can one therefore chart the fall or rise of those interests in these texts? And second, even if one could chart such interests, how would that serve a feminist approach? Is not the revealed fact of the relatively minor importance of the female victim's rights within the language of rape law throughout the period studied enough, as it indicates the continuity of patriarchal interests throughout the period examined?

To answer the first objection, it seems to me that what this study of the texts has shown is that although the construction of rape through language was never driven primarily by a desire to protect women's interests, those interests were served better by the earlier phases than the later. The first stage discussed here, which constructed the raped body as a bleeding and violently assaulted body, and in which the woman herself brought any appeal, is more likely to have protected her safety and sense of self-worth than the late phases. The second stage still served a woman's interests to a large degree, because one should not underestimate the extent to which preservation of virginity may have been important to young women as well as their families, but begins to swing away from protection of women to protection of the broader family and its patriarchal concerns. The final phase, especially in placing some control over the appeal process in male family members' hands, clearly and consciously replaces concerns about the female victim with concerns about those men with rights over her. It seems to me that though one can certainly not chart anything like an absolute process from strong concern over women's interests to little concern, some kind of veiled and limited process of this nature can be discerned.

But finally, to consider the second objection, how can recognition of such a veiled and limited process serve a feminist approach? Has not one merely revealed the broad continuities of women's oppression by such a study? Such questions are prompted by the arguments of Judith Bennett, who has claimed that women's history has been too prone to construct narratives of transformation in women's status from one period to another. She claims that actual changes are so minimal across history that one does better to construct narratives of continuity, which serve as a more powerful instrument to reveal women's subjection over time.[58] I am in sympathy with her anxiety about transformation narratives, but not reassured by the prospect of their replacement by an emphasis on continuity in which subtle changes are submerged. The project of feminist history is best served by approaches which can encompass both change and broader continuity, for without such recognition of complexity studies of patriarchy risk appearing caricatured or hackneyed. In the instance of tales of rape in English common law, I do not propose a narrative of transformation, but rather of slight but significant change. Bennett is right to condemn histories which chart women's status from good to bad, but perhaps these should be replaced with histories which chart changes from bad to worse. This is the picture which I see revealed by this essay's analysis of rape narratives. The process from the bleeding body, to the deflowered body, to the absent body, sketches the outlines of a complex picture of decline for women under the common law.

---

[58] She has explored this theme in a number of pieces, most notably 'Confronting Continuity', *Journal of Women's History* 9 (1997), pp. 73–94, and see the responses in the same volume.

'[S]he will . . . protect and defend her rights boldly by law and reason . . .':[1] Women's Knowledge of Common Law and Equity Courts in Late-Medieval England

EMMA HAWKES

CHRISTINE DE PISAN assumed that widowed women could 'defend [their] rights boldly by law', implying that they would have learned about the law earlier in their lives.[2] A close study of the ways late medieval northern English gentlewomen approached common law and equity courts suggests that these women were indeed informed and experienced legal agents. The related issues of late fifteenth- and early sixteenth-century women's participation in legal processes and their knowledge of the law are addressed throughout this work.

I consider women's knowledge of the law through both broad studies of the traffic through the Westminster courts and case studies of individual uses of the law. I am concerned with both women's actions in the courts – those legal undertakings which bore their names – and their knowledge of the law, tentatively defined as the extent to which they understood these actions and made decisions in legal matters. I examine the actions lodged in King's Bench by disputants from Yorkshire and Lincolnshire in the Trinity terms of 1480, 1496 and 1500 and the Common Pleas actions brought by Yorkshire and Lincolnshire litigants in Trinity 1479, 1500 and 1520, and compare these legal undertakings with those in the equity court of Chancery between 1461 and 1515. While this statistical information indicates that women made informed choices about courts, quantification of participation in legal activity can only

---

1 Christine de Pisan, *The Treasure of the City of Ladies, or The book of the Three Virtues*, tr. Sarah Lawson (London, 1985), p. 82.
2 Christine de Pisan addressed French noblewomen in the early fifteenth century, but her work was translated into English and her warnings about women and the law were applicable to fifteenth- and sixteenth-century English women.

indirectly address the issue of female knowledge of the law. For this reason, I conclude by examining some women's legal undertakings – especially litigation over land – in more detail. Since there is more anecdotal information about the better-documented gentry, the focus is on the ways northern gentlewomen participated in the courts and understood the law.[3]

This study considers differences in female activity in the common law courts of King's Bench and Common Pleas and the equity court of Chancery. The laws of England were far from monolithic in the fifteenth and sixteenth centuries, existing, rather, as a network of intertwined jurisdictions.[4] King's Bench and Common Pleas were part of the system of law established in England since the time of Henry II. The equity court of Chancery offered an alternative system to the common law courts.[5] It was intended to provide swift justice for those who, for various reasons, could not bring their cases to the traditional courts. Because these jurisdictions offered women different legal statuses and attributed them with different legal abilities and duties, a comparison of female undertakings in these courts suggests that women made knowledgeable decisions about the courts they entered into.

Baron et feme erunt animae duae et carne una. In common law, the married couple were but one legal person and that one person was the husband.[6] Writing in the eighteenth century, Blackstone noted that 'the very being or legal existence of a woman is suspended during the marriage, or at least it is incorporated and consolidated into that of the husband: under whose wing, protection, and cover she performs everything'.[7] Married women were *femes couvertes* and their husbands were both their sovereigns and their guardians. For this reason, during the period of coverture a wife could not own any chattels.[8] Any personal property she had owned as a single woman became the absolute property of her husband who could dispose of it as he willed during their lives. The wife's land was under the control of the husband for the time of the marriage, although the wife customarily had the power of veto over the

---

[3] A useful introduction to the legal status of other medieval women is provided by Caroline M. Barron, 'The "Golden Age" of Women in Medieval London', *Medieval Women in Southern England*, Reading Medieval Studies 15 (Reading, 1989).

[4] Amy Louise Erickson, *Women and Property in Early Modern England* (London, 1993), p. 5.

[5] Margaret E. Avery, 'The History of the Equitable Jurisdiction of Chancery, Before 1461', *The Bulletin of the Institute of Historical Research* 42 (1969), pp. 129–44.

[6] *The Laws Respecting Women* 1777; repr. New York, 1974), pp. 65–66, 148–83, 341–48; Basil Edwin Lawrence, *The History of the Laws affecting the Property of Married Women in England* (1884; repr. Littleton, Colorado, 1986); William Holdsworth, *A History of English Law*, 16 vols (1908; repr. London, 1942), vol. 3, pp. 520–33; J.H. Baker, *An Introduction to English Legal History* (London, 1971), pp. 258–62.

[7] Sir William Blackstone, *Commentaries on the Laws of England*, vol. 1 (London, 1829), p. 442.

[8] Ann J. Kettle, ' "My wife shall have it": Marriage and Property in the Wills and Testaments of later Medieval England', *Marriage and Property*, ed. Elizabeth M. Craik (Aberdeen, 1984), pp. 89–98; Barron, 'The "Golden Age" of Women in Medieval London', pp. 35–38; Erickson, *Women and Property in Early Modern England*, pp. 24–28.

alienation of land she brought to the partnership. And, most importantly, women could not bring cases to common law without their *barons*. *Femes couvertes* were liable for criminal prosecution but other litigation had to include their husbands. The situation was boldly summed up in *The Lawes Resolution of Women's Rights*:

> Every *Feme Covert* is a sort of infant. . . . It is seldom, almost never that a married woman can have any action to use her wit only in her name: her husband is her stern, her prime mover, without whom she cannot do much at home, and less abroad. . . . It is a miracle that a wife should commit any suit without her husband.[9]

King's Bench and Common Pleas were the major law courts of late medieval England. King's Bench had developed in the thirteenth century as the King's particular court.[10] By the end of the fifteenth century it was unusual for the king actually to sit in this court and the number of cases coming to the court may have been declining, but it remained one of the most important common law courts in England.[11] King's Bench Jurisdiction had authority to examine and correct all errors in law and in fact and in any other court except Exchequer. In the seventeenth century, Coke wrote that the judges of the court were 'called *capitales* in respect of their extreme jurisdiction throughout England'.[12] While Common Pleas also had authority to supervise and correct the older local courts, including the county court and the hundred court, the increasing importance of the work of justices of the peace acting in other local courts of assizes and gaol delivery had eroded the jurisdiction of these courts.[13] By the late fifteenth century, the largest and most important part of the jurisdiction of this court was over common pleas – that is to say, over actions between one private litigant and another.[14] The majority of actions taken to Common Pleas consisted of real actions, the peaceful transfer of lands through fines and recoveries, and personal actions, including those over debt.

Women went to the common law courts less often than men, but their litigation, like that of men, was mostly concerned with claims to land.[15] When

---

9 T.E., *The Lawes Resolution of Womens Rights*, The English Experience Series (1632; repr. Amsterdam, 1979), pp. 204–5.
10 Holdsworth, *A History of English Law*, vol. I, pp. 204–12.
11 Marjorie Blatcher, *The Court of King's Bench, 1450–1550: A Study in Self Help*, University of London Legal Series (London, 1978), pp. 10–33.
12 Sir Edward Coke, *The Fourth Part of the Institutes of the Laws of England* (1628; repr. New York, 1979), p. 75.
13 Holdsworth, *A History of English Law*, vol. I, pp. 198–202.
14 Margaret Hastings, *The Court of Common Pleas in England: A Study of Legal Administration and Procedure*, The American Historical Association (Ithaca, 1947), p. 16.
15 Susan M. Wright, *The Derbyshire Gentry in the Fifteenth Century*, Derbyshire Record Society 8 (Derby, 1983), p. 120.

Table One. Proportions of Men and Women in Common Pleas, 1479, 1500 and 1520

	Women	%	Men	%
CP 40 867	73	4	1563	96
CP 40 953	40	5	698	95
CP 40 1025	54	5	948	95
Total	167		3209	

the records of Trinity term of King's bench in 1480, 1496 and 1500 are examined, it is clear that very few women were engaged in litigation in this court.[16] Of the 274 litigants coming from Yorkshire and Lincolnshire, only 11 were women. That is, 5% of the litigants were women.

To exemplify the infrequency with which women were named in King's Bench records, the well-documented Plumpton family was involved in six actions which were brought to King's Bench eighty-five times between 1480 and 1530, but only one action mentioned one woman once. In 1483 John Roucliff esquire and Margaret his wife (née Plumpton) brought an action of illegal entry against Robert Plumpton.[17] This action, begun shortly before an arbitrated award between the two parties was made by Richard III, served partly as coercive litigation to force a conclusion to the dispute and partly as a means of highlighting the Roucliff claim to the lands.[18] Since this claim was through Margaret, the heir general of the Plumpton family, it is almost certain that she was named as a litigant only to strengthen her husband's position.

Women made up the same small proportion of litigants in the Yorkshire and Lincolnshire actions of Trinity 1479, 1500 and 1520 in Common Pleas. There were 167 women among the 3376 litigants who went to the court in those terms, again 5%. This figure was a surprisingly constant one in the common law courts, each term showing virtually the same proportion as the total. It appears that over forty years there was very little change in the relative number of women who went to Common Pleas.

The majority of the Common Pleas actions which involved women were over land. To give a handful of examples, in 1500 William Vavasour esquire and his wife, Isabel, defended an action brought by Roger Ask and William

---

[16] This database was compiled with assistance from Jennifer Smith and Anthony Briggs. I wish to offer them my thanks.

[17] King's Bench [Hereafter K B] 27 884/69. All manuscripts are held at the Public Record Office.

[18] Shirley Walker, 'The Plumpton Correspondence: An Historical and Social Survey' (unpublished Masters Dissertation, Leeds University, 1962); Keith Dockray, 'The Trouble of the Yorkshire Plumptons in the Wars of the Roses', *History Today* 28.7 (1977), pp. 459–66.

Ask esquires, over the manor of Whatson, four messuages and 130 acres of lands in Whatson and Gilling near Richmond.[19] Again, in 1509 William Plumpton and his wife Isabel accused Thomas Rokeby gentleman of breaking into a close called Hawnsley and pasturing cattle there illegally, an allegation frequently used to highlight claims to land.[20] In 1520 Alicia Lacy brought an action against Robert Slater, accusing him of entering the 'clausum ipius Alicia' at Warburgh and that same year Elizabeth Guy 'spynster' was accused of illegally entering lands in Yorkshire.[21]

Indeed, women were even more likely than men to be involved in cases concerned with land. Overall a third of the trafffic through Common Pleas in the Trinity terms of 1479, 1500 and 1520 dealt with various quarrels over land, but half of the actions in which women were named dealt with claims to land.[22] About a third of the 1500 actions were brought over land – 92 accusations of illegal entry of lands from a total of 253 cases.[23] Again, around one third of the entries from 1520 dealt with actions about land – 112 allegations of unauthorised claims to lands from 344 entries.[24] The figures for 1479 were slightly lower, around a quarter of the actions dealt with land claims – 123 accusations of illegal entry of lands from a total of 516 disputes.[25] The numbers of female claims to land were out of line with these otherwise quite constant figures. In the 1500 and 1520 actions 95 women were named and 49 of these women were involved in actions of illegal entry *vi et armis*, waste or claims to lands. That is to say, only one third of the male litigants, but half of the female litigants, were involved in claims to land. There were, of course, fewer women acting as litigants, but they were proportionally more likely to be involved in land cases.

Given the economic importance of land in a pre-industrial society, it is unsurprising that such a large proportion of Common Pleas litigation should have dealt with actions over land.[26] It is, however, interesting that women were more likely to engage in this sort of litigation than any other. It is possible that women were more likely to be named in actions over land, because under common law married women maintained some rights over lands they brought to the marriages, whereas control over the chattels they brought to

---

19 Common Pleas [hereafter CP] 40 952, 122d.
20 CP 40 986, 56.
21 CP 40 1025, 478d; CP 40 1025, 481d.
22 C.E. Moreton, *The Townshends and Their World: Gentry, Law, and Land in Norfolk, c. 1450–1551* (Oxford, 1992), p. 106.
23 CP 40 1025.
24 CP 40 953.
25 CP 40 867.
26 J.L. Bolton, *The Medieval English Economy, 1150–1500* (London, 1980), pp. 223–86; Christine Carpenter, 'The Fifteenth Century English Gentry and their Estates', *Gentry and Lesser Nobility in Late Medieval Europe*, ed. Michael Jones (Gloucester, 1986), pp. 36–60.

marriages passed to their husbands.[27] Any personal property they had owned as single women became the absolute property of their husbands who could dispose of it as they chose during their lives, but wives could veto the sale of lands they brought to their marriages. If the husband enfeoffed his wife's lands to others without her permission, then after his death the widow could recover the property with a writ of *cui in vita*.[28] Perhaps women were disproportionately represented in litigation over land because even *femes couvertes* retained some legal claims to land under common law.

In some cases a husband and wife litigated together, specifying that they were seeking the wife's inheritance or dower from her previous marriage. For instance, Robert Plumpton and his wife Grace brought two actions claiming twelve messuages and four hundred acres of land in Ripon, Westwick and Knaresborough 'ut dotem ipsius Gracie'.[29] On other occasions the pursuit of the wife's land claims was not explicitly stated but can be inferred. In 1515 William Plumpton and his wife Isabel (née Babthorp) defended an accusation that they had misappropriated lands in Lincoln.[30] The charge was brought by William Babthorpe and was undoubtedly part of the long running feud over Isabel's inheritance. It is possible that many of the Common Pleas cases which named women did so because the contested lands had been part of their dower or inheritance.

Women were, then, uncommon litigants in common law courts. The proportions of women in both King's Bench and Common Pleas hovered around 5% between 1479 and 1520. As well as going to the courts less often, women were particularly likely to engage in actions over land and it may be that many of these claims represented attempts to gain women's inheritances and dowers. If this is so, it is difficult to assess whether women were actively involved in these actions or if they were brought principally by their husbands. Female knowledge of the courts can be illuminated if the differences and similarities in the way women approached common law and equity courts are compared.

Female litigation in the equity court of Chancery was different in degree, though not in kind, to that in Common law courts. Female petitioners and respondents in Chancery were again a minority, though a larger one than in the common law jurisdictions, and their bills generally dealt with disputes over land, indeed, disproportionately so. Chancery had developed in the early fifteenth century to provide a forum for equitable remedy and a court in which strict adherence to the rules of common law was unnecessary.[31] Chan-

---

[27] Kettle, ' "My Wife Shall Have it" ', pp. 89–98; Barron, 'The "Golden Age" of Women', pp. 35–8; Erickson, *Women and Property in Early Modern England*, pp. 24–28.
[28] Holdsworth, *A History of English Law*, vol. 3 (1908), pp. 22, 245.
[29] CP 40 890, 415; CP 40 891, 391d.
[30] CP 40 1009, 116d.
[31] Baker, *An Introduction to English Legal History*, p. 51.

cery was concerned with cases which could find no remedy by the usual course of the law or which could be tried at common law, but where, owing to the power of the defendant or the unsettled state of the realm, the ordinary courts could not act.

Of the 1384 bills of complaint sent to Chancery between 1461 and 1515 by petitioners living in Yorkshire, 438 included women as petitioners or respondents.[32] That is to say, almost one third of the petitions included women as petitioners or respondents. These petitions involved a total of 3606 people, 3080 men and 526 women – 85% of the litigants were male and 15% were female. These numbers suggest that women were significantly more likely to participate in legal activities in equity than in common law courts.

The majority of these Chancery petitions were concerned with land. Of the 1384 bills lodged between 1461 and 1515, 273 complained about the illegal alienation of lands and a further 683 dealt with the detention of deeds related to lands. These two groups, when combined, made up two thirds of all the petitions sent from Yorkshire over this half a century. As with male litigants in equity, most of the petitions sent from Yorkshire presented by women were over land. Female litigants were named as sole or co-petitioners in 20% of all the Yorkshire petitions alleging the detention of land deeds and in 29% of the bills dealing with illegal entry. That is to say, women were named as petitioners in roughly one quarter of the petitions over land although they made up only 15% of the litigants overall. They were unexpectedly prominent in the significant area of land ownership.

This characteristic of female litigation was an exaggerated version of a pattern which can be seen in all Chancery litigation. Of the 3606 people named in the petitions, 2397 were named in bills dealing with the loss of lands or detention of deeds (67%). The percentages for some groups of women are out of line with these averages – 25 of 33 bills presented by daughters (76%) and 141 of 160 bills presented by wives in conjunction with their husbands (88%) dealt with these kinds of accusations. It appears that daughters' and married women's legal activities were exaggerated versions of the typical ones, although widows were marginally less likely to be involved in petitions claiming lands (69 of 110 bills).

Litigation over land was exemplified in the petition brought by Thomas Thwaytes and his wife, Emma, who were claiming a share of her landed inheritance from her father's feoffees.[33] John Hamerton and his wife Elizabeth, the daughter of Thomas, Lord Cliffford, brought a similar case against Sir William Plumpton, looking for the dowry which had been promised to her at the time of her marriage to William Plumpton who had died at

---

32 This database was compiled from the Lists and Indexes Series. I owe an immense debt of gratitude to David Emrich and Simon Oxwell for their help.
33 Chancery 1 [Hereafter C1] 246/14.

Table Two. Percentages involved in Land and Deeds
Cases in Chancery, 1461–1515

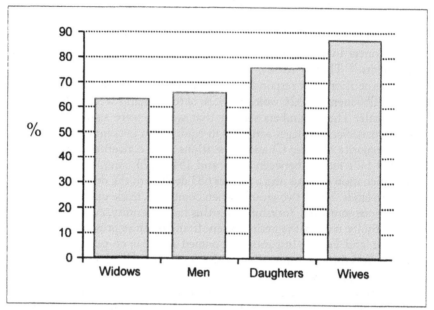

the battle of Towton.[34] Margaret Thomson, a widow, lodged a petition against Margaret Rayn over the detention of deeds relating to lands at Barnard Castle.[35] Likewise, Joanne Grenacre accused Margerie Oresby of appropriating a messuage in Kingston on Hull.[36]

The tendency for these women to be involved in cases over land may well have resulted, in part, from their weak legal standing which would have discouraged all but the most necessary litigation. Because married women retained some control over the landed dowers while they lost all claim to the movable possessions they brought to the marriage, they would inevitably have been more likely to litigate over land than chattels. Additionally, married women were unlikely to be involved in some other varieties of litigation such as disputes over broken financial agreements. The fact that married women could not enter into contracts meant that they were rarely named on bonds and hence were unlikely to go to court in disputes alleging that debts from bonds had not been paid.[37] The disproportionate presence of women in

---

[34] C 1 31/330.

[35] C 1 229/36.

[36] C 1 31/360.

[37] Some late medieval women in the urban trading communities could contract independently, but they were the exception. Gentlewomen could not contract as *femes soles*: Barron, 'The "Golden Age" of Women in Medieval London', pp. 38–41.

litigation over land was, then, the result of their exceedingly limited legal rights in other areas of late medieval law.

It is possible that these women were only nominally involved in this legal activity and that they had little understanding of the intricacies of the law. It is striking that none of the Yorkshire wives who sent petitions to Chancery did so independently. All 160 of the married women living in Yorkshire who sent bills to Chancery did so in co-operation with their husbands even though technically married women could act independently in this equity court. The implication of this is, of course, that these women had very little opportunity to establish separate legal identities and statuses. Their legal actions were invariably made in conjunction with their husbands. It is therefore difficult to distinguish between their nominal and their actual involvement.

On the other hand, female knowledge of law is implied by the fact that women were more likely to use equity courts than common law courts. They made up 15% of Chancery litigants and only 5% of those in Common Pleas and King's Bench over a comparable period. The unchanging proportion of female litigants in King's Bench and Common Pleas over a forty year period (despite significant changes in the law and in the overall numbers of disputes taken to these courts) indicated that gender was a very significant factor in determining the use of these common law courts. It seems likely that the comparatively large number of female litigants were taking advantage of equity as a more favourable jurisdiction.

By the eighteenth century Chancery was perceived as a court exceptionally favourable to women,[38] and there is evidence which suggests this trend had begun well before this period.[39] As Holdsworth wrote, 'The equitable rules were designed for the purpose of giving rights to the married woman. They therefore subjected her to very few liabilities . . . . The position, therefore, of the married woman became as unduly advantageous in equity as it was unduly disadvantageous at common law.'[40] In these circumstances the difference in the ratios of women in common law and equity jurisdictions is large enough to suggest that women, or possibly their husbands or advisors, actively made a choice of courts.

Certainly, by the end of the fifteenth century Chancery was seen as a court which showed favour to the dispossessed and the weak. It has been suggested that women who went to equity courts were more likely to claim poverty or inability to use the law than were men.[41] A theme that runs through these

---

[38] G.W. Keeton, *An Introduction to Equity* (1938; repr. London, 1961), pp. 153–59.

[39] Maria L. Cioni, 'The Elizabethan Chancery and women's rights', *Tudor Rule and Revolution: Essays for G.R. Elton from his American Friends*, ed. D. Guth and J. McKenna (Cambridge, 1982), pp. 159–82.

[40] Holdsworth, *The History of English Law*, vol. 3, p. 533.

[41] Tim Stretton, 'Women and Litigation in the Elizabethan Court of Requests' (unpublished Ph.D. thesis, Cambridge University, 1993), pp. 208–21.

Chancery bills is that women were especially pitiful figures who deserved a more favourable hearing from those in power.[42] Men in the same position, especially poor men, could sometimes use the same technique of playing for sympathy, but the descriptions of women are often particularly pathetic. In 1539, Elizabeth Gambylfelde sent a bill to the chancellor of the Winchester diocese, requesting the return of a bequest,

> having no thinge to help my self with but only my fathers beqwest beseching your mastershyp in the wey of pytte to helpe me your poore bedmaydyn or else am i but as a fren[d]les gerle lyke to be utterly cast away.[43]

This was an abject cry for help. Friendship was a valuable commodity in this time; it was difficult to bring a case without well-connected friends.[44] For example, John Hole, a Yorkshire contemporary, argued that his case against Thomas Savile deserved an equitable hearing because he was 'bott a poure man an hath small frendes' while his adversary was 'so frendyd and born in the contrey' that there could not be a fair trial.[45] To be a 'fren[d]les gerle' was plausibly represented as even worse.

It is unlikely that these women were entirely without agency or ability. And yet it was worthwhile for them to present themselves in this way, possibly because the admonition to succour widows and defenceless women in the courts had Biblical backing.[46] In Caxton's 1484 edition of Lull's *The Book of the Ordre of Chyvalry*, it was clearly assumed that women were pitiful creatures who had to be helped. 'Yf chyvalre which is so moche an honourable offyce were to robbe and to destroye the poure peple and not myghty and . . . doo wronge to good wymmen [&] wydowes that have nothyge to diffende

---

[42] Elizabeth Thomson Oakes, 'Heiress, Beggar, Saint or Strumpet: The Widow in the Society and on the Stage in Early Modern England' (unpublished Ph.D. thesis, Vanderbilt University, 1990), pp. 28–29.

[43] HRO CB7, 7 June 1539, cited by Ralph Houlbrooke, *Church Courts and the People during the English Reformation, 1520–1570* (Oxford, 1979), p. 106.

[44] Indeed, it is worth considering whether a woman could be a friend (as opposed to having one). The late medieval ideal of friendship was both affective and instrumental. Literary friendships, the ideals of friendship, were characterised by the combining of practical aid with genuine emotion. A woman as powerless as Elizabeth Gambylfelde was in no position to help anyone else. She was friendless in every sense of the word. Note Philippa C. Maddern, ' "Best Trusted Friends": Concepts and Practices of Friendship among Fifteenth-Century Norfolk Gentry', *England in the Fifteenth Century: Proceedings of the 1992 Harlaxton Symposium*, ed. Nicholas Rogers (Stamford, 1994), pp. 100–117.

[45] STAC 2 26/234 in *Yorkshire Star Chamber Proceedings*, vol. 3, ed. William Brown, Yorkshire Archaeological Society Record Series 51 (1914), pp. 152–53.

[46] James A. Brundage, 'Widows as Disadvantaged Persons in Medieval Canon Law', in *Upon My Husband's Death: Widows in the Literature and Histories of Medieval Europe*, ed. Louise Mirrer, Studies in Medieval and Early Modern Civilisations (USA, 1992), pp. 193–8.

then that offyce thenne were not vertuous but it should be vycious.'[47] John Trevisa wrote in his fifteenth-century translation of De Proprietatibus Rerum that 'a rigtful lord be wey of rigtful lawe makeþ ende of causes, plees, and strif þat beþ bytwene his subiectis . . . . And . . . defende[s] innocentes agenst yueldoers and deliueres smale children, fadirles and modirles, and widowis, of hem þat ouersettiþ hem . . .'.[48] Some of the bills which were sent to Chancery called on these chivalrous ideas and assumed that women could ask for protection. Given that the Chancellor was the representative of the king, these bills were calling on the idea that the king should be the friend to the friendless, caring for widows and children. The use of this ideology may have made Chancery a more attractive jurisdiction for women.

This knowledgeable choice of courts indicates that some women were relatively proficient in legal matters and that they merely lacked the opportunity to practise this on a large scale during their coverture. Judgements about the degree to which gentlewomen were active partners in litigation must draw on qualitative material such as letters. While some anecdotal evidence suggests that some married women were involved only nominally, other material indicates that these women were full participants in legal undertakings. In 1452 Osbern Mundford wrote candidly that he 'wol take an accion . . . of forsable entré in [his] name and my wifes for oure title, &c., and an accion of trespasse for dispoiling of [his] godes. . .'.[49] He clearly perceived himself as the real participant in the legal proceedings and his wife as at best the junior partner in the actions.

Another example which indicates that some late medieval women were only tangentially involved in litigation can be found in the Chancery petition which was presented in the names of William Vavasour and his wife, Isabel, against Piers Bank between 1461 and 1467.[50] Throughout the body of the petition, however, William was referred to as the sole plaintiff ('the said Will'm Vavasour your suppliant'). The claim to the deeds had come to the Vavasour family through Isabel's inheritance and it seems likely that her name was invoked in the introduction to the petition only to enhance William's assertion. It was, after all, a legal requirement that an action be brought in the names of both the husband and the wife if the husband held the property in right of his wife.[51] In this case Isabel was the conduit through which

---

47 Raymond Lull, *The Book of the Ordre of Chyvalrye*, The English Experience (1484; repr., Amsterdam, 1976).

48 John Trevisa, *On the Properties of Things: John Trevisa's Translation of Bartholomaeus Anglicus De Proprietatibus Rerum*, 2 vols. (Oxford, 1975), vol. 2, p. 317.

49 Norman Davis, ed., *Paston Letters and papers of the Fifteenth Century*, vol. 2 (Oxford, 1971), letter 485, p. 78.

50 C 1 41/157.

51 Stretton, 'Women and Litigation in the Elizabethan Court of Requests', p. 152.

land could be inherited and her name was the mechanism through which it could be claimed.

On the other hand, married women were described as active and involved legal agents in other late medieval sources. To give some examples, in the early sixteenth century, Dame Anne Rokesby was urged to make a letter of attorney to take up a dispute in which her husband had been involved.[52] In 1570 Lady Lawrence set out to go to the courts in London, but the particular jurisdiction she wanted was prorogued.[53] In fifteenth-century Norfolk, the redoubtable Elizabeth Clere interrogated an errant tenant in the technical language of the law.

> And I askyd hym if he wold a-bide be þat . . . my men come in-to his place with force and armes or noght, and þat he was betyn or noght, and he answerd ageyn with many crafty wordes; but at þe last he was a-knowe þat he had seide hem and it was untrewly seid, and þat he wold no more sey so . . .[54]

Elizabeth clearly understood the legal meaning of the phrase *vi et armis*. If this accusation of the use of force could not be made, her tenant could not bring his case to King's Bench. A similar understanding of the law is suggested in Sir William Stonor's insistence that Peter Marmion come to court with both his wife and his sons to guarantee the smooth transfer of some lands.

> First the forseyde Syr Wylliam . . . requeryth the forseyde Perkin Marmiun that he hym selfe come and cause his wyfe and hys sunys Tobard Marmyun and Jon Marmyun to come afore my lord Bryan, chefe jeuge of the comon place, and by fore the seyde lord Bryan that he and hys wyffe and hys ij sunys aforesayde do make and every of them do make a seure and a sufficient knowledge in lawe by fyne for the surcese of all the londes . . . to the forseyd Sir W. Stonore . . .[55]

William Stonor perceived that not only Peter Marmion but also his wife and his heirs had an interest in future claims to the land and that they were all capable of making a 'sure and a sufficient knowledge in law by fyne'. His assumption that Marmion's unnamed wife would have the ability to launch such a legal action suggests a respect for female knowledge of the law.

---

[52] Thomas Stapleton, ed., *Plumpton Correspondence: Written in the Reigns of Edward IV, Richard III, Henry VII and Henry VIII*, introduction Keith Dockray, Camden Society Series (1839; repr. 1990), Letter 6, pp. 227–28. Hereafter referred to as *PC*.

[53] *Calendar of the State Papers of the Reign of Elizabeth*, Addenda, cited by Stretton, 'Women and Litigation in the Court of Requests', p. 169.

[54] Davis, *Paston Letters*, vol. 2, Letter 600, p. 199.

[55] Christine Carpenter, ed., *Kingsford's Stonor Letters and Papers, 1290–1483* (Cambridge, 1996), Letter 323, p. 410.

A more detailed example can be taken from the experiences of Isabel Plumpton in mid-sixteenth-century Yorkshire. She was rarely involved in litigation during her husband's life, but she took at least two cases to the courts of Augmentations and the Exchequer in the four years between Robert's death and her own in 1551.[56] Around 1548 William Woodrif told her that charges against her in Exchequer had been dropped and that an order in the Court of Wards was in process and suggested that she should enter into a bond.[57] She wrote to her son, who was studying at the Inner Temple, telling him to complete business in the court of Augmentations that she had begun.[58] Strikingly, Isabel also acted as an administrator of justice at the manorial court at Sacombe. Robert Girlington wrote to inform her of the proceedings of the last session and to ask her what her 'commaundement' was for the following one.[59] Her contact with the court was, like that of most of her peers, at a remove, but it is clear that she was functioning as the 'lord' of the manor.

Further, Isabel was treated in these legal matters, at least on occasion, as the equal of the land-owning men of the gentry. Indeed, Christopher Twisleton, a Yorkshire gentleman, wrote to her proposing that they pool documents to deal with a threat to both their lands. He appealed to the patrilineal ideal, saying that it would be for 'the safte of us and our heires', ignoring the fact that Isabel was not a fellow patriarch.[60] Twisleton treated Isabel as another landowner, assumed her knowledge of the law and wrote that they might act 'as one gentleman and gentlewoman may use one another with favor'. It is possible that other women were equally involved in legal manoeuvres which have not been recorded.

The disproportionate presence of women in equity rather than common law, coupled with anecdotal evidence of female knowledge of the law, indicates that at least some gentlewomen understood the law and acted within the courts. Indeed, it is possible that women were engaged in legal activity outside the courts. Anecdotal evidence suggests that late medieval gentlewomen worked in an extra-curial world. By this I mean that they took part in the behind-the-scenes activity which was necessary to the functioning of legal mechanisms: legal work which did not take place in the courts but which was still an important part of all late medieval legal transactions. To give an example, each medieval bond named at least one person who was obliged to pay the bond and one to whom the money was due. The bonds did not, however, describe who drew the bonds up, who stored the bonds and

---

56 *PC*, Letter 12, pp. 234–35; *PC*, Letter 28, pp. 253–54.
57 *PC*, Letter 28, pp. 253–54.
58 *PC*, Letter 12, pp. 234–35.
59 *PC*, letter 30, p. 256.
60 *PC*, Letter 20, p. 245.

who ensured they were fulfilled. This necessary background work may well have been undertaken informally by wives and female relatives. So, for example, in 1447 Thomas, Lord Scales, Seneschal of Normandy, ordered his bailiff in Berton to deliver £12 10s 6d to Katherine, the wife of William Iwayn of Wireham as payment on a bond.[61] It was she who undertook the necessary (though usually unrecorded) administration of the bond. Again, a Paston letter of 1459 shows that Elizabeth Poynings was engaged in collecting money which had been promised to her husband by her parents and which was to be used by her husband to pay the surety on a bond.[62] Gentlewomen of this sort had some knowledge of the law and experience in the extra-curial world.

Evidence that women were involved in these extra-curial activities is, naturally, piecemeal and anecdotal, but some examples can be noted. John Paston matter-of-factly assumed that his wife was capable of overseeing legal processes when he wrote, 'I merveyll that I here no tidyngges from yow hough ye haue do at the assises.'[63] When Thomas Steward was brought before the Elizabethan Court of Requests he argued that 'hee cannot perfectly answere . . . before he have had conference' with his wife Margerie.[64] In these cases (and in how many others?), the wives were clearly involved in (if not making) the decisions about legal matters; but it takes such exceptional testimony to reveal this legal knowledge.

The extra-curial activities of Agnes Plumpton, the first wife of Robert Plumpton, a Yorkshire gentleman, are particularly well documented. If her efforts had not been recorded in a series of urgent letters to her husband in London, little would be known of this work as she did not actually go to court. In 1502 Agnes wrote that some cattle had been taken in an act of disseisin. She had responded by sending some men to get them back but they could not 'have them without a replevie'.[65] She was willing to act informally but did not apply to the sheriff for the replevin without discussing it with her husband first. Her retelling of the events shows a clear grasp of the complex procedures of distraint and replevin and indicate her general knowledge of the law.

Later that year, Agnes noted that they were having difficulty collecting the rent from some tenants and had ousted them. These men had complained at 'Colthorpe', the seat of Sir John Roucliff, indicating that this rent collection was part of the broader dispute between the Plumptons, Sotehills and Roucliffs. The rent collection was undertaken in the name of their son William, but the money was actually handed over to Agnes ('the names of

---

[61] Norfolk and Norwich Record Office, Hare MSS 261 (Box 85 x 6). My thanks to Philippa Maddern for this reference.

[62] Davis, *Paston Letters*, vol. 1, Letter 121, pp. 206–7.

[63] Davis, *Paston Letters*, vol. 1, Letter 76, p. 139.

[64] Stretton, 'Women and Litigation in the Elizabethan Court of Requests', p. 155.

[65] *PC*, Letter 133, p. 168.

them that hath payd me . . .'). In 1502, then, Robert, the head of the Plumpton clan, was in London, arguing his claim to the disputed lands in the courts and before the king, while William and Agnes were attempting to assert a Plumpton presence in some of the leased lands.

A fortnight later Agnes informed Robert that the dispute had escalated, the Archbishop of York was now involved and the sheriff had told William to 'sette in' the tenants. (I take this to mean that he was ordered to reinstate non-paying tenants whom he had ousted from contested lands.) Agnes' response was immediate and, once again, outside the formal structures of the courts.

> And so I sent one servant to the shereffe, and the shereffe shewed my servant that my lord [Archbishop] had wrytten unto him . . . But my sone [William] kepes them forth as yet, and therfor I trow my lord Archbishop will compleane of my sone and you; and sath, that he will indyte them . . .[66]

It is noticeable that while Agnes communicated with the sheriff informally and in non-legal circumstances, the two men of the family were named as the ones who might be indicted and taken to court. Agnes noted that Thomas, the Archbishop of York had 'indytt my sone William and XVI of his servants' for ignoring a replevin.[67] There was, in some sense, a division of their legal and interests and abilities. William was the one named in their official procedure of the courts although Agnes had been involved in both the conception of the idea ('ye, and I, and my sone, was content' with the plan) and the application of the distraint. Agnes' role was to gather information, to do the accounts, to encourage and urge her menfolk to go to court and to undertake the routine legal procedures which did not take her to court.[68] She was engaged in protecting the family estate just as Robert and William were, but her actions were directed to extra-curial settings and manoeuvres.

I tentatively suggest that women's extra-curial activities might be associated with the late medieval divisions of public and private spheres. In gathering information, pressuring neighbours, paying bonds and arranging legal services, women were assisting their families even though they did not actually enter the courts. They could, in this way, remain legally active within the confines of fifteenth- and sixteenth-century conceptions of public and private spheres.

The ideology of late medieval England confined women to the house-

---

66 PC, Letter 135, p. 170.
67 PC, Letter 136, p. 171.
68 In her next letter Agnes wrote that she was unsuccessfully trying to get a copy of the indictment to examine: PC, Letter 196, p. 171.

hold.[69] As was noted in *Dives and Pauper*, 'As þe sonne schynyng aillumynyth þe world in þe heiþe of þe day, so þe bewte of a good woman is confort & aray of hyr houshold.'[70] Sir John Fortescue, the English legal theorist, moved this general advice into a legal context when he wrote in *De Natura Legis Naturae*:

> For a man devotes his attention to affairs outside, the woman hers to the internal business of the family. Whence it is the duty of a woman . . . to keep quiet at home, and to look after the concerns of the household.[71]

While it is clear that medieval gentlewomen did appear in public and that they often had the ability to move legal procedures along, they were rarely found in the courts. It would seem likely that work in the extra-curial world was considered suitable for the wives and daughters of the gentry. Although such work meant leaving the household, it did not require going under the scrutiny of the county in the courts.

This suggests that a careful distinction should be made between legal activity and legal knowledge. Women's actions in the courts can be thought of as those legal undertakings which bore their names. It is relatively easy to trace women's participation in the courts; it is more difficult to say whether these women understood the law. Women's knowledge of the law could be defined as their ability to guide and direct competently their legal undertakings. It might also, and more meaningfully, be described as their understanding of their legal obligations and statuses in the different jurisdictions of fifteenth- and sixteenth-century England. Such a definition would encompass women's extra-curial work and would acknowledge the constraints placed on women's activities in the courts in the late medieval period. Late medieval women were not unfettered legal agents; their legal autonomy was limited by conceptions of appropriate behaviour and the ideology of the public and private spheres. As a result, legal activities and legal knowledge were overlapping but not identical categories.

This may explain the distinction between the relatively infrequent appearances of late medieval Yorkshire women in the courts and the anecdotal evidence of their knowledge of the law. Women were only rarely present in the courts, and yet their informed choices of jurisdiction and rare qualitative sources suggest a sure understanding of the law.

On the whole, women were rarely found in the courts. Even in the more favourable jurisdictions such as Chancery women only made up 15% of the

69 Judith M. Bennet, 'Public Power and Authority in the Medieval English Countryside', *Women and Power in the Middle Ages*, ed. Mary Erler and Maryanne Kowaleski (London, 1988), pp. 18–36.

70 Priscilla Heath Barnam, ed., *Dives and Pauper*, Early English Text Society, vol. II (London, 1976), p. 89.

71 Sir John Fortescue, *De Natura Legis Naturae* (London, 1980), p. 252.

litigants and in common law courts there was a consistently lower proportion of women. Additionally, in both common law and equity courts women were more likely to be involved in actions or petitions concerned with land. While land was undoubtedly significant to the late medieval economy, the association of women with litigation over land stemmed partly from their legal inability to enter into contracts or bonds which might have involved them in other sorts of litigation. The link between women and claims to land was, then, partly a result of their limited ability to own chattels and to enter into contracts. It was a sign of their constrained legal status.

On the other hand, these broad studies of the traffic through Common Pleas, King's Bench and Chancery nonetheless indicate that some women were familiar with the law. Women were disproportionately present in Chancery, a jurisdiction more favourable to women – 15% compared with 5% in common law courts. The fact that widows, independent legal agents, were as likely as married women to act in equity, suggests that women were actively choosing the more favourable jurisdiction. Individual examples suggest that women sometimes presented themselves as pitiful figures in need of equitable remedy, in accordance with the acceptable stereotypes for Chancery bills. Both the preponderance of women in equity and the skill with which some Chancery petitions manipulated legal categories suggest that women understood their legal obligations and statuses in the different jurisdictions of fifteenth- and sixteenth-century England.

Further, women's extra-curial activities hint at a knowledge of the law which was not recorded in the official court documents. The chance survival of the Plumpton letters means that we can view Agnes' actions and suggests that other gentlewomen undertook similar, unrecorded extra-curial work. Very few legal materials produced by women survive from the late medieval period, but this lack of information about women, especially married women, is in itself revealing as it demonstrates the extent to which women's legal activities were shadowed and hidden by the more obvious activities of patriarchs.

Some women participated in legal activities and probably more women understood the law. Indeed, it is possible that many more women than we know of acted behind the scenes, working in the extra-curial world. Such activities were generally unrecorded, but were necessary to legal undertakings and were based on women's manipulation of the law. Although all women in the medieval period were subject to some of the 'weaknes and debilities' at the law which a legal commentator attributed to *Femes couvertes*,[72] they nonetheless understood the law and were sometimes able to act in the courts.

---

72 Sir Henry Finch, *Law, or a Discourse thereof in four books* (1627; repr., Buffalo, 1992), p. 26.

Index

Index

Index

Burton, William de, draper, 48
Bushel, Thomas, 130
Byconyll, Elizabeth, 61, 75
Byconyll, John, 75
Byrtnoth, 9, 14, 15

Cammell, John, 75
Cammell, Sybil, 64, 75
Cardoni, Marti Aurelli, 19, 20, 21
Carter, Joan, 75
Carter, John, 75
Caxton, 119, 120, 154
Chaunterell, 64
Cheyette, Fred, 26
Chocke, Elizabeth, 75
Chocke, John, 75
Chocke, Margaret, xii, 63, 64, 75
Chocke, Richard, 63, 75
Chocke, Thomas, 75
Chichester, bishop of, 99
Child-swapping, 91
Chivalrous society, 115
Chrétien de Troyes
    Yvain, 114, 115
Christ, 66
Christchurch, Canterbury (Kent), 7
Christine de Pisan, 145
Churches
    All Saints, York, 50
    St Crux, Fossgate, York, 48
    St Giles, Stapleford, 61
    St Martin's, Coney Street, York, 50
    St Michael le Belfrey, York, 50
Clanchy, Michael, 7, 61, 63, 140
Clere, Elizabeth, 156
Clifton, Nicholas, 141
Clifford, John le, 137
Clopton, John, 61, 67
Cnut, 4, 9, 10
    Laws of, 2, 6
Coke, 147
Colshill, 70
Consent, 50, 105, 106, 114, 128, 135
Cornwall, 130
Crawe, Malot, 129
Cui in vita, 150
Cuthbert, St, 2

Dale, John, 50
Davis, Natalie Zemon, 126, 139
Degrevaunt, 116
Denmark, defence of, 11
Dependence, 55

Ditton (Ely), 14
Dives and Pauper, 159
Domesday, 17
Domna, x, 20, 21, 22, 24, 25, 26, 30, 33, 34,
    36, 37, 39, 45
    Agency of, 23, 26
    Construction of as powerful, 27
    In law, 27
Donahue, Charles, xi, 49
Dorchester, 61
Dower, 150, 152
Dowry, 32
Duke of Gerle, 116

Edith, Queen of Edward the Confessor, 4, 16
Edward I of England, 88, 140
Edward III of England, 99
Edward, son of Æthelred, 4
Edward the Confessor, 4
Ely, 10, 14
Elyot, Edmund, 64
Embroidery, 2
Emma, Queen, 4, 16
    Her son, Edward, 17
Encomium Emmæ Reginæ, 1, 4, 17
Erkedon, William, 64
Ethehmer, 15
European household systems, 51

Fabliaux, 87
Familia, 51
Family, 33
Fatherhood ideal, 82
Faukener, William, 92
Fell, Christine, 7, 106
Fellows, Jennifer, 84
Female
    Kinship ties, 46
    sexual appetite, 87
Feme Couverts, 146, 147, 150, 161
Feminism, 142–4
Feminist history, 144
Feudal ethos, 101–2
Feudal society, 99
Feudality, 79
Fine Rolls, 79
Fitz-James, Elizabeth, 71
Fitz-James, Isabel, 64, 72, 75
Fitz-James, John, 71, 75
Fitz-James, Lady, 71
Fleta, 132, 133, 142
Florence, 95
Floris and Blanchefleur, 116–17

Printed and bound by CPI Group (UK) Ltd, Croydon, CR0 4YY

13/04/2025

14656522-0005